# Touching the Face
# Of God

The Story of
John Gillespie Magee, Jr.
and his poem
***High Flight***

Ray Haas

First Edition

Paperback ISBN-10: 1941564003
Paperback ISBN-13: 978-1-941564-00-4

eBook ISBN-10: 1941564011
eBook ISBN-13: 978-1-941564-01-1

Library of Congress Control Number: 2014908666



Published by High Flight Productions, Wilson, North Carolina.
V1.3

Front cover picture:
John Gillespie Magee, Jr. with Spitfire MKVB, VZ-B, AD329, "Brunhilde."
Photograph courtesy of Robert Bracken.

Back cover picture:
John Gillespie Magee, Jr. gets his Wings from Group Captain Curtis, July 16th, 1941.
Photograph courtesy John G. Magee Family Papers, Record Group 242, Special Collections, Yale Divinity School Library.

Front cover design:
Brett Latta.

This book is dedicated to:

# Flight Lieutenant Barry Needham
# Royal Canadian Air Force
# 412 Squadron

... and to all of us who have found a home in the sky.

## *HIGH FLIGHT*

Oh! I have slipped the surly bonds of Earth

And danced the skies on laughter-silvered wings;

Sunward I've climbed, and joined the tumbling mirth

Of sun-split clouds,—and done a hundred things

You have not dreamed of—wheeled and soared and swung

High in the sunlit silence. Hov'ring there,

I've chased the shouting wind along, and flung

My eager craft through footless halls of air ....


Up, up the long, delirious, burning blue

I've topped the windswept heights with easy grace

Where never lark, or even eagle flew -

And, while with silent, lifting mind I've trod

The high untrespassed sanctity of space,

- Put out my hand, and touched the face of God

# Pilot Officer John Gillespie Magee, Jr.
# Royal Canadian Air Force

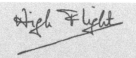

# High Flight

Oh! I have slipped the surly bonds of Earth
And danced the skies on laughter-silvered wings;
Sunward I've climbed, and joined the tumbling mirth
of sun-split clouds, — and done a hundred things
You have not dreamed of — wheeled and soared and swung
High in the sunlit silence. Hov'ring there,
I've chased the shouting wind along, and flung
my eager craft through footless halls of air ....

Up, up the long, delirious, burning blue
I've topped the wind-swept heights with easy grace.
Where never lark, or even eagle flew —
And, while with silent, lifting mind I've trod
The high untrespassed sanctity of space,
— Put out my hand, and touched the face of God.

3.IX.41

The original *High Flight* manuscript.

Original scan courtesy of the Library of Congress, restored by author.

# Table of Contents

# Notes and Introductions

## Crown Copyright, Canada and England

There are many documents and photographs reproduced throughout this book. Some of them were marked with "Crown Copyright," having been obtained from the National Archives of Canada and England. In reproducing them, I am using guidelines which state that Crown copyright protection in published material lasts for fifty years from the end of the year in which the material was first published.

## John G. Magee Family Papers Collection

A major source of information was the John G. Magee Family Papers Collection located at the Yale Divinity Library, New Haven, Connecticut. Some of the pictures in this book came from this collection, and will be marked with this citation:

John G. Magee Family Papers, Record Group No. 242,
Special Collections, Yale Divinity School Library

## Introduction to the First Edition

Without a doubt, there will be more editions of this book. I am certain that I will receive feedback from people who will be able to add missing pieces and offer corrections to this story. Try as I might, I cannot know everything related to John Gillespie Magee, Jr., and his poem *High Flight*. I had to stop at some point and get this book published, and go forward with what I had.

If you, the reader, have comments or corrections about this book, then please feel free to write to this email address:

feedback@highflightproductions.com

This book begins with the life story of John Magee. Following this, I relate what happened with John's most famous work, *High Flight*, tracing its journey from its inception to the current day, as well as reactions to the poem itself. The last part contains detailed information on the aircraft that John flew and other miscellaneous information.

I intend for this book, along with all subsequent editions, to comprise the "final" word on the life of John Gillespie Magee, Jr., and his poem *High Flight*.

# Introduction to the Story

For generations before it was possible, man dreamed of flight. That dream was first realized in balloons and gliders, then eventually in controlled, powered flight. Leonardo da Vinci invented many flying machines, including the parachute, ornithopter, and several types of gliders. Leonardo may or may not have actually flown himself, but certainly he envisaged flying; many of his maps and sketches of earth were drawn from an aerial perspective. If he didn't fly himself, he certainly belonged to the family of fliers, as Leonardo is purported to have said:

**When once you have tasted flight, you will forever walk the earth with your eyes turned skyward, for there you have been, and there you will always long to return.**

For those people who were apparently born to fly, it is often hard to describe exactly what it feels like while in the sky. It is like trying to describe the color blue to the blind. This inability has dogged aviators who have tried to express to non-fliers how they felt about flying. While many poems and stories were written to convey the experience of flight, they somehow fell short.

Then along came this certain young man.

Somehow, a mere teenager captured lightning in a bottle, and pilots past, present and future could breathe a sigh of relief. "What does it feel like to fly?" "Read this," they can say, and hand over a very special poem. In the space of 14 lines, the essence of flying was concisely, joyously and accurately described. What's more, the sonnet was an exercise in spirituality, for the poem demonstrated that, like da Vinci, one did not need an aircraft in order to escape earth and travel to a higher plane.

I'm going to tell you the story of this youth, who will be forever young due to fate's caprice. It is a true story, one of commitment, courage, love and sacrifice. For some, this story will be a tragedy; for others, uplifting and inspiring. And for yet more, the tragedy of a life cut short will be tempered with the inspiration that he left to future generations.

Indeed, for over 70 years, we have remembered him not so much for his accomplishments as an aviator, but for what he left behind in his writings. A poet and a scholar, he may have become a pilot and warrior; but being a warrior was what he did in that place and time, not who he was.

He was barely 19 years old when he gave the world an amazing sonnet; shortly thereafter, he gave the world his life. At a time when the world had been plunged into global conflict, he found beauty and a contentment in the sky above a war-torn land, captured that nearly inexplicable feeling, and managed the incredible feat of putting it down on paper. Nobody before or since has described the wonders of flight nearly as well as he had done in the summer of 1941. We read the words; we soar with him to a bright, shining place, leaving the earth and its troubles far below. We dare to go to that place where we, too, are one with the divine. And where we, too, can put out our hand to "touch the face of God."

In the decades since it was written, his poem has been read by millions of people all over the world. Its lines have been used in movies and books, on television, and have even been parodied many times. An American President has quoted it. Songs have been written using the words from the sonnet.

In this, the Age of the Internet, there is a profusion of inaccurate and misleading information regarding the author. The time is overdue for the complete story to emerge, setting the record straight and letting the world know just who this this remarkable person was.

The name of this certain young man is:

### *John Gillespie Magee, Jr.*

His most enduring sonnet is called:

### *High Flight*

And this is his story.

# PART ONE

## THE STORY OF
## JOHN GILLESPIE MAGEE, JR.

# The Magee Family

In order to really get to know John Gillespie Magee, Jr., it is necessary to go back a bit in history to understand his family background and the subsequent influence it would have on his life.

## Paternal Lineage

John Gillespie Magee, Jr., can trace his paternal lineage back to England, Scotland and Ireland. The Magee family came to North America early; Magee's American ancestors have fought in nearly every war in North America before and after the establishment of the United States. The Magee family was instrumental in establishing the city of Pittsburgh, Pennsylvania; family members included William Addison Magee (a mayor of Pittsburgh) and Christopher Lyman Magee (member of the Pennsylvania State Legislature, and founder of the Elizabeth Steel Magee Hospital and the Pittsburgh Zoo).

John's father, John Gillespie Magee, was born to Frederick McNichol and Hannah Gillespie Magee on October 10, 1884, in the city of Pittsburgh. (Henceforth, John's father will be referred to with a "Sr." attached to his name, in order to differentiate father from son.) Magee Sr. attended school at Shady Side Academy in Pittsburgh, the Hotchkiss School in Lakeville, Connecticut, and then went on to earn his Bachelor of Arts degree from Yale University in 1906.

Magee Sr. had three siblings: James McDevitt, Mary, and Margaret Louise. His older brother James had attended Yale several years before Magee Sr. got there. Both Magee Sr. and James were members of Yale's "secret" society, Skull and Bones; James in 1899, and Magee Sr. in 1906.

In the summer of 1909, John Sr. was sent as a missionary to Nebraska with the Winnebago Indian tribe (sponsored by the Dutch Reformed Church).

In what would appear to be a major deviation from the traditional Magee family path, John Magee Sr. continued his education, attending the Episcopal Theological School in Cambridge, Massachusetts, and earning his Bachelor's degree in Divinity in 1911. He then became a minister of the Episcopal Church and was promptly sent to Nanking, China in 1912.

For the next 28 years, John Magee Sr. would continue to serve in China, inadvertently becoming a part of China's World War II history. After the Japanese army invaded China, Magee Sr. joined forces with several others (including the "good" Nazi John Rabe) to establish the International Safety Zone in Nanking. This Zone was credited with saving the lives of thousands of Chinese as the Japanese Army ran amok.

An ardent letter-writer, Magee Sr. wrote letters to his family and friends detailing what he had witnessed. One can tell from reading these letters written in China that Magee Sr. was hard pressed to understand what was happening, and why. Many of the letters read like a journalist's dispassionate chronicling of horrific events, seemingly attempting to record them for posterity. Clearly, John Magee Sr., wanted to make sure that the world at large would know what happened there, and would never forget. The personal conviction and commitment that John Sr. showed during that terrible time would be echoed in his son's similar commitment later on.

Using a Bell & Howell 16mm film camera, Magee Sr. risked his own life to film some of the atrocities that took place in Nanking. These films are used to the present day as documentation of the horrific events that happened there during late 1937. [1] [2]

John Magee Sr. returned to the United States in 1938 and made a tour speaking about what he had witnessed in China. Most of "isolationist" America was not ready to hear about these events; it would take the Japanese attack on Pearl Harbor nearly three years later to awaken Americans to the threat of an imperialistic and expanding Japanese nation.

John Sr. permanently returned to the United States in the summer of 1940, reuniting with his family.

The tales of John Sr.'s sisters and brothers are interesting in their own right. In 1896, John Sr.'s sister Mary married James Vernor Scaife. Mary and James produced three children: Alan Magee Scaife, James Vernor Scaife, Jr., and Frederick Scaife (who was killed in an automobile accident while attending Yale). Alan Scaife then married Sarah Cordelia Mellon; their children were Cordelia and Richard. Richard Mellon Scaife became a billionaire and was a well-known conservative and also the owner & publisher of the Pittsburgh Tribune-Review.[3] Richard Scaife died in July of 2014, just before this book was published.

After getting married to James Scaife, Mary was often referred to as "Mrs. J.V. Scaife." "Aunt Mary" would come to play a large role in Magee Jr.'s life.

John Sr.'s older brother James McDevitt Magee was born in 1877 near Pittsburgh. After attending Yale, he became a lawyer, and was engaged in a successful legal practice when war broke out in Europe. When the United States declared war on Germany on April 6th, 1917 (the day after James's 40th birthday), James signed up for service, and was commissioned a first lieutenant in the fledgling United States Army Air Service. After the war ended, James continued his service in the Reserve, rising to the rank of lieutenant colonel. James was elected to the 68th and 69th U.S. Congress (1923-1927), acting as a Representative from Pennsylvania.[4][5]

In 1906, John Sr.'s sister Margaret Louise married Baron Franz Reidel de Riedenau, Secretary of the Austria-Hungary Legation in Washington, D.C. making her a Baroness.

## Maternal Lineage

On his mother Faith's side of the family, John Jr. could trace his maternal lineage back for hundreds of years. According to the book, *Plantagenet Roll of the Blood Royal*[6], Faith's mother, Mary Anne Emmeline Walford, was descended from King Edward III, the King of England from 1327 to 1377 A.D.[7], thus giving John Magee, Jr. royal blood.

Faith's father was Edward Batt Backhouse, Rector at Northwood Vicarage, Middlesex. Edward Backhouse and Mary Walford were married on September 17th, 1890.

Faith Emmeline Backhouse was born on October 1st, 1891 in Helmingham, Suffolk, near Stowmarket, England. Faith was the first child of Edward & Mary; she was followed by siblings Ruth Margaret (1893), Edward Henry Walford (1895), and Ellis Brockman (1897).[8]

Faith's brother Edward Henry Walford Backhouse joined the British Army around 1914, and was promptly involved in WWI. Edward was commissioned into the Suffolk Regiment, and served in France where he was wounded and taken prisoner by the Germans after only five days in action.[9] Continuing his service in World War II, Edward rose through the ranks to become a Brigadier General commanding the 54th Infantry Brigade in Malaya. The 54th was involved in the Battle of Singapore in 1942, and surrendered along with the entire British 18th Infantry Division on February 18th, 1942[10] (Winston Churchill has called this surrender the "worst disaster" and "largest capitulation" in British military history, with approximately 80,000 British, Australian and Indian troops surrendering to the Japanese Army). Thusly, Edward Backhouse was a German prisoner of war in WWI, and then a Japanese POW in WWII.

John Gillespie Magee, Sr. and Faith Backhouse Magee.
Both of the top and the lower left pictures are from John's photo album.

All pictures this page are from: John G. Magee Family Papers,
Record Group No. 242, Special Collections, Yale Divinity School Library

[1] http://www.nankingatrocities.net - accessed 5/9/14.

[2] http://www.library.yale.edu/div/Nanking/findingaid.html–accessed 8/28/12.

[3] http://en.wikipedia.org/wiki/Richard_Mellon_Scaife–accessed 4/22/10.

[4] http://en.wikipedia.org/wiki/James_McDevitt_Magee–accessed 4/17/10.


[6] *Plantagenet Roll of the Blood Royal: The Clarence Volume, Containing the Descendants of George, Duke of Clarence* by marquis de Melville Henry Massue Ruvigny et Raineval.

[7] http://en.wikipedia.org/wiki/Edward_III_of_England–accessed 8/15/12.

[8] According to the 1901 Census, the Backhouse family lived at the Vicarage, Ruislip, Northwood, along with several "Domestics–Governess, Parlour Maid, Lady Nurse, and Kitchen Maid".

[9] http://www.unithistories.com/officers/Army_officers_B01.html–accessed 4/15/12.

[10] http://en.wikipedia.org/wiki/Battle_of_Singapore–accessed 4/15/12.

# The Missionaries go to China

Faith and John Magee Sr. arrived in China by completely different paths. With her father as the Rector of Helmingham in England, it seemed natural that Faith would have an interest in the church and becoming a missionary. Under the auspices of the Church Missionary Society, Faith traveled to China as a missionary in January 1919. Faith's father, Edward Backhouse, wrote his daughter a letter on the eve of her departure, expressing how much he and Faith's mother would miss her "in distant China."

There had to be a certain amount of family puzzlement and consternation when one of the Magee family sons decided to give up the pursuit of power and money to become a missionary. Not only did John Magee Sr. become a missionary; as part of the Yale Divinity School, he wound up traveling to China in January of 1912  to join an Episcopal mission in what would become a 28-year odyssey (according to his passport application, Magee Sr. was a missionary for the "Domestic and Foreign Missionary Society of the Episcopal Church").

It seems that Magee Sr.'s brother James was not entirely in agreement with this expedition to China. In a farewell letter written on January 16th, 1912, James conveys his lack of understanding and at the same time his support and love:

> *Dear John,*
>
> *Just a word of goodbye... Only wish I was there to wish you Godspeed... I rejoice in your doing something worthwhile and almost envy you... Don't understand your motives exactly — not "having it," as you say — but I do know that you are sincere, dead earnest and happy... If I have hurt your feelings by misplaced foolery put it down to boorishness... Anyway, Kid, I'm with you right from the heart... Lots of love and the best of luck, James*

In the years before meeting Faith Backhouse, Magee Sr. was kept busy building up the ministry in China, mostly in the Nanking area. He traveled back to the United States several times, including a trip in 1916 to the U.S. via Austria to see his sister Louise (the Baroness) who was seriously ill with tuberculosis.

While in China, John Sr. met and fell in love with fellow missionary Faith Backhouse. John and Faith were married on July 19th, 1921, at the Church of the Ascension in Kuling, China. Not quite a year later, the Magees were to become parents.

# China — 1922 to 1931

## Nanking, China — June 1922 to November 1931

In June of 1922, Faith Magee traveled the roughly 180 miles from Nanking to the Victoria Nursing Home in Shanghai to deliver her first son.[1] At 10:48 p.m. on June 9th, the Magees welcomed their child into the world. They named him John Gillespie Magee, Jr., after Magee Sr. (with the "Jr." suffix that would follow the younger John through his entire life). During his early years in China John Jr. was called "Ian," reverting to "John" after moving to England in 1931.

On the occasion of John's first birthday, Faith sent a newsletter to her family, dated August 1923.

> *And what of Baby John? What has he done, and what*
>
> *can he do? He, too, has certainly helped, by drawing his*
>
> *mother closer to these loving Chinese mother-hearts, and by*
>
> *his happy laugh and baby ways with those who have come*
>
> *to see him and us.*

From the beginning, it was clear that John Gillespie Magee, Jr. was a special child. Born in China to an American father and a British mother, he was different from the outset. At age four, young Magee asked his father, "If we ask the Lord not to let me be afraid, and I *am* afraid, what?" John's divinity school trained father did not have a ready answer for such a seemingly simple question. How do you explain to a boy of four why some prayers are apparently answered, and some not?

Young John Magee was just at the beginning of his questions. For all of his life, John would ask questions of himself, of God, of his parents and friends, of authority, and of life itself. Sometimes the answers would not immediately appear, or be immediately understandable, but that didn't stop the questioning. John would read, study hard, have long discussions and write letters, all in search of the answers.

John would also avoid the mundane like the plague. If life did not provide him with challenges that he liked, John would invent his own, at times to the consternation of his elders and those who were charged with supervising him.

Born in China, becoming bilingual was a necessary step. John immediately started learning Mandarin Chinese (and several other

Chinese dialects) along with English. He also started learning Greek and Latin, and eventually added French to his repertoire. He demonstrated a talent for being able to learn any given subject very quickly when he set his mind to it, and John did not just learn a little bit—he generally went all out and learned as much as he could about whatever had caught his interest. In addition to the languages, John would learn how to play the piano, sail a boat, fire a rifle, play tennis & golf & football (English), build model airplanes, fly a fighter aircraft in combat (with all the subjects implied by learning how to fly and fight), drive a car (for a long time, John was the only person in his immediate family who held a driver's license), write prose, poetry and plays (even acting in some of them), publish a book, and so on.

Early on, Magee started developing a dual nature: on the one side he was extraordinarily intelligent, creative, studious, and well-behaved, while at the same time having an unexpectedly mischievous and devil-may-care side. All of this combined into a volatile intelligence; early on, John started playing pranks on his teachers (especially the ones that he didn't like) and fellow students. However, in a pattern that would repeat itself throughout his entire life, Magee's family, elders and teachers had a hard time becoming or staying upset with him because he was so tremendously apologetic, and... John did have that *other* side, that amazingly well-behaved side, which could not be easily ignored.

Being an American growing up in China undoubtedly helped inject John's native intelligence with flexibility and adaptability. John needed to function in two completely different cultures, and so early on he learned *how to learn* things very quickly.

At age two John travelled to Goodnestone, England, home of his mother's family, staying for nearly a year. From there, the family went to the U.S., and stayed with John's Aunt Mary in Pittsburgh. After four months there, the Magee family returned to China.

In 1925, life in the Magee household became a little more complex when John was joined by new brother David Backhouse Magee. David was born on the 6th of July in Kuling (where Mr. and Mrs. Magee had been married in 1921). More brothers were to follow: Christopher Walford was born on August 19, 1928 in Karuiza, Japan, and Frederick Hugh, born in England on August 23rd, 1933.

John's first school was a small school for Chinese children in Nanking, where he was forced to learn Chinese very quickly! At age five, John attended the Hillcrest School in Nanking, a school for American children living in China (they even had a Boy Scout troop; it's not clear if John was involved, but his younger brother David was). There, teachers quickly learned that young Magee needed to be kept occupied; otherwise chaos would likely ensue, generally in a manner that nobody would expect. Not only teachers, but Magee family housekeepers were also kept busy trying to keep their young charge under control; it is dubious whether they were ever entirely successful.

April 1927 brought the start of the Chinese Civil War[2], between forces of the Republic of China (led by the Kuomintang) and the Communist part of China. The Soviet Union was also heavily involved, and it was during this period when Chiang Kai-shek rose to power. This war would go on, in one form or the other, until 1950, and resulted in the creation of the Republic of China in Taiwan.

Not for the first and certainly not for the last time, Magee Sr. sent his family away for safety's sake. In 1927 that place of comparative safety was St. Paul's University near Tokyo, Japan. (St. Paul's, also known in Japan as Rikkyo University, was formed by Episcopalian missionary Channing Moore Williams.)

His family relatively safe in Japan, Magee Sr. did what he always did in times of trouble: he wrote. His letters, written from the perspective of a person in the thick of events, remain an amazing record of what happened. (Later, John Sr. would add movies to his record.) Here are a couple of excerpts from Magee Sr.'s letter to his brother James, written on April 4th, 1927:

> It was on Monday afternoon, March 21st, at about 4:00 P.M. that we heard the first sound of firing in the attack on the City. I was at a meeting of the Nanking Church Council over in the City about four miles from our place at Haiakwan. It seems from the story of the Northern soldiers who two days later came into our compound, that was one regiment of Northern soldiers did not want to fight and the regiment behind them did.

> I did not know at what moment someone would take a shot at me. This was about 5:00 P.M. ... Dr. Price, one of the older missionaries in Nanking was in their hands for five hours, alternately being beaten and threatened with death. Most of the people had everything stripped from them except their underclothes and their houses were completely wrecked. A great many more would have been killed than

*were killed if it had not been for the wonderful loyalty of servants and Chinese friends who hid them away, putting their own clothes upon them and in some cases ransoming them off. We have heard that about six Chinese who helped the foreigners were killed. From the evidence of many people I think that it was the intention of a good many of the soldiers to kill all the foreigners, though I do not think this was the plan of all the soldiers. They first wanted to get all the money possible from them and then kill them.[3]*

The Magee family traveled again to Japan for a period of time, where Christopher Walford Magee was born on August 19, 1928. In late 1928 all three of the Magee boys were sick, diagnosed with pertussis, otherwise known as whooping cough. Bronchial ailments would follow the boys through their lives, especially while young.

Events in eastern China started heating up again in 1931. Japan, starved of natural resources, restarted its imperialist drive. The invasion of Manchuria, starting on September 19, 1931, was just the beginning. Magee Sr. must have understood, perhaps more clearly than many others, what this particular event heralded. Taking action, he made arrangements for his wife and three sons to travel to England with the intent of leaving the boys there.

John Magee Sr. would stay in China and tend his Chinese flock the best he could. As events would prove, John Magee Sr.'s "best" was nothing less than incredible. In the ensuing years of Japanese invasion and occupation, Magee Sr., along with others, would risk everything to establish the International Safety Zone, thus saving the lives of tens of thousands of Chinese civilians. Using a 16mm movie camera, John Sr. also documented the extreme brutality of the Japanese army, knowing full well that if caught he would forfeit his life. These films, along with letters and the testimony of John Magee Sr. and other witnesses, were used at the post-war trial ("Tokyo Trial"[4]) of accused Japanese soldiers. (There are many videos available on sites such as www.youtube.com which show Magee Sr.'s testimony).

Throughout his stay in China, John Sr. would keep his family apprised of events. These letters form a picture of the awful brutality of the Japanese soldiers:

> *They not only killed every prisoner they could find but*
> *also a vast number of ordinary citizens of all ages.... Just the*
> *day before yesterday we saw a poor wretch killed very near*
> *the house where we are living.[5]*

Here is an excerpt from a letter John Jr. wrote to his father in response, dated Sunday, March 20, 1938:

> *You have given me a picture of a Nanking I never knew*
> *and I hope never to see. I have not realized (to date) how*
> *terrible things are out there. I am showing your letter to Mr.*
> *Lyon as he is very anxious to hear about you. It certainly*
> *makes me proud to think of the wonderful work you have*
> *been able to do among the refugees. It is certainly not the*
> *Christian spirit to be revengeful but I cannot help wishing*
> *that something will come along to repay the Japanese for*
> *such brutal, such excessive cruelty, and their horrid manner*
> *of adding insult to injury. Even if I can't say much about your*
> *letter it certainly impressed me very much, and I shall never*
> *forget some of the things you said.*

Up to the present day, the films taken by John Sr. continue to stand as a testament to what happened in China during the grim days preceding World War II, events which some attempted to deny had even occurred. The film *Witness to the Nanking Incident* by Jiro Takidani portrays what John Magee Sr. did during what came to be called the Nanking Massacre. Author Iris Chang wrote *The Rape of Nanking* (Penguin Books, 1997), a book which mentions some of the actions of Magee Sr. and others during the Japanese invasion and occupation of China. The Yale Divinity School contains many of the records, photographs and documents relating to this event.[6]

In getting his children out of China at the end of 1931, John Sr. did what he felt he needed to do, even though it meant that he would be separated from his boys for long periods of time. This separation would have a great effect on the boys, especially John Jr.

## Shanghai, China to Kent, England — November 1931

It might be argued that John Magee, Jr. was mostly Chinese, since China was where he spent nearly half of his life. But that time came to an end during late 1931. According to the November 13th 1931 issue of the newspaper *Singapore Free Press and Mercantile Advertiser*, a "Mrs. J. Magee 3 children and governess" were leaving Shanghai aboard the P&O liner *Naldera* (the Magee's fourth son Frederick Hugh would be born later in England). The ship was headed for "Penang, Columbo, Bombay and Europe."

Nine-year old John was undoubtedly sad at leaving his father behind, but had to be at least somewhat excited to be on another long sea voyage. Traveling south through the Eastern and South China Seas, the ship passed Hong Kong, went around Singapore and then turned north. The ship transited the Suez Canal and found its way into the Mediterranean Sea. The Magee family disembarked in Marseilles, France, headed for the northern shore and departed from the French town of Dunkirk. Crossing the Channel and landing at Dover, England, Faith Magee and her boys travel the remaining short distance to the Backhouse family home named "Foxburrow" near Kingsdown in Deal.

Baby John's First Birthday Party, June 9th, 1923.

American Church Mission,
Hsiakwan,
Nanking, China,
August, 1923.

Dear *Father & Mother.*

Sea views and sea air are inspiring me to write a letter which I wish
could have been sent off months ago. I love to keep you all in touch
with our work out here, but sometimes it is so hard (I might say impossible) to keep things going and at the same time get letters written.
However, a short time ago we came up to this wonderful holiday resort
of Peitaiho (Chili) where there is every opportunity for rest and recreation,

And what of Baby John? What has he done, and what can he do?
He, too, has certainly helped, by drawing his mother closer to these loving
Chinese mother-hearts, and by his happy laugh and baby ways with those
who have come to see him and us.

I cannot close without loving thanks to the many who are praying
for us, and for the work in Hsiakwan. We truly rely on your prayers,
and we know that in answer to them God "is able to do exceeding
abundantly above all that we ask or think."

Yours gratefully,

*Faith B. Magee*

A newsletter from Faith Magee, with a picture of John Jr.
(wearing the hat), and his Chinese family at his first birthday party.

The Magee family in Tsingtao, China.

John at Hillcrest School in Nanking, China.
In the stack, John is in the third row on the left.

[1] Magee Sr. corrects factual errors concerning his son contained in an RCAF press release in a letter to L.M. McKechnie of the RCAF Dept. of National Defense, dated February 2nd, 1942.

[2] http://en.wikipedia.org/wiki/Chinese_Civil_War - accessed 8/10/13.

[3] Letter from John Magee Sr., to his sister Mary.

[4] http://en.wikipedia.org/wiki/Tokyo_Trial –accessed 8/10/13.

[5] http://www.newworldencyclopedia.org/entry/Nanjing_Massacre#cite_note-16 – accessed 4/5/12.

[6] http://www.library.yale.edu/div/Nanking/Magee.html - accessed 8/10/13.

# England — 1931 to 1939

## St. Clare's School—1932–1936

In 1932, Faith, David and Christopher returned to China, leaving John in England to continue his schooling. (John Sr. and Faith Magee decided that primary schooling would be best done in China, where they could keep a closer eye on their younger children, and that England would be the best place for the remainder of their education). And so John resumed his schooling at St. Clare's, a boarding school in Walmer, Kent, just north of Foxburrow, their grandparent's home in Kingsdown.[1]

At St. Clare's, John wasted no time in resuming his boisterous ways, exploding a blank cartridge in the class of a teacher he didn't like and mimicking in public the same teacher (both actions resulted in sound beatings; English schools were generally not tolerant of such actions). The "other", studious and intelligent side of John continued to offset his behavior, though, and it was hard for his teachers to be too hard on the boy.

In family letters, the Magee family stopped referring to John as "Ian" and thereafter he was most often referred to as "John Jr." or "young John." Magee himself signed his early letters (1932) as Ian, but by at least 1937 he was signing them as "John."

Around this time, the Magee family grew again with the addition of Frederick Hugh on August 23rd, 1933. John, who spent most of his time at boarding schools, was never able to become tremendously close to his brothers, with the exception of David. (David returned to England and attended St. Clare's along with John; their closeness was evident throughout the rest of John's life).

In what appeared to be an experiment in living in the United States, John Jr. and his family briefly visited in 1934, where John attended school in Pittsburgh. There are references in some of John's letters to this "failed experiment."[2] John returned to England and the rest of the family went back to China.

John visited his family at Foxburrow often, but it always seemed that he was more of a visitor there than a member of the family. St. Clare's was but the first of several boarding schools that John attended. Headmasters at St. Clare's and Rugby (which he would attend later) served as substitute fathers; at Rugby the wife of the Headmaster also served as a substitute mother. Even John's uncle Edward Backhouse filled in as a parental surrogate at times. John suffered from the lack of a regular family structure, and missed his family while at school. In later years, this lack manifested itself in a continual searching for a family and a home.

Even at the young age of 10, John's qualities made quite an impression on not only the headmaster, but also on his classmates. One of John's best friends at St. Clare's was Robert Dawson, who wrote about John:

> At school, John was an extraordinarily bright student of Latin and Greek.
>
> He [John] may have been a year younger than I was but he was way ahead of me in countless ways... including the pursuit of girls.
>
> One afternoon, during the weekly [boxing] training sessions we had with a retired Sergeant of the Royal Marines, John was put into a one-round session with another boy (as we all were) and he <u>pretended</u> to be knocked out. He fell quite spectacularly to the floor, where he lay spread-eagled on his back... Anyone, who went through the English boarding school system in those days, knows how easily such an original experiment (in what? Psychology?) could have been misinterpreted as "funking." But that never bothered John in the slightest. We chatted about it later and he said he had simply wanted to find out what it felt like to be knocked out. It wasn't a very realistic experiment, of course, because he was not in fact knocked out at all. But the point I want to make is that it was a classic example of John's bold and cavalier disdain for conventional behavior.

John had somehow acquired a dinghy while at St. Clare's. It was characteristic of John that he felt no fear in venturing out by himself into the English Channel. Dawson writes:

*... he [John] would sail it out into the channel on long forays that were infinitely more adventurous than our little bike rides... The channel, as you know, is notoriously and unpredictably rough and it is fair to say that John was literally taking his life in his hands. I'm quite sure he didn't stay close inshore because he once told me that he had tried actually to get across to Cap Gris Nez [note: the closest point to Dover, across the Channel in France] and had to turn back because it got rough and because "it was obviously going to take too bloody long." ... What I'm getting at is that John was a real caballero.*

Decades after attending St. Clare's with John, Robert Dawson continued his reflections:

*Of course, John was a natural aristocrat who didn't need wealth to be "cool" in the presence of it. I use "cool" in the contemporary, American sense: casually composed, completely self-confident. Well, I guess that is the classical meaning, too.*

*We both learned about drinking and something about girls at deb parties but John was an advanced student of both booze and girls... John was brilliant and charming, and surely knew it...*

With regards to certain matters of education, the lack of a present father was apparent. James Vincent (J.V.) Hitchcock, the Headmaster at St. Clare's, wrote to "Mr. Backhouse" (John's Uncle Edward) in March of 1936:

*As to the subject of the Private paper [note: it is not clear what "Private paper" refers to, but it seems clear what the subject might be] — we urge parents to do this themselves, but in cases where parents are abroad or, as not infrequently happens, they are diffident about it, we always make a point of talking quite plainly to the boy & if you would like us to do so, we most certainly will talk frankly with John…*

Perhaps "the talk" was never accomplished. The following year, Rugby's Headmaster Hugh Lyon wrote a similar letter to Colonel Backhouse (John's uncle); this time the subject was clear:

*I had a talk the other day with John on the subject of sex. He was very interested and appreciative, & I think knew very little. He clearly has the right attitude towards the whole question, and will I am sure keep his standards high in this as in other things.*

John continued his schooling at St. Clare's. Much later, reflecting on John, Headmaster Hitchcock wrote:

*From the earliest days that we knew John Gillespie Magee — in January 1932 — he was always aiming at the stars. At that time he was not in his teens & had not realized that the way was difficult. As his knowledge gradually came to him, he was not deterred, though many a backsliding, many a fall, had to encountered, he climbed.*

Hitchcock seemed to understand John's duality:

*We like to remember John as a younger boy serious and foolish in turn, reading, and reading very well, a Lesson in Chapel and immediately after having to have a lesson read to him, laughing and crying almost in the same breath… What one admired in John was his readiness to admit and, what is more, recognize failings & his effort to overcome it*

*genuinely & not merely to please those in authority.*

John graduated from St. Clare's with flying colors (6th out of 34 graduating boys), and was ready for Rugby. His "percentage marks" were: Latin 83, Math 71, French 83, English 65, and Greek 58. According to Headmaster Hitchcock, "This is really very satisfactory, & his place will give him a good start [at Rugby]."

## Rugby — 1936 to 1939

In 1936 Magee started at the venerable Rugby School in Warwickshire. Formed in 1567, Rugby was instrumental in producing the standards for a "Victorian Gentleman."[3]

Rugby, the game, is named after the school. There is an anecdotal tale concerning William Webb who, according to the story, invented the game.

The school at Rugby is comprised of several "Houses." Magee stayed at School House, which is still there today. When John attended, Rugby was an all-male school.

John adapted quickly to Rugby. He started reading and writing poetry, which lead him to Rupert Brooke. (Or perhaps it was the other way around. Brooke, being a local legend, may well have inspired John to write more poetry.) Brooke had attended Rugby 36 years before John arrived (Rupert Brooke was born in the town of Rugby, with a father who was also a Rugby schoolmaster). The influence of Brooke is evident in much of John's poetry. One of John's poems (*Sonnet to Rupert Brooke*) was dedicated to him (Brooke died due to septicemia in 1915). Douglas Eves, a friend of John's at Rugby, wrote:

> *John was a fecund and productive poet but most of his*
>
> *work at School was influenced more by Rupert Brooke than*
>
> *by the harsher realism of the school of Auden, Spender,*
>
> *MacNiece and Day Lewis.*
>
> *After all, we were nurtured and educated in the self*
>
> *same scene and surroundings as Brooke, and his [Brooke's]*
>
> *photograph and a facsimile of the MS of The Soldier was*

*placed near the entrance of the Library and caught our*

*attention whenever we left.*

Another person who would have a significant impact on John's life at Rugby was Hugh Lyon (aka P.H.B. Lyon, or Percy Hugh Beverley Lyon). Lyon was a military veteran, poet, and had been Headmaster at Rugby School since 1931. John and Hugh would form a strong bond that would last for the rest of Magee's life. In a way, Lyon could relate well to Magee, having been born in India and shipped to England at age nine for his schooling. John could not have had a better mentor than Hugh Lyon. John was so comfortable with Lyon that he often called him by his first name, "Hugh," much to the consternation of John's elders.

Hugh Lyon had several children; one of them was to have a tremendous influence on John Magee. Elinor Lyon was older than John, but not by much. She was herself a fledgling poet, and it was to John that she showed some of her earliest poems. Since Elinor was the daughter of the Headmaster of an all-boy school, it is not surprising that John fell for Elinor; probably many of the boys did.

The Lyon family would take the boys to family picnics and outings, so there was plenty of opportunity for John to take more and more notice of Elinor. One such holiday outing was in the summer of 1938, taken at Robin Hood's Bay. Hugh and his wife Nan had rented Fyling Hall School, located on the moors near the beautiful Yorkshire coast (the school still exists there today). The Lyons invited their entire family, along with several groups of boys from Rugby. John was present during one of those trips, and undoubtedly enjoyed being close to Elinor.

Rugby would be considered a "prep" school (roughly equivalent to a high school in the United States) for English boys wishing to attend Oxford or Cambridge. John would stay there during the school year, same as he had when he had attended St. Clare's, visiting home during holidays. There was plenty to fill John's days, both academically and athletically.

A quick learner, Magee found out where the lines were that he could not cross, both at school and at home. Though he seemed to calm down a bit as he got older, he still had the occasional misadventure. However, his likeability and scholastic achievements combined to serve as effective countermeasures to getting into truly deep trouble.

While at Rugby, John continued his letters to his family. Just after starting at Rugby, he writes on School House stationery (wherever he went, John would try to write or type his letters on nice stationery, preferably personalized):

*The subjects I am taking for the School Certificate are:—French, English, Math, Latin, Greek, History, and Scripture. Of course, there are several papers on each subject — about 20 altogether. I may have to drop off the Scripture at the end, as I have such a lot to read up (particularly Roman History 14 AD to 83 and English 1485 — 1714).*

John enjoyed being at Rugby in the beginning. In his later years, he started becoming discontent with the course that seemed to be shaping up for him. Adding to his disquiet were the events on the European continent; war appeared to be coming back. The Great War had just ended in 1918, only 20 years prior. Even though John was too young to remember what turned out to be the First World War, the British wouldn't soon be forgetting those events, and young people were reminded by the many wounded survivors of the price paid by their forebearers in that conflict. John began questioning what exactly life was all about; was the purpose of life to attend school, become a merchant, and have business rule his life, or was there a different course for him?

Throughout this time, John would continue writing to his family, keeping them up to date. On October 26th, 1937, John wrote to his father:

*Every day I read of bombing attacks on Nanking, and hope you are safe & sound. Have any bombs landed in the compound? I hope you got into a bomb-proof shelter or something during the attacks. I don't know what the outcome of all this will be but I certainly hope it will end soon!*

*I ... am now in the Upper Fifth [approximately 11th grade in America]. I shall try for the School Certificate this term — it should not be very difficult. I have not yet decided what subjects I am going to take, but hope to get the matriculation as well.*

Rugby students and teachers discussed the rise of Adolf Hitler and the Third Reich. In general, the boys knew what it meant; they knew that war was likely to come again, and that they would more than likely be involved. A sort of fatalistic hold took place on Magee. It was at that time that he began to feel that he wouldn't live long. John shared these thoughts and feelings with his teachers, fellow students and, via letters, his family. His poetry also reflected his questions and growing concerns.

Growing up with missionary parents, John had developed strong views on religion. He concluded that killing was wrong, and that if war did come, he would serve by joining the Pacifist Corps. John felt that this was what Christ would have wanted, that not killing his fellow man was the ultimate expression of Christianity. The senior Magee agreed with John in principle, if not in fact. Faith Magee, however, believed that fighting for a cause was not in conflict with Christianity. Faith's brothers were serving in the British Army, so Faith understood what the fight was about, and had seemingly come to terms with the paradox — that taking the life of another in a righteous war was compatible with her Christian faith.

John had to have been somewhat conflicted. In his third year at Rugby, his grades began to slip. He started losing interest in his studies; if he and his generation were to be drawn into the war and likely killed, what was the point of education?  Why take time away from enjoying some of the beauty of life, while he could?  John, at age 16, poured out his feelings in his poetry and letters to friends and family:

*Now is the time that a boy sees life at its best, untainted by the sordidness of age. Then why can't he have time to enjoy the beauties of bird, beast, and flower?  If I were to die tomorrow, how much of Beauty would I have seen?  Pathetically little. When I shall probably never be more appreciative, more happy, more able to see a thing in its natural beauty, without having to think of its position with regard to 'autres choses', its significance in life, etc. And how do I spend my time?  Sitting before a pile of books and trying to concentrate on Demosthenes to the exclusion of all the thrills I might have at beholding something beautiful, something real, something natural. School consists of the worship of man and the things he has made; his books, his letters, his thoughts. Plenty of time, we say for Beauty afterwards. Suppose there is no 'afterwards'?*

Prophetic words. And strong thoughts for a boy of sixteen. Even at this age, John had a gift for expressing himself, and often his letters would reference other poetic and literary works (above, in passing, John references Demosthenes, the Greek orator and statesman, as well as phrases from other languages such as 'autres choses,' which is French for 'other things').

John's thoughts, questions and feelings all came boiling out in a torrent of words. Throughout his entire life, Magee would question so much, not take anything for granted, and try to dig out the essentials. John would question his friends, teachers, faculty, always trying to arrive at a good understanding of whatever was occupying his mind at the moment.

In his quest to know his own mind, John would document the process via his writings. Like his father, John turned into a prolific writer of letters, sending them to his family and friends. John was extremely verbose, sometimes describing in great detail his experiences, thoughts and feelings. Sometimes John would tell different versions of the same experience, depending on who his audience was, and was not above embellishing certain events.

In 1939, during the spring break at Rugby, John was invited to a "Reading Group" hosted by a professor at Cambridge's Trinity College, The Reverend Charles Franklin Angus. The meeting was held in the village of Mortehoe, Wales, a scenic village located about 200 miles from Rugby.

The others in the group were students at Cambridge, and all older than John. However, John was accepted as an equal, and quite possibly for the first time in his life, John could speak his full mind and be seriously considered. In a way, this was John's "intellectual" high flight.[4]

At the very start of this vacation, John developed a close friendship with Geoffrey Sergeant from South Africa. Both of them would visit rocky Morte Point, with its breathtaking vista of the coast and the ocean, and hold long, in-depth conversations. On Easter Sunday the boys attended the Communion Service at the Parish Church of St. Mary Mortehoe.[5]

One of the many things that Geoffrey, John, and the rest of the reading group discussed was the seemingly inevitable war that was coming and what part they would play in it. In this rarefied atmosphere, it seemed to John that the Christian ideal was to act as Christ might act, to be a pacifist and not to kill his fellow man.

Throughout his life, John was somewhat of a chameleon, adapting to and taking on the colors of his environment. Most likely, in the company of several idealistic young men at Mortehoe, John did feel that he *should* be a pacifist, and he most likely shared that view with the reading group. However, it is doubtful that John, at heart, truly felt that way. At least part of him understood that there might come a time when he, John Magee, would be called to serve, and that he would go. He had previously enrolled in the Officers Training Corps (O.T.C.) at Rugby, complete with rifle and gas attack practice, and had certainly been interested in the Royal Air Force. John wrote his father in March of 1938:

> I have passed my preliminary shooting test and aim to
>
> fire on an open range (.303) at Warwick for the first time
>
> next Thursday, which I am, of course, looking forward to very
>
> much indeed.

Apparently the OTC took its job seriously, providing, among other subjects, an introduction to several types of poison gas. John continues in the letter to his father:

> Yesterday the 'Intelligence Section' of the O.T.C.
>
> [Officer's Training Corps] of which I am a member (it is
>
> reserved exclusively for the intelligentsia!) had to attend a
>
> demonstration at the Rugby A.R.P Centre[6], during which we
>
> all had to go into a gas chamber, but none of us believed
>
> there was any gas in there until we were made to go in
>
> without our masks! The room was filled with Tear Gas — a
>
> more persistent gas, and there was enough gas in that room
>
> to 'lay out' 50 people — it was quite a large room, and it had
>
> all come from a minute fluid about this size [about ¾"] —
>
> which brought home to me more than ever the horrors of
>
> warfare. We also had a 'whiff' of mustard gas, various

*'arsenic smoke gas'* — *phosgene, chlorine, and, lastly, the most dangerous of them all—Lewisite. It smelt of geraniums.*

John's dual nature found no contradiction in trying to simultaneously be a "true" Christian and also preparing for war. He saw the benefit of both approaches, and could live in both worlds.

## Poetry Prize

Inspired by his time at Mortehoe with the reading group and in conversations with Geoffrey Sergeant, John finished his poem, *Brave New World*. This poem won John the prestigious Rugby Poetry Prize, the same prize won by John's idol Rupert Brooke 34 years before.

In a letter dated July 20th, 1939, Magee Sr. wrote to his son with some comments about the poem:

> *The prize poem and the latest issue of the New Rugbeian came several days ago and I thank you for sending both. I found both very interesting, and was especially interested in the prize poem which somewhat astonished me. It is certainly the most ambitious thing you have ever done along this line, and showed a real development on your part, showing powers that I hardly realized you possessed.*
>
> *The whole thing showed a wealth of imagination, not only in the many figures and thoughts in individual lines but in the concept as a whole. There is real beauty of diction and a depth of feeling that show you have it in you to be a poet. Your portrayal of the mood of disillusionment, so common in life and even in youth, is very good. And the thing that makes me so happy about it is that you have a really constructive, positive message at the end. I remember one of the conversations I had with you at Foxburrow, when I was urging you to be constructive in all that you should write and not be merely clever; that the world was full of clever writers*

*who were not contributing anything to the real problems of man, if anything the reverse. If you keep on this positive, constructive note, you will have an increasing joy in your work and will bring happiness to others as well. I rejoice that you were able to produce this unusual work, and think it should be an encouragement to you to keep on with your writing.*

John had gotten praise for his *Brave New World*, both in public (Poetry Prize) and in private (letters from his father and encouragement from Hugh Lyon). However, this was not enough to reignite the spark he once felt in attending Rugby.

The stage was set for the next chapter in John's life, one that would forever alter his life's journey.

St. Clare's School Picture — 1935.
John is fourth from the left, right behind the staff.

John at St. Clare's.

Magee family picture, 1934.

John while at St. Clare's.

John with James V. Hitchcock,
Headmaster at St. Clare's.

*Taken at the Spa Hotel, Tunbridge Wells by Aunt Mary, 1937.*

*After croquet at Tunbridge Wells.*

John and David Magee, Tumbridge Wells,
near Kent, England, 1937. (From John's photo album).
(Note the airplane that David is holding.)

Magee family Christmas card,
from John Magee Jr.'s photo album.

John, on the right, with the Lyon Family and others
on a vacation in the Lake District.
Photo is from John's album with a note at the bottom:
"Udge", Arthur, "Dandy", Aunty Nam [Hugh Lyon's wife], "Babe", Uncle Hugh,
Bar, Dermott, Ennor [John's name for Elinor], Michael, Self.

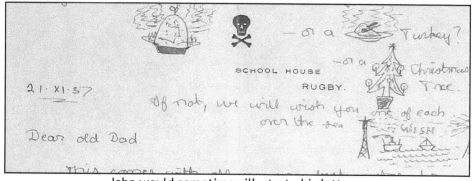

John would sometimes illustrate his letters.
This is the heading of a November 1937 letter to his father.

Ennor, Dermott, Sill, Ban. (Windermere)

John, Dermott Magill, and Elinor Lyon.
Photos are from John's photo album.

School House, Rugby

Rugby Chapel

No. 3 Dormitory at Rugby.
From John's photo album.

John, stylish as always.

John showing his mother his Poetry Prize, won at Rugby for his poem, "Brave New World." Speech Day, 1939.

John and friend Dermott Magill in a Rugby class picture.

All pictures this page are from: John G. Magee Family Papers, Record Group No. 242, Special Collections, Yale Divinity School Library

John on the Mortehoe Downs, Easter, 1939.

[1] http://www.walmerweb.co.uk/history/history-upperwalmer-1920s-1930s.html – accessed 3/5/12.

[2] Letter from John to his family dated February 15th 1940:
"Dad has written suggesting the possibility of his returning soon to make a home for us in America. Do you remember our last visit there as a family? It is not exactly a very happy memory for any of us…
… there was something the matter with all of us. Life in a big city, where virtue is the number of cars one possesses and Love is wanting, never did and never will suit us. We have lived simply, and with the exception of some moments, have at times been almost divinely happy. We are simple people,–and are cut out for a simple life."

[3] http://en.wikipedia.org/wiki/Rugby_School–accessed 3/5/12.

[4] Mortehoe is not far from Llandow, about 35 miles as the bird flies. Llandow is where Pilot Officer Magee would, a couple of years later, take off on the flight that would inspire the writing of his sonnet "High Flight." It is quite possible that Magee flew over Mortehoe during that flight which could have provided additional inspiration.

[5] St. Mary's Church has been around since the Norman times. A table-tomb of a church rector is dated 1322. http://en.wikipedia.org/wiki/Mortehoe–accessed 3/5/12.

[6] Air Raid Precautions (ARP) Centre–
http://en.wikipedia.org/wiki/Air_Raid_Precautions–accessed 5/12/12.

# United States — 1939 to 1940

## England to the United States—Summer 1939

At Rugby, the 1938-1939 school year finally came to an end. There were successes and high points during the year, but John seemed increasingly disenchanted with the entire educational process. What was the point? The world was headed for another war; that much was clear. John believed that many of his generation would not have long to live; considering what had happened just a few short years before, John and his contemporaries might have had many reasons to believe this.

John's poetry reflected his feelings. Even his Rugby Poetry Prize winning poem, *Brave New World* was somewhat melancholy. And what of his feelings for Elinor? She continued to be as elusive as ever, remaining a friend and nothing more. John remained hopeful, though, since the Lyon family had invited John to accompany them on a trip to Scotland during the upcoming summer.

It was in this atmosphere that John's parents suggested that he take a break; travel to the United States for the summer, get better acquainted with his American relatives, then come back refreshed for his final year at Rugby. (This would not be the first time John had visited America; he had done so at least twice before, once in 1925-1926 when he was three and again in 1934, at age 12.)

In addition, Magee's Aunt Mary had set her sights on getting the younger Magee back into the American fold. It is probable that the Magee family had still not quite recovered from Magee Sr.'s moving overseas as a missionary; here was an opportunity to at least get one of his sons back. She offered to fund the trip, for both John and one or two of his friends. Apparently the offer was sufficient to change John's mind.

Aunt Mary wrote to John's father:

> *After writing you the other day that he had decided not to come to America, I received a letter from him. I immediately cabled him to come and bring his friends, and I am really perfectly delighted to have them. [I am] glad that they are landing in New York instead of Boston. It is a much more impressive way to arrive in America for anyone making his first trip. We shall see the [World's] Fair before starting to New England.*

Indeed, it would be a good time to visit the States, since the 1939-1940 World's Fair in New York was underway. And John clearly needed a change of pace. Though reluctant at first, John agreed to travel to the U.S., fully believing that he would return to Rugby in the fall to complete his course of study. Little did John know that it would be nearly two long years full of trials and tribulations before he would return to England.

For unknown reasons, John's U.S. passport was cancelled on July 21st, 1939, in England. As an American citizen, John could legally enter the United States, but would need a passport/visa to return to England. The Neutrality Laws in the United States were becoming more prominent and were likely to be enforced more frequently as war came to Britain.

The journey to America was made aboard the R.M.S. Queen Mary[1], departing Southampton, England, on August 2nd, 1939 and arriving in New York on August 7th. Accompanying John on the trip was his good friend from Rugby, Dermott Magill. On the trip, John apparently completely immersed himself in the company of several attractive young ladies; Elinor, it seemed, was a case of "out of sight, out of mind." He arrived in New York and had to have thoroughly enjoyed the World's Fair.

John spent the month of August with family friends (the Corcoran's) on Martha's Vineyard. Once again, Magee had his affections captured by several local girls. John pursued them with such vigor that his Aunt Mary wrote to Magee Sr.:

> When I arrived I was quite amused to learn that Johnny and Dermott were spending their entire time at Edgartown with the young Lasell girl. You had mentioned you wanted John to be sure to meet Mr. and Mrs. Remington and believe me he has fallen <u>desperately</u> in love with the girl. It all amuses me very much when I consider how worried you and Faith were about the girl in England and he has fallen for every girl he has met here.

After Martha's Vineyard, Dermott returned to England, and John traveled with his Aunt Mary to New Haven, Connecticut, and on to Pittsburgh.

While staying in Pittsburgh with his Aunt Mary, John had the opportunity to visit the exclusive Rolling Rock Club[2] several times. The Rolling Rock Club, located about 50 miles outside of Pittsburgh, belonged at that point in time to the Mellon family (which was part of the extended

Magee family).[3] It was at this club where John would be exposed to what could be considered "American royalty." During the summer of 1939, John rubbed shoulders with the children of the powerful and wealthy. For perhaps the first time, he was exposed to the reality of what money could do. It had to be a huge cultural shock, coming from an England that was facing a war to an America that was doing its best to ignore that very same war.

For a while, John joined wholeheartedly in the fun, glitter and excitement. His Pittsburgh family had to be excited to have John back in the fold. The extended Magee family boasted its share of wealthy and influential people in Pennsylvania, and Aunt Mary seemed determined to have John meet all of them.

While in Pittsburgh, Magee Jr. and his uncle James McDevitt Magee (a former pilot during WWI) undoubtedly had many discussions about flying and aerial combat, adding a dose of realism to the flying movies that Magee Jr. had seen, such as *Dawn Patrol* and *Hell's Angels*.

As John's passport had been cancelled in England before he left, and since he was an American citizen, he required a visa to return to England in order to complete his final year at Rugby. Due to the neutrality laws that had gone into effect barring American citizens from entering war zones designated by the President, Magee's visa application was summarily rejected by the U.S. State Department.

This turn of events must have upset John's plans considerably, for he was beginning to tire of the fun and games in the United States, as well as becoming increasingly concerned about events back in England and Europe. Hitler had begun his quest for world domination in earnest, and if England was not first on the list of countries to be conquered, it surely was not going to be the last.

John was certainly listening to the radio news broadcasts and watching the newsreel footage at the movie theaters. John had an insight as to what was happening in Europe that most Americans did not have. The United States, by and large, did not want to get drawn into another disastrous European conflict; over 116,000 Americans had been lost in the Great War, the "war to end all wars." Luminaries such as Charles Lindbergh were outspoken in their opposition to U.S. involvement; Lindbergh truly did not feel that England had a chance against the Nazis, especially in the arena of aerial combat.

With his return to England seemingly barred, John was coming to realize that he might be stuck in America, against his wishes. His family was sympathetic, but what could they do? It was not them, after all, preventing his return; it was the Neutrality Laws and the U.S. State

Department that were standing in his way. But since John was stranded, he felt he might as well make the best of a bad situation.

Through family contacts, a place was found for John at the all-boy Avon Old Farms School near Hartford, Connecticut (about 45 miles from Yale); here John could finish up what would have been his final year at Rugby. As Rugby was a prelude to schools such as Oxford and Cambridge, Avon was a prep school for college, especially nearby Yale.

## Avon Old Farms School—Fall 1939 to Summer 1940

Thanks to his Aunt Mary, in the fall of 1939 Magee started classes at Avon. It seems that John was ill-suited to an American school. At 17 years old, he was near six feet tall, spoke with a decidedly English accent, and could read Latin like it was the morning newspaper. At Rugby, John had learned Greek, Latin, the classics, and other subjects that were just not emphasized in the U.S. at that time. At Avon, he was referred to as a "peacock among pigeons." Life could not have been very comfortable for John, due to his somewhat peculiar ways.

However, there were some bright spots; in his own way, Magee found a way to endear himself to his fellow students. Brooks Stabler recalls:

> Magee and a chosen group of four or five used to do
> their Latin together during free periods. Magee would say,
> "Well, what have we today?" They would hand him the
> assignment in Latin, which he would proceed to read at sight
> in easy, perfect English, and the rest of the period would be
> spent in cheerful bull sessions or discussing semantics or
> whatever they were interested in at the moment.

Academically, there was at least one subject that Magee had more trouble with than others. He writes to his Aunt Mary:

> Year exams coming up in about two weeks and I am
> having to do a great deal of work in my spare time —
> particularly in American History, in which I am handicapped
> in that I have never done it before.

In fact, John was more comfortable with his teachers than with his fellow students. Brooks Stabler, Avon Provost during the time John attended, recalls:

> *He [John] used to solace himself by going frequently to the room of one of the masters, where he would drink China tea and read the master's books. The tea, he said, connected him with his early days in China and with the time he spent at Rugby.*

In the above quote, Stabler may have been referring to art instructor, Paul Child, a worldly and well-traveled man. Stabler goes continues to describe John:

> *This master's impression of Magee was one of charm; the boy had a humorous, twinkling eye, exceptionally good manners; he liked to talk about philosophy and religion, and later in the year about girls...*

Yes, life at Avon was not without its charms. John continued to enjoy American girls, and explained one particular dilemma in a letter to his Aunt Mary:

> *Well, anticipation fills the heart of every Avonian as the week-end, and the subsequent school dance draws near.*
> *I still don't know whom I am going to have to the dance. Possibly Misty Anderson (from Miss Porter) or Roberta Martin (also from M.P.S.) — or again, alternatively, Sue Smith, whom I invited to the dance last term.[4]*

"Miss Porter's School" is an all-girl school located in Farmington, CT, only five miles from Avon (this school, along with Avon Old Farms School, still exist in the same locations as they were in 1940). John dated some of the girls there, including a Miss Peggy Gould (John would dedicate one of his Poetry books to Peggy.[5])

Provost Stabler recalls an incident involving John:

> *After one of the school winter dances, Magee climbed*
> *a tall tree to rescue a cat; before he had come down out of*
> *the tree, there was a circle of admiring and exclaiming girls*
> *watching him from the ground; it is possible that his first*
> *taste for being a hero came with this incident.*

John was called to account for some of his extravagant spending while at Rolling Rock the previous summer. He was apparently guilty of going to every hunt, ride, party, and dance that he was invited to, not realizing that these events were being put on Aunt Mary's bill. (Or perhaps John did actually realize it, but chose to ignore it.)

In a letter to his father, John tries to explain:

> *... you [John Sr.] speak of my causality. I agree with you*
> *that this is going to be one of the major difficulties of my life.*
> *I don't know <u>why</u> I should have this trait, or where it came*
> *from — my up-bringing was rigorous and fine — at any rate*
> *up till the time when I was left in England on my own.*
> *Perhaps that was the time I grew careless in this regard.[6]*

In this (and other letters) John alludes to the fact that he felt somewhat abandoned being left at boarding schools, and that his less than desirable actions might be chalked up to this.

In one particular letter to his father, written on January 21st, 1940, John launches into a five-page explanation of what his feelings are relative to America and England, as well as John's attitude toward religion. The letter ranges far and wide, and is a quite amazing product coming from a 17 year old teenager:

> *My Dear Dad;*
>
> *... I am settling down on a Sunday afternoon with a*
> *pipe to tell you something of myself...  I will try to answer*
> *each paragraph in order or I will never get straightened out...*

The letter is in response to one sent to him by his father, which talks about some of the expenditures incurred by John during the previous summer. Magee Sr. also expounded at some length about the virtues of America versus England. It is notable that John feels comfortable enough with his father to express himself freely:

> ... you go on to speak of the relative virtues of American and English education; I agree with much of what you have to say; that this country is far, far more democratic, both Idealistically and also Practically, than any other country in the world, including England; I concur with that most heartily, from what I have seen of this country so far.

Magee goes on to address other statements made by his father:

> I quote [from the letter Magee Sr. had written]: "In America... we are in advance of England along technical education and in many branches of applied science and in the important field of medicine. I want you to learn to appreciate this..." Now of course I am ready to appreciate, objectively, facts in trying to persuade me that America is the right place for me in which to finish my education; but I could very easily riposte with the statement that England preserves everything which holds both intellectual interest and spiritual attachment for me (by that term I mean 'personal' rather than 'godly').

In the next few lines, John explains exactly why he feels compelled to return to England:

> It was there [England] that I developed, as you know, an impassioned love for poetry, which was accompanied by a sort of awakening of interest in life, and people, and things, that I had never known before; this could, I suppose be

*ascribed rather to the fact of adolescence than to its environment, but I know, deep down, where it hurts to know, that I must go back to find that certain stimulus, in which I find this country [America], though it be Great and Noble and Up-to-date, and though it holds Wealth and Prosperity and Democracy, and everything else that is considered conventionally to be Fine and Virile — in fact, all the qualities which historians declare as being the Great Essentials of a Great Nation, etc., but, to be perfectly frank with you, none of these are what I am looking for in life. American Interests in general do not lie where mine do, and I say that not only because I have been here six months and met a pretty fair cross-section, I think, of American Life, but also because I find myself to be particularly sensitive to people and surroundings, more so, perhaps, than you will ever know.*

In this extraordinary letter, John then invokes Plato and Socrates to explain his views about religion. John truly starts lecturing his father, with much of the last part of this letter reading more like a scholastic term paper:

*To express myself properly I must revert to Plato, who says that a man's first duty is toward the Tendance of his Soul. We should, by reading, thinking, and conversing with people of his intellectual choice, think out for himself the most profitable way to live (profitable, of course, for his soul). (Here let me insert that I am not still arguing for England versus America, but am trying to show you my attitude toward Religion — my religion, of which there is, I think, possibly, but by no means certainly, more across the Atlantic).*

*Thinking, he says, is the essential thing. I quote:*

*"Must it not then be by reasoning, if at all, that any of the things that really are become known to it (the soul)?"*

*"Yes"*

*"And surely the soul best reasons when none of these things disturb it — neither hearing, nor sight, nor pain, nor pleasure... (etc.)... but it retires as much as possible within itself, taking leave of its own body and the bodies of those around it, and, as far as it can, not communicating or being in contact with it, it aims at the discovery of that which is (i.e. Reality)..."*

*This is an extract from the Phaedo, perhaps the greatest work on the subject of the soul ever written, as you must know, whether or not you ever read it.*

John goes on to quote the Phaedo some more, laying the groundwork for his conclusions.

*Now I am certainly not endowed with any 'divine reason' — and therefore to my mind the only way for me to live is to think out my best course with regard to the right way to live, and never to allow myself to be satisfied, but to think endlessly in the hopes of attaining a more logical conclusion. (I believe I have something in common there with the Oxford Group Doctrine — don't they say that you should 'start with yourself'?). Goethe would call this "Divine Discontent", which is the term he gave to this continual seeking for the Truth that the Platonic Socrates so urgently advocated..."*

In a passage seemingly written to antagonize his father, Magee continues:

*.... the Christian doctrine speaks of Peace and Contentment; there is something almost defeatist about casting your problems upon the deity, as being things too profound for human solution! —And I <u>cannot believe</u> that God has a plan by which our lives are so regulated and pre-ordained that all we have to do is to approach Him in the submissive spirit, and ask Him to reveal it to us; and I cannot say that I <u>want</u> to particularly find 'peace of God which passeth all understanding' for according to Goethe 'Peace and Contentment are Death' — or, as Nietzsche wrote: "If you have not chaos in your mind, you cannot give birth to a dancing star" Remember that it was Chaos from which the world was created!*

Continuing his diatribe against established religion, John goes on to quote from Browning, Faust, Goethe, and others. It is unclear what John is trying to accomplish in one of his last paragraphs, for it seems the very antithesis of what his father believes in:

*Another point about the Christian Faith: it has undergone the most amazing metamorphosis since Christ began it....*

*So many people are quite content to go regularly, or irregularly, to Church, as the case may be, and listen for half an hour to some member of the clergy set down for them his particular interpretation of the Gospel, and imagine that it is thus that they will find Immortality, or whatever it is that they may be looking for. Rather I think the deity will consign these to damnation before all the murderers of this world...*

Towards the end of this letter John seems to attempt an overall explanation of what he had written:

*I don't know what your reactions will be to this letter. I don't want you to think it is easy for me to cast aside the traditions of my upbringing, as it must seem to you that I am doing; but I want you to believe that these problems have been in my mind for a long time, and this is the first opportunity I have had to write about them....*

*Let me conclude by saying that, though I do not concur with all your views, at any rate I respect them, and the greatest thing I respect you for is that you both, above all else, have the courage of your convictions — your whole lives testify gloriously to that; and I feel that it has been a bit of a victory for me to be able to come out before you, with all your experience, and express myself freely, rather than if I had just sat back and accepted all you might say. Open discussion never harmed a subject, whether religion or the Best Method of Raising Newts in a Goldfish Bowl!*

*Much Love, John.*

In a somewhat similar letter to his mother written about the same time as the above letter, John tries again to explain himself and his actions:

*... I have just dispatched a long letter to Dad giving him all my thoughts about returning to England. I have talked to Dr. Kammerer[7] on the subject, but cannot help feeling that life here is sort of a regression to what I had at Rugby; the work is trifling compared to what was done there, and though it is possible to go beyond what is being taught to a certain extent on one's own it is hard to effect anything worthwhile without either a definite goal or supervision of any kind; I suppose the Yale Examination, for which I am provisionally working, is a sort of a goal; but it is the*

*American equivalent of School Certificate in England, which I took a good two years ago; and I am finding it rather hard to believe in myself; Of course, I am deriving certain enjoyment from the strangeness of life over here, but that is not everything; as far as I can see I am just wallowing in a sort of intellectual backwater after the rushing stream of Rugby...*

Magee explains what happened during his last term at Rugby. At Rugby he had decided to do things *his* way in true John Magee fashion:

*I never explained to you with regard to my last term at Rugby; I had for some time been a little dissatisfied with the system at Rugby, whereby everyone worked for material reward, whether it be in the shape of a prize for good work; or a high mark; or a move into the next form; that seemed to me to be wrong, so in true Faustian spirit I decided to renounce that system and work for what I considered to be my own good, without regard for the competition of others; of course if I had known it was to be my last term there I would not have done it; and it was not a very great success; but I feel that I profited by the experiment.*

In this letter to his mother, John expresses his dilemma and confusion:

*I just wanted you to know that I am rather worried as to whether or not I am doing the right thing over here; even if I return to England I have neither the desire nor the ability to join up, as I am an American citizen; all I want to do is to find my kindred spirits, of which this country has, as yet, yielded none!*

At the end of John's letter, he seems to arrive at a conclusion. He misses his mother, wants to help her, and desperately wants to return to the land that he loves:

> But I want you to know that there will always be moments like this, when I am thinking of you remorsefully. Particularly at this moment, as I am feeling terribly homesick for you. I want to cry out to everyone here that I love you, and want to get back to your side. I think you will find me changed in some ways. I have had a good time. Now I want to see you have a good time, and I am so longing to get back to help out. I know things are twice as difficult as they are for me. And for that very reason I shall never be really happy over here. Don't you believe a man should live by his convictions? I am convinced that my place is in England, and if ever I see the opportunity, *I'm coming*. Much love to you, dearest Mother — John

At this time, reality intrudes upon John's wishes. Since it was not clear when, if ever, John would be able to return to England, he was persuaded by his parents and the staff at Avon to take the Yale admittance exams. It is not surprising that some accounts say that John Magee achieved the highest scores ever recorded for the Classics portion.

Whether or not John would have been given a scholarship to Yale without the influence of his father and uncle is unclear; but the fact is that John was given a very generous scholarship, and was scheduled to start attending Yale as a freshman in September, 1940.

Magee Jr. never stopped looking for a way to return to England, continually applying to the State Department but encountering a stone wall every time. The long dreaded war had finally come to England, and the epic Battle of Britain was being fought during the summer of 1940. Knowing that his family and friends back in England were being bombed on a daily basis was driving John mad. Long gone were his initial pacifist beliefs; the Nazis were threatening Elinor and his friends, and that was not going to stand.

On weekends, Magee and friends visit New York City. Magee sees the movie, "Dawn Patrol," starring Errol Flynn and Basil Rathbone. The movie further inflames his resolve; he becomes convinced that joining the Royal Air Force is the ideal path he should take to break his American exile. Frank Wylie, a classmate of John's at Avon, tells John's father in a letter that the decision to join the RAF came to John while at Avon, and that he (Frank) was one of the first to hear of it:

> … his [John's} great feeling of responsibility or duty,
>
> was his joining the air force. I was with him the day he first
>
> gave it thought…

Avon Provost Stabler gives this account that is consistent with Wylie's:

> One afternoon, after lying on top of a tower for a
>
> couple of hours in the sun, Magee turned to his companion
>
> and suddenly announced, "Well, I think I'll join the R.A.F."

However, the RAF in England was a long way away, and Magee thought he would need to be in England in order to join, even if he could (which was not at all certain). But then, John learns of an alternate path to England: via Canada. If he could manage to join the Royal *Canadian* Air Force and become a pilot, he would almost certainly be sent to England. And it seemed that there were few barriers to this path.

## *Poems* Book

While at Avon, John, with the assistance of Instructor in Printing Max Stein, published a small book of poetry on Avon's Washington Hoe press. A few copies were printed; surviving copies give us a record of what John created.

The process of composing, printing and binding this book was long and arduous. In one of his many letters to Aunt Mary, John wrote about having to get back to the difficult process of binding his book. He anticipated the day when the book would be finished:

> Am again getting to work binding the rest of my books.
>
> What an endless task! When I finish the last one (which is to
>
> be in natural Pigskin!) I shall coin a medal — I haven't

*decided whether it will be gold or silver — which I shall wear*

*on my chest, which will by then have been pushed out 6*

*inches in honor of the occasion!*

Simply named *Poems*, the slim volume contained what John considered his best poetry. The book is very well put together with excellent typography.

The first pages are fairly standard for a book. (All the images below are courtesy of Erl Gould Purnell, and are used with permission. Erl's mother attended Miss Porter's School and dated John. John apparently used his book of poems to impress the girls, and gave Erl's mother a copy.):

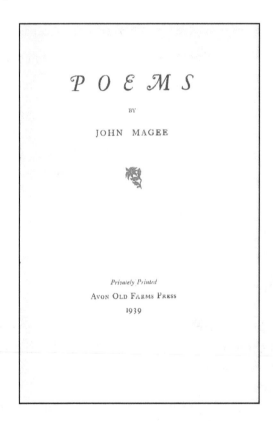

The third page is the most revealing, indicating the person who was the inspiration for many of the poems contained within the book:

*For E. B. L.*

*Forsan et haec olim meminisse iuvabit*

"E.B.L." could only mean Elinor Bruce Lyon; she might have been far away, but clearly was still in John's thoughts. The phrase "Forsan et haec olim meminisse iuvabit" is from *The Aenid*, by Virgil, Book 1, line 203:

*Forsan et haec olim meminisse iuvabit.*
Perhaps, one day, remembering even these things
will bring pleasure.

John's Foreward to the book:

*This little book is thrust upon the world, not as being in*

*any sense a work of art, but rather as a potential object of*

*interest for those of sufficient curiosity to read it; and the*

*sole reason for the publication of these immature verses is*

*that they may possibly be acceptable to the more indulgent*

*as representing various emotional conflicts occurring in the*

*life of a boy between the ages of thirteen and sixteen, and*

*that they may, perhaps, bring back to the reader, if readers*

*there be, something of his or her own youth, when Wonder*

*was fighting for life in the teeth of Pride, and Love lay*

*shivering under the howling winds of adolescent Cynicism.*

John further asks that the reader not be too critical, something that anybody who has written anything has prayed for:

*The fact that I printed them myself, with the invaluable*

*help and advice of Mr. Max Stein, will, I hope, be no great*

*impediment to their acceptability. However, all I ask is that*

*they be read not too critically, and that they be permitted by*

*the Muses to give some pleasure to my contemporaries, but*

*more particularly to those for whom Youth is but a laughing*

*ghost of Long Ago...*

The production value of this little book is quite amazing. In this day of computer-generated fonts and typefaces, it perhaps doesn't seem like much. But back in 1939, it was considerably more difficult to self-publish a book.

It was clear that John wanted to sell the book. In a letter to his mother, John doesn't seem to be very hopeful about his prospects:

*As yet, I have had no opportunity to do anything about*

*getting an option on my insignificant, but extraordinary*

*book of verse. I shall visit a few unsympathetic publishers*

*during my visit to the Big City, who will, no doubt, throw it*

*back in my face. Poetry, I am afraid, has no commercial value*

*unless written for the public. And when I sink as low as that,*

*I shall stop writing it altogether.*

John presents another side of himself in a letter to his Aunt Mary, seeming to hope that his poems will, indeed, have commercial value:

*Mrs. Riddle, the founder of this school [Avon], was very*

*pleased with my book and was very encouraging when I told*

*her I thought of selling it. I am half hoping that she will be willing to do some "string-pulling" with any publishing*

*connections she might happen to have! I am planning to*

*take the book with me when I go to New York and see if I can*

*get an option on it.*[8]

John was never one to pass up opportunity when it presented itself. On a trip to New York, with the help of Charles Meyer, a friend's father, John was actually able to meet with Charles Scribner at Charles Scribner's Sons Publishing. In a letter to his father, John describes what happened during part of his 1940 Spring Break from Avon:

*First of all I went out to Long Island to stay with a*

*school friend, Willet Meyer, where I spent six days. Mr.*

*Charles G. Meyer, his father, is a prominent N.Y. lawyer and*

*a good friend of Charles Scribner to boot. He gave us a letter*

*of introduction to the latter, and I strode in there one*

*morning, feeling utterly minute! He was very nice to me, and*

*treated me with the utmost courtesy. I showed him my book*

*(did you even receive your copy?) and he seemed delighted*

*with it. I left it with him, and spent a very nervous week-*

*end wondering whether or not he would take it.*

John spent not only a "very nervous week-end," but also a few more nervous week-days before getting the word:

*On Tuesday I left for Wallingford ... and it was there*

*that I received final word of the book. In short, he rejected it,*

*saying that he had, however, been very interested in the*

*verses, and would like to have the honor of publishing them*

*for the first time, etc., but that the output of such a small*

*volume would be a pretty expensive affair, and that he*

*couldn't at the moment afford to take the risk on it, and that*

*he could not quite see the way to putting out a large edition.*

The "official" rejection letter from Charles Scribner is succinct and yet encouraging:

> *I have just received a report from our reader on the book of poetry that you left with me, which I am enclosing as that it may interest you even if you do not agree with it. I am sorry that we cannot see our way to making you an offer but I wish to congratulate you again on the lovely piece of typography you did in printing the book.*

Attached to the rejection letter was the review by one of Scribner's "readers:"

> *These poems are skillful and show the feeling of the poet without, in our opinion, being in any way outstanding. They are somewhat immature in mood and technique and, in the sonnets certainly, strongly under the influence of Keats and Rupert Brooke. The influence of Rupert Brooke particularly extends into the other poems, not only in their method but in their substance.*
>
> *There are beautiful lines here and there, and there is always a certain level of craftsmanship. These make the reading of this slim volume very pleasurable. Perhaps if this poet went on with his work he might develop a note of his own.*

"Might develop a note of his own." Indeed.

It seems that Mr. Scribner still would have liked to publish the book, but found it too small to warrant a print run. John writes to his father:

> *However, he [Charles Scribner] wrote me a very nice letter, saying that he would like to have had 'the honor' of*

*publishing it, but it being a <u>small</u> book the cost of output*

*would be very great, etc,. etc.*

Perhaps Mr. Scribner was more impressed with the production of the book itself than by its contents.

John expresses to his father the disappointment he felt and his determination to try again, perhaps next time adding his prize-winning poem "Brave New World" to the mix.

*Of course I was very disappointed, though why I don't*

*know, as I didn't really think he'd take it in the first place!*

*However, the letter he sent should be of some use at a*

*smaller Publishing office. I think before I try it again I'll try*

*and get hold of my 'Brave New World' and put that in with*

*the others, which will more than redouble the size of the*

*book.*

In a letter to his Aunt Mary, John gave a somewhat more abbreviated version of what happened:

*Be it known that I drew a final and totally expected*

*blank at Chas. Scribner's. Not that I really expected any*

*more. (Sour grapes?!!)*

*If, however, I decided to add to it he would be honored*

*if I were to present it to him again. Before I send it up again*

*I think I'll put my 300 line effusion from Eng' [England —*

*"Brave New World"] and put that in too. Of course I'm sort*

*of disappointed, & I feel that I've let you all down, raising*

*your hopes the way I did. Still, I've got to learn how to fail!!!*

John was very proud of *Poems*. He would sign and give copies to friends and, especially, to girls who to whom he wanted to impress. John seems to have totally forgot Elinor, to whom he had dedicated the book. Not long after Magee joined the RCAF, he wrote to Max Stein at Avon, who had helped him publish the book:

*What I want to know is, could you possibly send me*

*two copies of the Book (bound or unbound) with all possible*

*dispatch? I want one for my fiancé[9] and another wherewith*

*to establish myself as a sort of barrack-room poet laureate!*

Later in this book there is a discussion of who this "fiancé" might have been.

## Graduation from Avon Old Farms School

Without a tremendous amount of effort, in June of 1940 John graduates from Avon Old Farms School with honors. He has experienced part of the American school system and has found it wanting. Never seriously challenged at any time while at Avon, John used his spare time to investigate the surrounding areas of New Haven and New York.

John's father attempted to return to the United States from China to witness his son's graduation, but was not able to due to the many demands on his time in China, as well as the distances involved.

(Not long after Magee departed Avon, his teacher and mentor Paul Child also left and joined the U.S. Government's Office of Strategic Services (OSS), eventually arriving in Ceylon. While there, he met Julia McWilliams from Pasadena, California. Paul and Julia were married in 1946, whereupon Julia took on the last name of her husband, thusly making her... Julia Child. *The* Julia Child who would become a famous cook, author, and television personality. In the 2009 movie *Julie and Julia*, Magee's former mentor and friend Paul Child was portrayed by the actor Stanley Tucci, while Meryl Streep played Julia Child.)

## World War II begins — Decision Time

Prior to the Japanese attack on Pearl Harbor, the citizens of the US were polarized about involving the country in yet another war outside American borders. It had been only 20 years since the end of the "War to End All Wars," and it was increasingly apparent that the previous war did not accomplish anything for the average American, and amazingly, the entire process seemed to be happening all over again.

In general, the world was stunned as Nazi Germany began its conquest of Europe, even if this should have been expected after the utter economic and cultural humiliation handed to the German people after WWI at Versailles. Perhaps in denial or holding to a belief that the peace process would avert war, most people did not want to believe that another world-wide conflict was fast approaching.

After the first World War, Germany was plunged into a deep depression, with rampant unemployment and an economy that was near hopeless and indebted. Shrewd leaders such as Adolph Hitler took advantage of this dire situation in their rise to power. Improving the economy, making the trains run on time and giving jobs to a desperate populace were relatively benign acts that began to win over the German people. Even the early military incursions were called annexations or acts of defense; Germany was either defending itself or re-taking what it rightly owned. Over time, the real purpose of world domination was revealed, but the coming war was not started overnight; it was a slow and, to the German populace, natural extension of years of progress since Versailles.

When the Nazis began their overt drive of conquest, it was supported by these many years of secret preparation. This was especially the case with training of the Luftwaffe, Germany's Air Force. Combat aircrew training was done in Russia or under the guise of training for Lufthansa, the commercial airline of Germany.

In 1936, Germany took full advantage of the Spanish Civil War to test new weapons and tactics in support of the fascist Nationalist forces. German fighter pilots and technologists gained invaluable experience in combat operations, experience that would give them a decided edge in the opening stages of the upcoming World War.

On September 1st, 1939, Germany invaded Poland. Britain and France declared war on Germany on the 3rd of September, marking the "official" start of World War II. The British Commonwealth had read the signs more accurately than the German populace and had known that war was likely to come for some time—Britain also knew that much of the war would be fought in the air. Demand for pilots was expected to grow by leaps and bounds, and a place to train them was needed. Locating a proper training-ground for RAF pilots sufficiently far from the upcoming conflict so that training could proceed without interruption and also offered reduced risk of espionage was vitally important. Canada became a natural choice, being one of the oldest dominions in the British Commonwealth and being an ocean away from the brewing conflict in Europe.

Soon the ambitious British Commonwealth Air Training Plan (BCATP) was conceived to train British, Australian, New Zealand and

Canadian pilots in air combat (it was realized from the outset that non-Commonwealth pilots would also be trained).

It was clear from the beginning of the conflict that England would need all manner of assistance from the "neutral" U.S. in order to defend against a highly mobilized and veteran German combat force. While resources such as petrol, steel, armaments and foodstuffs were going to be needed, one of the most vital resources needed would be people, especially trained pilots. However, there were laws that prevented a citizen of the United States from joining the armed forces of another country without forfeiting their citizenship. To circumnavigate this, WWI Canadian ace Billy Bishop (a Canadian national hero) joined forces with American Clayton Knight, a fellow pilot from the Great War. The pair created the Clayton Knight Committee (CKC), and hatched a plan that would recruit pilots from the U.S., train them in Canada, and send them to England as trained pilots.

Of course, at that time this process could not happen in the open. Recruiting for the armed forces of any other country was frowned upon in the U.S., even if the armed forces were Canadian. Billy Bishop and Clayton Knight used their connections to arrange a meeting with President Frankliln Roosevelt in the United States. Roosevelt was sympathetic to the aims of the two men, and gave tacit approval. Though, strictly speaking, what Bishop and Knight wanted to do was against the law, Roosevelt made sure that there would be no enforcement of that particular law.

The CKC set up a recruiting station at New York City's luxurious Waldorf-Astoria Hotel. Fortunately, Bishop and Knight had the support of Homer Smith, another Canadian WWI pilot who had inherited a large amount of money, allowing the group to establish recruiting locations in several major American cities, usually in nice hotels.

Magee was known to travel from Avon to NYC with his friends on weekends, and possibly visited the recruiting station at the Waldorf at some point (John did write at least one letter during his spring 1940 visit to NYC using Waldorf-Astoria stationery). The Committee could not actually directly enlist pilots and would-be pilots into the Royal Canadian Air Force (RCAF) in the U.S., but they could direct them to Ottawa, Canada, where the potential recruits were assured they would be greeted by a support network ready to receive and train them.

Initially, the CKC[10] was specifically looking for men who had actual flying experience, as the RCAF was in desperate need of trained instructors. RCAF standards were not nearly as strict as those of the U.S. Army Air Corps (AAC), so one of the first places the CKC looked was those who had previously applied and been rejected from the AAC. They didn't have to look far. Some who applied were adventure-seekers, some were anxious to join the fight against Hitler, some had washed out of flight training, and some were just plain eager to fly. The RCAF offered the tantalizing possibility of flying two of the most advanced fighter aircraft of the day: the Hawker Hurricane and mythic Supermarine Spitfire.

Flying experience or no, the men who joined were not guaranteed to become RCAF pilots, let alone fighter pilots. They could become ground support or even cooks for the RCAF once deployed. Assuming the recruits passed the qualifications for pilot training, they might not make the grade to advance to training for fighters, and then might be relegated to becoming bomber or cargo pilots. Assuming one was accepted into fighter pilot training, there were many ways to wash out, not least of which was death during training exercises (many were killed during flight training).

Ever more desperate for pilots by summertime of 1940, the RCAF (via the Clayton Knight Committee) was ready to offer "ab initio"[11] pilot training, taking men who had never even been in an aircraft and turning them into pilots. The Battle of Britain was being fought during that summer, and the attrition rate among pilots was staggering. England was on the verge of losing the Battle, not because of a lack of aircraft (aircraft production actually exceeded losses during that summer), but because the Royal Air Force was losing too many trained pilots. As a result, pilot training was reduced to an absolute minimum; which, just like in WWI, gave green fighter pilots a very short life expectancy during aerial combat.

In the previous year, Magee had gone from being a pacifist to earnestly desiring to join the Royal Air Force. During his time in the rarified intellectual atmosphere of Mortehoe, John was drawn into a concept of what he conceived of as pure Christianity: turning the other cheek. He believed that it was wrong to kill a fellow human being for any reason.

Magee's initial pacific tendencies were soon to fade. Whether it was from learning of the horrors that the Nazis were perpetuating throughout Europe, or the excitement of watching such movies as *Dawn Patrol* and Howard Hughes's epic *Hell's Angels*, John Magee Jr. performed an about-face at Avon and committed himself to join the Royal Air Force and enter the fight against Germany. Much like his plans to return to England to finish schooling, this plan was derailed by the U.S. State Department, who told Magee that there was no way he was going to be allowed to travel to England.

After talking to the CKC, it turned out that there was actually a way. There was apparently nothing stopping John from joining the Royal

*Canadian* Air Force, which would almost certainly post him to England. In doing so, John would, in one move, maneuver around both the U.S. government *and* any objection his parents might have.

Magee must have found out about the RCAF recruitment efforts, either through a newspaper ad, an accidental encounter at the Waldorf-Astoria Hotel, or another source. At Avon, John certainly must have made it known that he wanted to return to England, and it is conceivable that a fellow student or Avon faculty member heard about this roundabout way to get to England and passed the information on to John.

Here is an ad that was posted in many newspapers, an ad that would have been certain to catch John's eye:

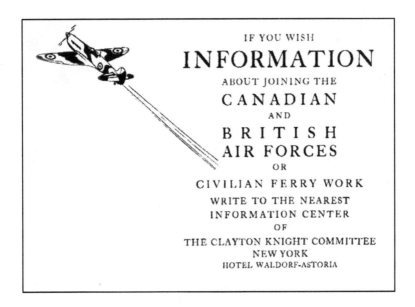

IF YOU WISH
# INFORMATION
ABOUT JOINING THE
## CANADIAN
AND
## BRITISH
## AIR FORCES
OR
CIVILIAN FERRY WORK
WRITE TO THE NEAREST
INFORMATION CENTER
OF
THE CLAYTON KNIGHT COMMITTEE
NEW YORK
HOTEL WALDORF-ASTORIA

When Magee visited the CKC in New York with the possibility in mind of joining up with the RCAF, he was undoubtedly informed that there was no guarantee that he would become a pilot.

It was the summer of 1940. John was at an important crossroad in his life as the Magee family came together at the home of a family friend on Martha's Vineyard. John had graduated from Avon, Mother had brought herself and John's three brothers from England, and on or near John's 18th birthday (June 9th), Magee Sr. had finally returned from China.[12] The reunion, though undoubtedly joyous in many ways, was overshadowed by the conflict engulfing England, Europe and China.

Before the reunion, there had been some trepidation on John's part, knowing that he had to confront his parents with his thoughts and feelings regarding his future.

Even with the personal tumult surrounding him, John did have an enjoyable time with his brothers on the Vineyard. John, the only one of the family with a driver's license, had obtained a car which he had brought to the island. John took his brothers for wild rides, and, for a brief moment on one memorable drive, had his entire family airborne after purposefully zooming over a bump in the road.

It is likely that there was some indecision on the part of John's parents regarding the best route to recommend to their son. Father, recently returned from the horrors of the Japanese invasion of China, had to be thoroughly against sending his eldest son to war. Mother, on the other hand, currently had a brother serving in the British Army, and several generations of her family had also served in the military. (To be fair, members of the Magee family had fought in nearly every conflict in America, before and after the establishment of the United States.)

During that time in the United States, there was an unseen battle being waged for the "hearts and minds" of the American public. There were those who believed it was only a matter of time before the U.S. was drawn into the war. Winston Churchill was desperately anxious for the U.S. to get involved, since England, by itself, could not possibly survive long without help. But the majority of people in the U.S. had been badly affected by the previous world conflict, and had no desire to get involved with another war that didn't seem to directly affect them. In addition, President Roosevelt had, at one point, promised the American people that he would not get the United States involved in another European war:

> "I assure you again and again and again that no American boys
> will be sacrificed on foreign battlefields."
> —Franklin Delano Roosevelt,
>    October 31st, 1940

The opposite was true at Rugby, where the looming war seemed much closer, right across the Channel. All the boys at Rugby sensed that Hitler's dagger was pointed straight at the heart of England, and without an ocean to provide a sense of distance from the growing conflict, there was no escaping it. In the United States, the European wars were more of an abstract concept. Citizens heard about the war indirectly on the radio, saw it in the theaters on the newsreels, and read about it in the newspapers. Many had seen war all too directly during the previous conflict, where many Americans had given their lives.

People were not sure that the U.S. had any business going "over there" in the first place. America was in the grip of isolationism, "Let the Europeans fight about whatever they wanted to fight about, and keep our boys at home," seemed to be the general sentiment. In 1940, most

Americans could not have picked out a place named Pearl Harbor if their lives had depended on it.

John had probably made up his mind that he was going to join the RCAF before the Martha's Vineyard family rendezvous, so he threw himself into making up time with his newly-reunited three brothers. It was also a time for serious discussions with Mother and Father. Even though John might have been able to have joined the RCAF without their permission, he felt it was his responsibility to get their blessing for this important life decision.

It is important to realize just what John Magee's decision meant in the context of the times. That very summer, the Battle of Britain was being waged, and the outcome was still seriously in doubt. All of Europe had fallen to the might of the Nazi Wehrmacht and Luftwaffe, and few believed that tiny England could remain standing. People such as Charles Lindbergh and Joseph Kennedy, the American Ambassador to England, had publicly declared their belief that England would fall, and fall soon. The attack at Pearl Harbor by the Japanese was still a year and a half away, so U.S. involvement in the European war was minimal at that point.

All throughout this summer, daily reports reached the United States public via radio about the progress of the battle. CBS reporter Edward R. Murrow's "This Is London" series of broadcasts brought the fight right into the living room of many Americans. John, with relatives and friends in England, had to be appalled at what he was hearing and seeing in remote America. He often went to the movies, where he saw newsreels which portrayed the conflict, adding an additional dimension to John's horror. Any pacifism remaining in John was burned away after watching Hitler's rampage across Europe.

Even with all this build-up of conflict and emotion to support England, the younger Magee was not completely sure about enlisting in the RCAF. John's father must have used many different arguments against going: there were strict neutrality laws that prohibited American citizens from joining the armed forces of another country (John could possibly lose his American citizenship), and John had already been awarded a scholarship to Yale.

Magee Sr. proposed that perhaps John could take a "wait and see" attitude. He could start at Yale, attend classes for a year, see what became of England, and then decide. This was a compelling choice for young John. He had a wonderful opportunity to attend a great school which, in all likelihood, would manage to challenge him. John's father and Uncle Jim had both attended Yale and would be a great help. And he would have a chance for long-term reunion with his mother, father and brothers.

John's Uncle Jim also had extensive experience for John to consider in making this important decision. James McDevitt Magee had served as an aviator during WWI, and had continued representing aviation during his time in the U.S. Congress. Whether Uncle Jim's input was for or against joining the fight is unknown.

There were other factors of this decision to be considered. During the Battle of Britain, England was getting bombed every day, and, along with other family and friends, Elinor was there. John had not left his feelings for Elinor fall entirely by the wayside; they were only dimmed momentarily by the glitz and glamour of American girls. Although Elinor and her family did not live in (or even near) London/southeast England (which was bearing the brunt of the Luftwaffe's aerial attack), it was not unknown for some attacks to be conducted far inland. John had reason to be worried.

In addition, in the United States, Yale itself was at the epicenter of the isolationist movement. In September of 1940, the *America First Committee* (AFC) movement was officially formed there. This would become the largest anti-intervention movement in the United States. Many prominent people counted themselves among its members, including Charles Lindbergh and numerous other luminaries.

Charles Lindbergh, whom John might have looked to as an inspirational figure, was one of the more outspoken people against U.S. intervention. Long before the AFC was born, Lindbergh was speaking out against the war. During one speech, Lindbergh alienated many people (including some in the AFC) by blaming the European war on the British, the Roosevelt administration, and the Jews.[13]

It was in this atmosphere that John contemplated his choice to either go to Canada and join the air force, or to stay in the U.S. and go to college. Perhaps more than most, John was aware of what was happening in Europe and England. He had come to the realization that in all probability, the only way to stop Hitler from consuming all of Europe and perhaps even the United States was the direct application of military force. For Magee, the very thought that his family, friends and Elinor were being bombed had to be very hard on him.

If John decided to go, the decision would certainly be hard on John's parents. Having just returned to America, his father surely did not want to lose his oldest son to fight in a global conflict. However, both Mother and Father recognized that John's commitment was not a passing fancy. Clearly, John was committed to return to England via the only way that was possible, with all the inherent risks associated with it.

Deciding to join the RCAF, become a fighter pilot and return to England is one thing, and quite a different thing to accomplish. It was not a sure bet that the RCAF would even accept John; and if they did, it was not certain that he would be selected for pilot training, let alone *fighter* pilot training. And if John beat the odds and successfully underwent fighter pilot training, there was always the possibility that he would be kept in Canada as an instructor. The only way to find out where his decision would lead was to travel to Canada and find out.

In August of 1940, John was already taking preliminary steps to joining the RCAF. He wrote a letter, dated August 16th, to "His Excellency the Secretary of War, Canadian National Gov't., Ottawa:

> *Not knowing to whom I should write in order to secure*
>
> *the information I need, I have presumed to trespass upon*
>
> *your time, which I am sure is not over-bountiful at this time,*
>
> *in the hopes that, should you not find the time to read this*
>
> *missive yourself, you will yet be so kind as to see that it*
>
> *reaches the appropriate department of the Canadian War*
>
> *Office.*
>
> *I am half English (my father being an American) and*
>
> *indeed think myself half English in everything but actual*
>
> *birth, having lived the best part of my life in England...*

The letter goes on to state John's educational history, emphasizing time at St. Clare and Rugby, and his participation in the Officers Training Corps. John even quotes part of the OTC certificate which appears to make him eligible for a commission in the Supplementary Reserve of the Territorial Army.

It is not known whether this particular letter helped John or not.

There was one final consideration. Since John had received a scholarship from Yale, he needed to speak to the school if he was considering not attending. This would lead John to the office of the president of Yale, Charles Seymour. President Seymour was good friends with both John's father and Uncle Jim. There had to have been some communication between John's father, Uncle Jim and President Seymour; perhaps Seymour could help John see that there was another, equally viable path.

John did indeed meet with President Seymour. In a letter written to John's father[14], Seymour explains what happened during the meeting:

*He [John Jr.] came in this morning and again this afternoon after lunch. He told me that he had practically reached the decision last night in his own mind, but that he did not want to make it final until he had talked to me. He was extremely courteous in expressing the hope that I did not feel that he was belittling the opportunity offered by Yale in admitting him. He said that the decision would have to be his own but that he would be grateful if I could throw any new light on his problem which might lead him to alter the decision he had reached.*

Charles Seymour himself had been educated in England and might have had a good grasp of what John was struggling with.

*In all honesty I had to tell him that this was a personal problem which he would have to decide himself, that in general I thought that young men in his position, or in positions similar to his, would do greater service if they accepted the educational opportunity offered, but that if his inclination against college at this time was so strong that he could not concentrate happily upon his work here, I on my side could not urge him to undertake it. He said that after balancing all the factors, he was quite clear that he would not be happy this year in New Haven and that the only peace of mind he could find would be by seeking his commission in Canada...*

John seems to have decided to hedge his bet, and try to leave the door to Yale open:

*He went on to say that he had also decided that it would be better for him to ultimately come to Yale rather than to go to Oxford, and he asked what arrangements could be made for admission in a later year. I advised him that if he had definitely made up his mind he should inform the Chairman of the Board of Admissions that he wished to defer matriculation and that later, when the opportunity offered, he should apply again for admission. In the circumstances such admission would be certain to be granted.*

President Seymour then presented his final analysis of the conversation, as well as an apology to John Sr. for not making a more concerted effort to persuade John Jr. to attend Yale:

*I was so taken with him and his approach to his problem that I am deeply disappointed in a personal sense that apparently he is not to be with us, but there can be no question of the depth of his feeling. I think that it is entirely likely that he would be unhappy here under present conditions...*

*I can understand your own feelings with regard to the immediate future of your boy. I hope that you will not feel that I let you down in not bringing the strongest sort of pressure to bear upon him, but in all conscience I believe that this is the kind of problem which can only be settled by the man himself.*

Amidst all this conflicted opinion and in the pressure of seeing his adopted homeland viciously attacked, John made up his mind suddenly and finally: *he had to return to England.*

John had decided to give up a generous scholarship to Yale, give up the relative safety of his family and of the United States, and to go into harm's way.

John Gillespie Magee, Jr., age 18, was going to war.

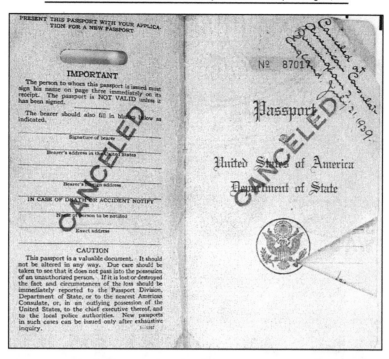

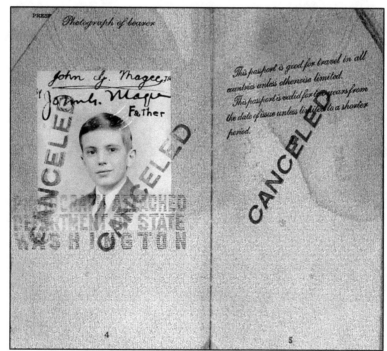

John Magee's cancelled U.S. passport.

John's Avon Old Farms School graduation picture.

John G. Magee Family Papers, Record Group No. 242,
Special Collections, Yale Divinity School Library

John always seemed to be neatly dressed.

John, David, Hugh and Christopher Magee.

John and his father visit the Nathan Hale house and statue on the Yale campus.

Magee family portrait, 1938.

YALE UNIVERSITY

*This certifies that*

*John Gillespie Magee Jr.*

*has been admitted to the Freshman Class*

*entering Yale University in* 1940.

*Edward S. Noyes*
Chairman of the Board of Admissions

*New Haven, Connecticut* *July 17,* 1940.

*The Class will meet for organization in Woolsey Hall, Saturday, September 21, 1940, at 10.00 A.M., daylight saving time.*

John's certificate of admission to Yale.

Courtesy of the Library of Congress

[1] After John's trip, during the return voyage to England the Queen Mary was escorted by the battlecruiser H.M.S. Hood. QM made one more trip to New York, after which she was converted to a troopship.

[2] The Rolling Rock Club is still a very exclusive place. In 2007, then Vice-President Dick Cheney hunted there.

[3] The Mellon family is related to the Magee family: Father's sister Mary had married James Vernor Scaife, and their son Alan Magee Scaife had in turn married Sarah Cordelia Mellon. Sarah's family owned the Rolling Rock Club. (Alan and Sarah's son is the billionaire Richard Mellon Scaife, a current-day prominent resident of Pittsburgh).

[4] Letter from John to his family, 2/7/40.

[5] Author's personal correspondence and conversations with Erl "Puck" Purnell, Peggy Gould's son.

[6] Letter from John to John Sr., 1/21/40.

[7] Dr. Kammerer, Avon's Provost, resigned in January of 1940, and was replaced by The Reverend W. Brooke Stabler.

[8] Letter from John to Aunt Mary, 1/25/40.

[9] The "fiancé" mentioned above is likely Tanya Davis, a Czechoslovakian woman John met soon after coming to Toronto. Apparently John did not continue this relationship after his return to England.

[10] http://en.wikipedia.org/wiki/Clayton_Knight_Committee–accessed 2011_12_14

[11] Ab initio – Latin for "from the beginning."

[12] Magee, Sr. left Shanghai, China on May 18th, 1940 aboard the SS Empress of Asia, and arrived in Victoria, British Columbia on June 3rd. Traveling across Canada, Magee Sr.'s official Port of Entry into the United States was at St. Albans, Vermont.

[13] Wayne S. Cole, *America First: The Battle against Intervention, 1940-41* (1953).

[14] Letter from Yale President Charles Seymour to Rev. John G. Magee, dated 9/16/40.

# Canada — 1940 to 1941

## Per Ardua: From Student/Poet to Pilot/Warrior
## Washington, D.C. to Montreal, Quebec, Canada
## October 1940

After the family reunion at Martha's Vineyard, Father was appointed assistant rector at St. John's Episcopal Church[1] in Washington, D.C., located across the street from Lafayette Park and the White House. The Magee family rented a house on Bancroft Court in northwest D.C.

With John's decision to join the RCAF, he did not start school at Yale in September. He made preparations to travel to Canada, spending just a little more time with his family prior to his departure. Shortly before John left for Canada, he and his father traveled to New York City. During this trip, all pretenses were stripped away and it was just a father and a son, facing the uncertain future together, united in their faith. They attended the Sunday service at Grace Church; father asking God for his son to be safe, and son asking, perhaps, not to be afraid.

Before leaving for Canada, John gathered several letters of recommendation. All of the letters are addressed to the Royal Canadian Air Force, and have similar things to say.

Here is an excerpt of a letter from Harold O'D Hunter, Aide to the Provost, Avon Old Farms School:

> *This letter is written to you with reference to John Gillespie Magee, formerly a resident of this School, who is now making application to join the Royal Canadian Air Force. He attended this School for one year — the only year recently of residence in the United States. He was graduated with honors in June and left here at the close of his senior year with special recognition for scholarship and with honorable dismissal.*
>
> *I understand that he has postponed his further studies, which were to have been carried on at Yale University, until his return from Service and that this has been done with the consent of the college authorities. I understand, also, that he is entering the Service with the consent of his father.*

Another letter of recommendation from John's cousin Alan Scaife gives the RCAF a background not only on John, but also on John's mother and father:

*I understand that John G. Magee, Jr. is anxious to enlist in the Royal Canadian Air Force.*

*In recommending him for admission to the service I might point out that he has been educated in England and as a consequence has very pronounced British sympathies. At Rugby he was an exceedingly brilliant scholar, while only recently he was awarded a scholarship in Yale University as a result of the excellence of his work during the time that he attended school in the United States.*

*His mother is an Englishwoman and comes from a British army family. Both of his uncles are in the British army and one of them is a Brigadier-General.*

*His father is a minister in the Episcopal Church and has spent most of his life in China since graduation from the Theological Seminary. He is an outstanding man in his profession and the family background that the applicant has on both sides is splendid.*

The President of the Bank of Montreal, Huntly Redpath Drummond, was a Magee family friend and had also attended Rugby. He wrote:

*I know the bearer, John Gillespie Mage; he was born in China, the son of the Reverend J.G. Magee, and was at school in England at Rugby from 1935 to 1939; afterwards he entered Yale with honours in all subjects. He was in the Rugby Rifle Team for two years and has an O.T.C. Certificate "A".*

*He is anxious to enlist and has come to Canada for that*

*purpose.*

*I can recommend Mr. Magee with confidence in his*

*ability and character.*

John finally departed to Canada, probably by train. Apparently, he did not share his decision to join the RCAF with his brothers before he left. It was only on September 26th 1940, after his arrival in Canada, that John wrote this to his brother David (who was away at school when John left):

*I expect you are rather amazed to hear that I am in the*

*British Empire (Hrrmph!!) — Also to hear that I am about to*

*enlist as a pilot-gunner in the R.C.A.F. (Royal Canadian Air*

*Force.) But there it is. I have lots to tell you, but not the time.*

*I hope to be called up on Monday, the 30th. If not, I'll have to*

*wait another two weeks. I'm scared to death at the prospect*

*of my M2 Medical Exam. I'm sure I'll flunk. (1 out of every 10*

*men gets in!) ... Sorry I didn't get down to say goodbye, but*

*as you can imagine everything was rather hectic.*

Later, John writes to his mother, describing the first part of his enlistment process:

*Having gone to Ottawa and had an interview even with*

*Air Marshal Breadner himself, I came back to Montreal and*

*put in my application for the Air Force.*[2]

It is uncertain how Magee obtained this interview with Air Vice Marshal (AVM) Lloyd Samuel Breadner. Breadner's responsibilities at that time included the air defense of Canada, the development of the British Commonwealth Air Training Program (BCATP), and the provision of RCAF personnel in all areas. He had to be a tremendously busy person, and the question arises whether Breadner would have had time to meet with an 18-year old American who wasn't even a pilot at the time. However, it may have been routine with pilot candidates, and there is the fact that John came well-equipped with many strong letters of recommendation.

During the interview with Breadner, John may well have been asked some of the same questions that John's father, uncle, and even President Seymour at Yale might have asked: Are you sure you want to do this? How committed are you to this course of action? Do you realize the implications of becoming a fighter pilot and going up against a talented and stubborn enemy; that you stand a good chance of getting seriously injured, taken prisoner, or even killed?

A memo dated September 28th, 1940, from Wing Commander A. deNiverville (office of the Chief of the Air Staff, AVM Breadner), to the Commanding Officer of the RCAF Recruiting Center in Montreal leaves no doubt that John Magee made a great impression during the interview:

> To: Commanding Officer, R.C.A.F. Recruiting Centre, Montreal,
>    Quebec
> From: Chief of the Air Staff
> Subject: Application for Enlistment (Air Crew)—MAGEE, John
>    Gillespie
>
> The above named applicant who is of English birth, but at present living in the United States was interviewed today.
>
> As he is living with friends in Montreal in order to enlist in the Air Force, it was suggested he submit his application at your Centre.
>
> In view of the candidate's high standard of education and good references, you are to include him, please, in your early selections. This is, of course, provided he is medically fit.

With this powerful recommendation in hand, John sets out to Montreal to pursue his dream of joining the Royal Canadian Air Force.

# Montreal
# October 1940

John stayed the path following his interview with AVM Breadner, and traveled to Montreal to officially put in his application to join the RCAF. While in Montreal, John stayed at the YMCA and with family friends.

After successfully navigating a virtual obstacle course consisting of the Canadian government, parents, other family members, the President of Yale, the Air Vice Marshal of the RCAF and initial interviews and medical exams, John Magee's forward progress in joining the RCAF came to a crashing halt. He was stopped literally at the gate due to something totally unexpected. He explained in writing to his mother:

> *Terrible misfortune has befallen me....*

During his medical exam of September 28th, John is found to be *underweight* by 16 pounds (at that time, he is 6 feet ½ inches tall and 137 pounds). Of all the things that could happen to him, to be stopped by something so trifling had to be extraordinarily frustrating. He was told to gain weight and come back in two weeks.

> *... I have been eating myself sick at every meal, drinking milk, stout, etc., ad infin., given up smoking and all forms of exercise and sleeping 10 or 11 hours at night. Have gained half a pound...*

John appeals to his mother, clearly in anguish about this scenario:

> *What on earth am I going to do? I've simply got to get in, I'll die of chagrin if I don't. If determination will get me in, I'm in.... I can't tell you how miserable I am. Give me some hints about getting fat!*

A very determined John Magee underwent a crash diet to gain weight. True to being John Magee, he had written not only to his mother but to other friends and acquaintances describing his woes. John received an encouraging letter in return from RCAF WWI ace, Squadron Leader Kenneth Burns Conn:

> *I am extremely sorry that your first effort to get into the Royal Canadian Air Force did not meet with more success. I trust, however, that by this time you have acquired the necessary poundage. After looking over your program, I feel that if I were the subject, it would either produce enormous weight or a corpse.*
>
> *I certainly hope that you will make the grade and will look forward to seeing you again.*

His weight-gaining efforts were rewarded, and on October 10th, 1940, a 152 pound John Magee becomes AC2 (Aircraftsman, 2nd Grade) John Gillespie Magee, Jr., Royal Canadian Air Force, serial number J/5823. John had firmly started his way back to England at last.

There was a problem at that time faced by the RCAF in recruiting non-Canadians into its ranks. There is a U.S. law that prohibits its citizens from joining the armed forces of another country. Generally, recruits into the RCAF had to swear allegiance to the King of England. By doing so, an American would be, in effect, breaking the law, as well as risking their American citizenship. Recognizing the problem, the RCAF developed a solution: American recruits into the RCAF had to swear to obey orders from superior officers for the duration of their service, without swearing allegiance to the King.

In June of 1941, when Magee was already getting his wings, President Roosevelt publicly declared, "… any man wanting to join the Canadian or British armed forces has a perfect right to do so… Neither the British nor Canadian Governments require an oath of allegiance to the British King…". Thus Magee winds up in the clear regarding his citizenship, which was not at all the case at the time of his decision to enlist.

With so many hurdles jumped, if John now thought that he was going to immediately go and learn how to fly fighter planes, he was in for a rude shock. Any military force has its own particular way of doing things, and John Magee was going to have to endure much more than he bargained for.

In 1939 and into 1940, the RCAF was still getting its training plan organized. With a tremendous influx of students from all of the British

Commonwealth and its allies, the training effort was a huge project from the outset. Airfields had to be built, aircraft purchased, instructors located and trained in how to teach students who had never been in a plane how to fly.

After his enlistment, Magee waited to get to his first duty station. Living at the YMCA in Montreal, John managed to spend a weekend with friend Patrick Stoker at Lac Paquin, in the beautiful country north of Montreal. In an update letter to his mother, John explained what was happening:

> I have some good news for you — I passed my medical test with flying colours, having gone from 137 to 152 pounds in 6 days. I am actually <u>overweight</u> the second time! So now I am A.C. /2 Magee, His Majesty's Royal Canadian Air Force. I really can't believe it, it's all happened so quickly — but it's true! ...
>
> I have not as yet been stationed anywhere and am still living at the Y.M. in Montreal. I am expecting any day now to be sent to my initial training school in Brandon, Manitoba, 45 hours west by train. If everything goes well I should be overseas by May — still I suppose I should not count my chickens.... I am week-ending with Patrick Stoker, a boy of about my age at his mother's heavenly place up here in the mountains about a hundred miles north of Montreal.

John concludes his letter, reflecting the enthusiasm he feels after joining the RCAF:

> As I said, I am on tip-toe to be off. Can't stop for more. Life is wonderful!

## Montreal to Toronto
## No. 1 RCAF Manning Depot
## October 1940

Shortly after John writes the letter quoted above, he is moved to Toronto (not Brandon, where he thought he was going to go). John, the inveterate letter writer, keeps his mother informed:

*Since I last wrote to you I have been moved to Toronto.*

*I arrived here on Friday morning with a snorting cold, and*

*feeling very miserable after sitting up all night on the train.*

*The first thing we were told on arriving was that we were*

*automatically C.B. [Confined to Barracks] for 72 hours. So*

*since then I didn't even see the sky, until this morning, when*

*we were allowed out on the grounds.*

At No. 1 RCAF Manning (as in "manning the plane") Depot in Toronto, John received his first taste of life in the RCAF. The year before, this Manning Depot was known as the Canadian National Exhibition (CNE), where Canada had held its famous annual fair since 1879. After Canada declared war on Germany, the buildings which once housed prize livestock were converted to barracks, and the entire grounds were given over to one huge perimeter where new recruits could be properly inducted into the military. A massive effort converted the General Exhibits area into sleeping quarters; 500 double bunks both upstairs and downstairs, for a total capacity of 2,000 new recruits. (After the war ended, the CNE resumed its original role as a fairground, a role which continues to the present day.)

At the Manning Depot, new uniforms are issued and fitted, and the new recruit is supplied with all the "stuff" necessary for their new military life. All the medical miscellany of being in the military must be attended to, such as examinations and vaccinations. Apparently John does not tolerate one of the inoculations well and suffers for a bit:

*The barracks here are situated on the grounds of an*

*obsolete exposition and we are living in the actual exposition*

*buildings, which is all very well except for the fact that it is*

*so terribly overcrowded. The Air Force is terribly congested*

*and disorganized just now, and it's a matter of luck as to*
*whether we spend a week or a month here. This is simply*
*what is known as a Manning Pool where we are issued with*
*uniforms, inoculated, etc. I took my first inoculation rather*
*badly and have felt like the devil since yesterday. Still the*
*thought of escaping confinement tomorrow, and being at*
*liberty to look at my militarized and be-uniformed reflection*
*in shop windows! I sleep in a large hall with about 1500*
*other men in two-layer berths but they are not too bad,*
*really.*

As with many other military endeavors, not much thought was put into the quality of the food that was prepared ad hoc for such a large number of recruits, John writes family:

*The food is not designed for the most sensitive palates,*
*as you can imagine, but that is just one of the Ardua before*
*the Astra come in sight.*

John's play on words reflects the official motto of the Royal Canadian Air Force: *Ad Astra per Ardua* (By Effort to the Stars).

Anybody who has served as an enlisted person in any branch of the military just about anywhere in the world can relate to what Magee is going through. The conversion from civilian to a member of the armed forces is, by necessity, a tough road. John undergoes training in military customs and procedures, including how to march, salute, recognize the different officer and enlisted ranks; a hundred details must be taken in before pilot training can even be considered.

Then there are the multitudes of indignities that must be endured. Privacy is non-existent. In the barracks, long troughs are provided where you urinate. There are also all manner of medical inspections which are, at the very least, very uncomfortable.

For young John Magee, perhaps living in boarding schools helped. But even that experience could not have prepared him for the reality of living in close quarters with thousands of other young men. One day you're at a very nice school in Connecticut with a nice room and good meals, and the next you are crammed in with hundreds of other young men from all over the world, eating mass-prepared food. There had to have been some doubts on Magee's part about the wisdom of joining the RCAF, but he pressed on, even managing to make friends:

> *I have made one good friend here, a young Polish artist from Yonkers, who is a particularly intelligent and interesting character.*

Many of the recruits were very young, and most likely were away from home for the first time. Magee appears to have written an amazing number of letters to family and friends during this period of time, and received many in return.

One letter in particular had to be somewhat difficult to write. Magee had not yet told Geoffrey Sergeant, his good friend from Mortehoe, that he had given up the idea of pacifism and joined the military. John wrote this to Sergeant:

> *It has been difficult to write you since I took this rather final step. I know, Geoff, how sorry you will be that everything has not worked out for me in the way we had hoped. But I think that convictions, however zigzag and contradictory a course they run, should be followed at any price. Hence my presence here. I decided that the things of democracy are worth fighting for, though I feel no antipathy to the Germans. And that's that... Apologies, dear Geoff, for a fallen ideal, but I hope it will not come between us.*

In South Africa, Geoffrey is working in a military hospital, holding true to the ideals that he and John had talked about not so long ago at Mortehoe in Wales. Though remaining a pacifist himself, Geoffrey recognized that John needs to be true to himself, and continues to hold John in the highest regard. Geoffrey, however, implored John to try and keep faith with the ideals they had discussed. In a letter written to John the previous October, Geoffrey tries to keep John on the straight and narrow path:

*But at all extents, remain loyal to our ideals. They are more likely to be right than anything born in these days of poisonous hatred & propaganda.*

*John — I entreat you as my friends in England are entreating me: if you can, keep clear of the hell. Good surely cannot come of it. And, anyway, you wouldn't be much use to the military. You are too sensitive to evil to have any faith in killing your fellow men — men who, when all the ramifications of cause & effect are allowed, are no more to blame than we all are for the consequences of unforgiving, unyielding, greed & the jealousy which it begets.*

Geoff paints a picture of what he hopes will happen after the war:

*The big job is to avoid now the poison of hatred, and, after the war, to share in the huge task of reconstruction.*

*Then—there will be the time for our idealism.*

*Do not give way to disillusionment and cynicism. It will be hard.*

*But please try. Afterwards—by Jove. Conserve yourself for then. It is your duty, for your strength lies not in destruction but in creation.* [3]

As difficult as the way was, with some opposition from his parents, family and friends, John persisted on the course he had charted for himself. And the way was going to be tough in ways that John could not possibly have foreseen. There were going to be many highs (literal ones!) and lows, many obstacles to overcome, before John would even be given a chance to return to his beloved England.

## Toronto to Trenton
## RCAF Station Trenton
## October 1940 to December 1940

With the influx of new recruits, there is a waiting period before getting to the flying portion of training. The RCAF needs to do something with these men to keep them occupied, and thus John is assigned guard duty in Trenton, Ontario, awaiting posting to Initial Training School (ITS). John writes to his mother again, with all the angst that is prevalent with new recruits in the military (not knowing what is going to happen, "hurry up and wait," rumors, and the like):

*I am so terribly sorry to have let so long go by without writing you, but since you last heard from me I have been drafted from Toronto to this place, which is the biggest R.A.F. Aerodrome in Canada. I am here on "Security Guard" that is, sentry duty, until there is a place for me at I.T.S. (Initial Training School). None of us were told anything about this long and tedious ordeal when we joined up, and even at Manning Pool they told us we would only be here about two weeks at the outside, but now we find that we shall be lucky to be in I.T.S. by Christmas...*

It is nearing winter now, with very low temperatures in Canada, and some of John's guard duty is at night. John writes to his mother one icy cold night:

*I am writing this on sentry duty between one and five a.m. at night; it's bitterly cold, I'm writing in gloves, which is why this is so illegible. Strictly <u>Verboten</u> and all that!*

The RCAF has given 18-year old John Magee possession of a machine gun, and John is duly impressed with this new-found power:

> *I'm in a sand bagged machine gun post, with a Lewis*
> *gun in front of me filled with 500 rounds of incendiary*
> *ammunition. From my vantage point I can rake the whole*
> *aerodrome, if need be. This is indeed a symbolic and*
> *powerful position.*

It is the first experience Magee has with being entrusted with a powerful weapon. It will not be the last. And as with many young men who are handed powerful weapons, it is somewhat intoxicating ("a symbolic and powerful position.")

It is telling that even here, in the frozen tundra, John is still tremendously excited about where he is and what he is doing. He has begun to realize that he has, perhaps, found a home, a place among like-minded people, embarking on a common cause. The poet in John finds expression in his letters.

Some of Magee's letters foreshadow not only the creation of *High Flight* but also of his own death:

> *I have become one of a group of men, who are all, to*
> *the last man, resigned to death and even anxious for it — or,*
> *if not for death, at least for the chance of showing their*
> *mettle....*
>
> *The whole place thrills to the vivid, eager living of men*
> *who realize that they are almost certainly in their last year*
> *of life.*

Such self-awareness and introspection are rare even among older people. John, barely past 18 years old, not only thinks about such imponderables as service to country and death, but also puts his thoughts down on paper in an extremely descriptive fashion. Less than a year later, it is not a surprise that John creates his sonnet *High Flight*, as he has been practicing expressing himself, on paper, for years.

John closes his letter in typical John Magee fashion:

> *And now, my good mother, I bid you a cold good*
> *night.—Your Cold, but Loving son.*

## Trenton to Toronto
## No. 1 Initial Training School (ITS)
## December 1940

Moving from Trenton to Toronto, John officially starts his flying-specific training at No. 1 Initial Training School (ITS). This ITS is located on Avenue Road on the grounds of the Toronto Hunt Club (the Club is still there today).

Magee begins to fly the Link ground-trainer, an extremely basic primary flight simulator. Moving the controls causes the tiny plane to move appropriately, and is a great way to learn the functions of stick and rudder without risking a large, expensive airplane.

Sometime during his time at Toronto, Magee becomes an Aircraftsman First Class, with Leading Aircraftsman (LAC) next up, assuming John manages to stay with the program (which is not at all guaranteed, as many trainees either wash out, quit, or are hurt or killed during training).

Unexpectedly, Magee is given a short leave for Christmas. He flies home to Washington, D.C., on Christmas Eve, where he presents to his family a John Magee far different from the one who left home just a few months before. Generations of families have been astonished when a newly-minted member of an armed force comes home after initial training, and John is no exception. "What has happened to John?" ask the three Magee brothers. With his uniform and bearing, John appears years older and much more mature. However, John wastes no time in reassuring his brothers that he is still the same old John, and engages in much rough-housing.

John decides to receive Holy Communion during Christmas service while at home. Not only that, but he will receive Communion from his father, assistant rector at St. John's. Without a doubt, this had to be tremendously moving for both father and son.

John's mother Faith tells of John's Christmas leave in a letter to her own mother:

> *When we last wrote John Jr. had gone to Canada and*
>
> *was training at Trenton, Ontario. To our great joy he was*
>
> *able to get short Christmas leave, and we all went out to the*
>
> *Airport to meet him on Christmas Eve. We were all together*
>
> *at the Christmas Service the next morning, and we had him*
>
> *with us at the Holy Communion as well which was a great*

*joy. It was not quite so much fun to see him off again that*

*same afternoon about five o'clock.*

All too soon, Christmas leave is over and it is time to return to Canada. But this time, John heads toward the known instead of the totally unknown; he is an official member of the Royal Canadian Air Force, and he has work to do.

After John returns to Toronto, he writes to his family. Apparently, the same old John is still flirting with the ladies:

> *Just a line to thank you for a marvelous Christmas and*
>
> *to apologize for running off inadvertently with the car key.*
>
> *The trip back was most successful. The hostess was*
>
> *even more entrancing than the one on the way down, and*
>
> *we got on so well that she took me to her home to meet her*
>
> *family who gave me dinner.[4]*

Catching German measles stops John's training for 10 days, forcing him into isolation. John writes his family:

> *Just time to dash off a letter in between exams. I got*
>
> *German measles soon after New Year's and spent 10 or 11*
>
> *days in the Riverdale Isolation Hospital just outside of*
>
> *Toronto. I couldn't write as paper would be infected. Now*
>
> *fully recovered. In the pink, working at tremendous pressure.*
>
> *Still haven't had my medical exam. Math finale on Monday.*
>
> *Doing very moderately in Link Trainer. Am easily upset by the*
>
> *machine. It is so sensitive and temperamental...*
>
> *Am now "Aircraftsman — First Class" and when I*
>
> *graduate from here on the 28th (if) will be L/A/C (Leading*
>
> *Aircraftsman) — then a long wait before becoming either*
>
> *Sergeant-Pilot or Pilot Officer. But that's in the very distant*
>
> *future![5]*

For all of his young life, John seems to have had a questioning attitude towards religion. His curious and inquisitive mind loved to consider, debate, and challenge the norm. John wrote to his mother from Toronto:

> Thank you very much for Biblical book. My religious views shifting again, but have not crystallized.

In a letter dated January 21st, 1941, John updates his brother David:

> Well, at last I am about to graduate from this mathematical madhouse, having yesterday passed:
> My Maths final
> My Armament and Navigation final
> My final "M2"
> (The toughest medical a flier gets)
> Personal interview with the C.O. out of whom I managed to extort a recommendation for a commission which I shall get, D.V.W.P, in June with my Wings — that is, if I am not caught looping an Avro Anson over Camp Borden or spreading orange-peel all over the heart of Toronto for want of an aeronautical waste-paper basket!
> I shall be posted to Elementary Flying School at the end of this week. God knows where. I applied for Vancouver by rather doubt if I shall get there as it is not in No. 1 Training Command, to which I am attached.

In this same letter, John relates a story which contains quotes from Shakespeare's *Romeo and Juliet* and *The Rubiayat of Omar Khayyam*:

> This morning the Squadron Bugler was sick and the grimmest Flight Sergeant-Major on the station burst into the

*barracks raging as to why we were not up. Suddenly he stopped and said:*

> *"Night's candles are burned out, and jocund day*
> *Stands tiptoe on the misty mountain tops . . .*
> *Awake! for Morning in the bowl of Night*
> *Hath flung the stone that put the stars to flight."*

*And so we get up.*

In due course, Magee's time at No.1 ITS is finally complete. Although he predicts the timing accurately, John has no idea which school he is going to next. In fact John is to be transferred to a location directly south of Toronto, across Lake Ontario:  No. 9 Elementary Flying Training School in St. Catharines, Ontario. John has proven himself on the Link trainer (getting a final score of 92%, where the record was 94%) as well as all the other ground school topics.

Finally, it is time to fly.

## Toronto to St. Catharines, Ontario
## No. 9 Elementary Flying Training School (EFTS)
## January 1941 to March 1941

*What was once a flying noisiness, an incomprehensible*

*machine, has become... a live and poised animal that*

*breathes; it is a dizziness, an eager and sensitive thing; it is*

*power; it is speed, and ecstasy. In fact, my dear old friend,*

*the worst has happened, and I wish you to forget and cast*

*me off; for I have become air-minded!*

> *- JGM*

RCAF No. 9 Elementary Flying Training School (EFTS) was formed at the St. Catharines Flying Club's airfield on October 15, 1940. The nationwide system of Aero Clubs in Canada provided the initial training impetus when in the late 1930s it became apparent that another war was looming. Murton Seymour had provided pilot training to Canadians since the first World War, and had founded the St. Catharines Flying Club for that purpose in 1928.

Through its closing at the end of 1944, No. 9 EFTS accepted 2,498 students, and graduated 1,848. Today, the airfield is known as Niagara District Airport, with one of the original BCATP/EFTS hangers still standing. (Today, there is a monument to the EFTS and John Magee at the airport. See the Memorials section of this book.)

In January 1941 Magee traveled from Toronto to St. Catharines. AC2 John Magee joins Course #25, and he is ready to fly. In a letter to his family on February 5th, he relates what happened between leaving Toronto and getting to St. Catharines:

*Much has happened since I last wrote. I graduated*

*from I.T.S. on the 28th... We came here by train as far as*

*Hamilton, and then on by bus, which broke down at 11:30*

*p.m. and we didn't arrive until 1 a.m. Having worked hard to*

*make the grade, and thinking that the worse was over, I was*

*vastly disappointed to learn on arrival that 79% of the*

*preceding class was "washed out" in a period of 3 days, and that you have to be a born and literally flawless pilot to make*

*the grade.*

*This has the reputation of being the toughest station in*

*the whole of Canada. Not knowing this, I chose it because it*

*is only 9 miles from Niagara and 30 m. from Buffalo [NY].*

*However, we don't get any leave at all so I don't suppose I*

*shall be going States-wards.*

Being at No. 9 EFTS was like being in a melting pot of different nationalities. So many Americans were there that many are calling the RCAF the Royal *California* Air Force. Local Canadians were, in turns, amused and terrified by the influx of instructors and students from Canada and all over the world.

In essence, the school itself was a private enterprise: St. Catharines Flying Training School LTD., in the case of No. 9 EFTS. Even though they wore uniforms somewhat similar to the ones worn by RCAF pilots, the instructors at No. 9 EFTS were civilians, and were supervised by Chief Flying Instructor George B. Dunbar. Some of the instructors were Americans, among the first Americans recruited by the RCAF because of their prior flying experience. The flight instructors were among the unsung heroes of Allied aviation, teaching young men how to fly safely and yet effectively in combat. In many cases, instructors would apply to fly in combat, but by and large would be denied due to the criticality of their flight instruction.

The de Havilland Fleet Finch is the trainer aircraft in use at No. 9 EFTS. The Finch was built in Canada, and along with the de Havilland Tiger Moth, provided most of the primary pilot training done in Canada. The Fleet had a 125 hp Kinner B-5 five-cylinder radial piston engine, producing a top speed of 104 mph and a cruise speed of 85 mph.

John is introduced to a real aircraft for the first time. Before arrival at St. Catharines, he has undergone ground training at Initial Training School, so he is familiar with the various components of an aircraft. A pre-flight inspection of the aircraft is demonstrated, as a pilot is always responsible for making sure that his airplane is ready to fly.

Magee first takes to the air on January 28th, 1941. This momentous 40 minute flight was made in de Havilland Fleet Finch Mark II biplane number 4688. The instructor for this flight is named Putnum (Magee logged only one flight with Putnum; this initial flight was to see if the prospective pilot should even begin flight training).

Every pilot has their very first flight as a student. Even if the pilot has flown before as a passenger, when you are intending to learn how to actually fly the airplane, this time it is different.

Magee and Putman fly for only about 40 minutes during that first flight, covering flying syllabus topics 1 and 1A (Familiarization with cockpit layout). There is no other notation in Magee's logbook, nothing unusual or extraordinary about this first flight. Date, type and serial number of the aircraft, name of instructor, what was done, and the time spent aloft are all duly noted.

The Fleet Finch is a very docile, forgiving aircraft. Soon Magee will be flying Spitfires, which make the Finch look like something from the Wright Brothers, but John, like all pilots, will always remember his first flight.

Evidence that John was doing well as a fledgling pilot is shown in the time it takes for him to solo. He goes from having never flown an airplane to flying one by himself in seven flights and 6.5 hours of aerial instruction (the average was around ten hours). A student's first solo flight is one of the hallmark events of a flying career, a flight that will forever be remembered. Magee's solo flight occurred on February 3rd in Fleet Finch #4609 and lasted a mere 20 minutes, enough for a takeoff and landing, perhaps a touch-and-go ("circuits and bumps" in RCAF/RAF parlance).

There was no special notation in John's logbook, just a recording of the facts of Magee's solo flight, very businesslike.

John's primary instructor is A.K. Paterson, and they will fly 25 flights together, the most flights John will ever have with an instructor.

In his February 5th, 1941 letter to his family, John gives this update:

> We started in flying at once and after six hours I soloed
>
> (Feb. 3rd). I was the first in my class of 24 to solo, and beat
>
> the record for this station which was 6:50. The average is 10
>
> to 11 hours. My instructor was most encouraging. Said I was
>
> the most exceptional pupil he had ever had, and he thought
>
> I would be a valuable man in the service, etc. Result,—J.G.M.
>
> cheers up a bit.

Apparently the instructors didn't waste any time demonstrating what is now, sadly, the lost art of spinning an aircraft:

> Do you know what a spin is?  It is a horrid, sickening spiral dive towards the ground (_ghastly_ and terrifying sensation) — in the last war they didn't know how to recover from them and consequently they took hundreds of lives. However, we do know now theoretically (Full opposite rudder, stick back, then forward, and full throttle). Well, I asked my instructor if we could do one. He demurred, but I really wanted to, so we did.

Terrifying as spin are, John decided that he must master them. To give some perspective, in the present time it has been decided that pilots should not be taught how to spin aircraft; they are, instead, taught spin-avoidance. It's not that spins are more inherently dangerous than any other aerial maneuver, but if the recovery is not prompt and proper, one can spin the aircraft right into the ground. John relates exactly what happened when he tried, too soon, to attempt a spin while flying solo:

> Soon I learned — or thought I learned — to do one myself (you can do one purposely to practice getting out of it) and he was very pleased, but warned me never to do one alone. That was yesterday. Last night I realized they had a sort of morbid fascination for me — possibly because they _were_ so terrifying (N.B. the engine is off and all you hear is the wind screaming in the struts) and today I was told to go to 3,000 feet and practice steep turns. On the way up a little devil kept tell me that I could easily do a spin if I got out of sight of the aerodrome, and nobody would be any the wiser. But it also taunted me for being _afraid_!  I fought the thing during the long climb skywards, and finally in a fit of impatience decided to do one. So instead of leveling off as instructed I continued climbing for 20 minutes until I was at

*the tremendous height of 6,500 ft., when I thought it was safe to try, and let her go. As soon as I was in it I realized something was wrong. I had the feel of being slightly <u>upside down</u> yet still not spinning. The ground was whirling before me when suddenly my safety belt snapped, and in the same moment I realized I was in an <u>inverted</u> spin, something I have only read of in heavy black type in flying manuals. My head hit the cockpit cowling and I came out of the seat. All the time I was hurtling like a corkscrew towards the earth. I had <u>no idea</u> how to get out of the thing. I applied full opposite rudder, but it made me spin all the faster. By this time my eyes were bulging out of my head and my ears blocked. I heaved on the control (joystick) column frantically but couldn't move it as I could not pull very hard with my safety belt bust. I think I became unconscious then. The next thing I remember is making one last effort and feeling myself pressed back into my seat as the nose came up. I remember my altimeter needle trembling between 700 and 800 feet. I had dropped almost <u>5000 feet</u> in about 20 seconds! As the ship leveled out, I relapsed into a state of semi-fogginess, and when I regained full use of my senses I headed straight for home but had to circle the field twice before plucking up the guts to land.*

There is a saying that if it doesn't kill you, it makes you stronger. John narrowly escaped death trying a spin by himself before he was ready. Somehow, John's instructor Paterson saw everything, and had to decide just how to respond. John relates what happens next:

*My instructor came running out and started to give me a good going over (He had watched the whole thing) but I was too dazed to listen. But he climbed into the rear cockpit and took me straight up again and immediately put me into*

*two consecutive spins, later explaining that if he hadn't I*

*probably would never have been able to fly again. When I*

*finally staggered out of the plane, he put an arm around my*

*shoulder and said: 'Laddie, you've got what it takes.' I am*

*simply dreading that it will get to the ears of the C.O. as it*

*would be certain to wash me out . . .*

Apparently John's escapade either didn't reach the C.O.'s ears, or the powers-that-be turned a blind eye, and Magee's training started in earnest. Formation and instrument (blind) flying, navigation, and cross-country trips were all practiced, again and again. In between flights, ground school subjects occupy his time. There is so much to learn in the classroom: aerodynamics, meteorology, navigation, engine operation, hydraulics, and radio (called "R/T" for radio-telephone) for air-to-air and air-to-ground communications. There are also topics related to fighting in the air, such as enemy aircraft recognition, armaments, and principles of aerial combat.

During those heady days, the student pilots were taught flying in a total immersion program. They ate, breathed and slept aviation, flying often; and when they weren't actually flying, they were *learning* about flying. The program was designed to take a young man who might have never even seen an aircraft, and turn him into a fully capable combat pilot in as little time as possible. The program was also designed to separate the wheat from the chaff; one would only stay in the program if one was 100% committed. Anything less, and pilots would either voluntarily or involuntarily wash out, or get injured or killed because they were not paying 100% attention.

There were opportunities for setbacks, not only imposed by his flying, but those caused by his body. Early in his training, John got sick again. He wrote to his family in mid-February:

*I never had my 20 hour check as the next day I had a*

*fever — it is really most annoying. This is my sixth day in bed,*

*and I still have a moderately high fever. The M.O. doesn't*

*seem to know what I have got. At first he thought it might*

*be scarlet fever, but I never got any rash. Still my*

*temperature will not go down, and all the time I am losing valuable flying time. But more important I am missing Ground School lectures. These cover very difficult subjects for which I have little aptitude. If I stay in bed much longer I shall be too far behind to think of trying to catch up, in which case I would have to wait about a month for the next class going through, besides losing all the ground I have made.*

However, John did manage to recover and continue his training, seemingly without missing a beat. During February in Canada, there are many days when flying is impossible, so Magee did not miss as much time as he would have during warmer weather:

*Normal today at last... I begin to realize where I got my fever. I got lost in the clouds for about 45 minutes the last days I was flying, and my cockpit cover wasn't properly closed. Hence, a leakage, damp air at high altitude, not so hot. Result — fever. That's the only explanation I can give. I hope to be up and about by tomorrow, then I will see where I stand. Snowing again today,—everybody grounded, so I am happy! I have 21 hours, 10 minutes flying time now. If I hadn't come here I should be at about 40. We graduate at 50 if we are ever lucky enough to reach that number!*

Magee's logbook does indicate a period from February 12th through the 22nd marked as "Inactive." Before getting sick, he had logged 10 hours five minutes dual instruction, and 11 hours, 40 minutes solo time (for a total time of 21 hours, 45 minutes).

The instructors know that a good fighter pilot is going to stretch his limits, find the places where he and his aircraft can and cannot go. This cannot be 100% taught; every pilot needs to go into the sky to find out his own personal boundaries and then always try to respect them. A student pilot who does not do this is never going to find excellence in his flying. So, though the instructor never lets the student know he's watching, the instructor is almost always indeed watching, looking for that spark, that certain mixture of rebelliousness and creativity, and that ease in the air that marks the natural pilot. John Magee had all of it, in abundance.

During the first three months of 1941 Magee learns the art of flying. He always flies the Fleet Finch, and his dual instruction is usually with A.K. Paterson. His 20-hour Test is given by Flight Lieutenant Dewey, and his 50-hour Test by Flight Officer Vincent; these two flights appear to be the only ones at St. Catharines that John flies with regular RCAF pilots rather than civilian instructors.

Nearing the end of the course, John looks forward to the next phase of instruction. At this point, the training has been common for both single-engine fighter pilots, and multi-engine bomber pilots. John expresses his concern about being a bomber pilot:

> It looks as if we shall be leaving this place soon — April 10th — also _unfortunately_ it appears to be Brantford we are being headed for which means bombers. We shall all be most irked if so, but there's still a chance.

John's update letter to his brother David of March 9th shows the same concern about flying bombers:

> We are all hoping against hope that this course will cinch us for Fighter Units, but we're really scheduled for Brantford, where we fly Ansons, and that will mean we'll all be condemned to fly Long-Range Bombers till the end of the war, or until —. What a Fate! Rather like being made to play a cinema-organ having learnt the art of music on a Mouth-organ-or driving a charabanc [tour bus] in Devon!

At long last, after so many pitfalls and basic training programs, John was finally able to start training in aerial combat. Naturally he does what any budding fighter pilot would do, and seeks out extracurricular opportunities to find out who is the *best* fighter pilot! It is during times like this that Magee's "other" nature, the reckless, mischievous, devil-may-care side of him, asserts itself. Magee takes advantage of a cross-country flight to Mt. Hope (another flight school in Ontario) in a Finch to engage in not one, but two unauthorized dogfights. John, never one to keep this kind of adventure to himself, described what happened in the March 9ᵗʰ letter to his brother David:

> *I went with another chap on a solo cross-country flight to Mount Hope, another E.F.T.S. in Ontario. All the way there we did rolls, loops, Immelmans, stall turns, etc, and had one magnificent dog-fight (strictly against orders!), finally arriving about 2 hours later. Got a going over from the C.O. there, and took off for home.*

John had just gotten a dress-down from the Commanding Officer at Mt. Hope, and is heading home. Did this slow down Magee, even one little bit?

> *I was ahead, so looped over him [his fellow student from St. Catharines] and sat on his tail, about 50 yards behind, pouring imaginary tracers into him like the devil. Suddenly out of the blue a Harvard (advanced trainer) dove down between us, just like a yellow blur. (They go about 200 to our 90). The other chap went on home, but I stayed to grapple with the Harvard, despite the disadvantage of speed and maneuverability. Needless to say he outflew me all the time, but whenever I got him turning round me I could turn inside him and drill him. Finally I saw him coming down on my tail again so I half-rolled on my back, and looped out but held her in the dive till I had about 180 m.p.h. Pulled out at 500 feet, and when my vision returned he had already passed me and was circling a field.*

Now at this point, Magee could have counted it good, chalked up some great experience, and felt satisfied at having held his own against a far superior aircraft. Did he?

*After taking a good look around (we would be washed out on the spot if caught), I landed and taxied over to him. He turned out to be a Flying Officer from Dunville, where we hope to get eventually, and complimented me on keeping him in my sights as long as I did. Finally he started out again.*

If the mock combat had ended there, Magee would've probably gotten away with it. But naturally, if one fighter pilot dares to make a scene, any observing fighter pilot is honor-bound to try and do him one better. So after the Harvard pilot decides to buzz a farmhouse, Magee must try to one-up him:

*... But there was a farmhouse at the windward corner of the field, so he decided to 'skim' it. This is another thing we are not allowed to do — that is, to fly low along the ground, then, almost in front of some fence, tree, etc., to yank back on the stick and zoom upwards at terrific speed. I did the same thing and, if he missed the house by five feet, I missed it by two.*

There it is, in John's own words... *if he missed the house by five feet, I missed it by two.* Gotcha! No way for the other pilot to know that John came closer to the house that he did (if John really did... who would be measuring?), but what was important was that John *believed* he had.

Here is an excerpt from John's letter, with the illustration of "skimming":

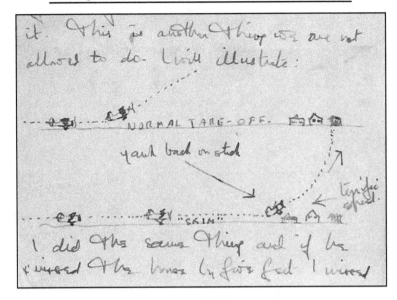

Not stopping there, the aerial gamesmanship continued:

> *We climbed up and then dove on the unfortunate*
> *inmates again and again. Finally I dipped my wings to him,*
> *thinking it was about time I got back. Besides, the ceiling was*
> *dropping rapidly and there was nasty looking weather to the*
> *N.W.*

Another major rule of such activities: Don't Get Caught. Don't get caught exceeding your abilities. Don't get caught going beyond your aircraft's capabilities. And don't get caught by your superiors (especially in the military) violating regulations. This time, the odds catch up with Magee:

> *Imagine my plight when, arriving back at the*
> *aerodrome, I was told to report to the Chief Flying Officer's*
> *office immediately. I went there, shivering in my boots, to*
> *face both the C.O. [Commanding Officer] and the C.F.I. [Chief*
> *Flight Instructor]. Apparently the poor benighted farmer had*
> *lodged a complaint against me (the Harvard was going too*
> *fast for him to get his number), and what could I say in my*
> *own defense? Of course it was useless to plead engine*

*trouble, as they obviously knew I had been deliberately 'low-*
*flying', the greatest crime you can commit in this outfit.*

However, Magee somehow manages to dodge the bullet. It seems that John had out-performed all the other students on a critical test, and the brass couldn't quite throw him out after such a fine performance!

> *... the C.O. said he was probably going to wash me out,*
> *and went over to the Administration Building to see how I*
> *came out in our Ground School Finals, which had just been*
> *posted. I sat in silence with the C.F.I. who was just civil*
> *enough to offer me a cigarette. Almost 10 minutes later the*
> *C.O. came back into the room, slapped me on the back, and*
> *said "Sorry, laddie, we haven't a hope of washing you out.*
> *You came in first!" This was really fantastic news as our*
> *subjects covered everything I've never been any good at —*
> *Aero engines, Armament, Navigation, Air-frame*
> *construction, Theory of Flight, Signals, Morse, etc, most of*
> *which I thought I'd flunked. So I escaped with the skin of my*
> *teeth.*

The C.F.I. and C.O. knew they had the makings of a first-rate fighter pilot on their hands, and didn't want to break his spirit. Magee sums up the entire incident:

> *His [the C.O.'s] final words to me were: "And for God's*
> *sake, remember that the crime is not in the doing, but in the*
> *getting caught!"*

John is very fortunate to have had such wise leaders, experienced pilots who recognized that fine balance between insubordination and benevolent rascality. As important as learning the stalling speed of a Fleet Finch, or what to do if your engine quits in mid-air, is learning when and where to bend or break the rules.

Aviation in itself is not inherently dangerous. But to an even greater degree than the sea, it is terribly unforgiving of any carelessness, incapacity or neglect.

—Captain A. G. Lamplugh, British Aviation Insurance Group, London. circa early 1930's

Perhaps in no other field can one learn so much from the experience of others; indeed, the job of flying instructors is to not only teach what is on the syllabus, but also impart their own personal experience. Inadvertent lessons are also important. Magee had a couple of opportunities to benefit from the experiences of others. He tells his family about them:

> Yesterday a chap called M—who had of late rather a high opinion of himself as a flier — landed upside down on a fence at the far end of the landing field. Plane caught fire but we got him out. Apart from burns, most noticeable result in M—: MODESTY!

In the same letter, John relays another lesson about the function of luck, divine guidance, and/or guardian angels:

> Last weekend a Harvard (our next type, if we go to Fighter School) flew over the aerodrome at low altitude in a blinding snowstorm. We couldn't see him and he couldn't see the ground. We sent up Very Lights to bring him in, which fortunately he saw and somehow realized that he was over an aerodrome; came in and landed, heaven knows how. Much excitement, inspection of the Harvard, etc. He had twenty minutes gas left and was headed direct for Lake Ontario. If he hadn't seen our lights he would have run out of gas half way out — very lucky.

Another adventure happened to John himself when his engine quit after performing aerobatics:

*Today I learned how to do a stall turn and a chandelle, both rather exciting manoeuvres. We had to keep below 1500 feet as the visibility was practically nil. Finally the engine froze up and we had to make a forced landing just beside the Welland Canal. Fortunately it was only a stone's throw from the aerodrome.*

All in a day's work as a student pilot. John would have at least one more forced landing later on in training.

It is imperative that instructors and examiners try and make absolutely certain that the student not only can be, but should be, advanced. John handles this test during his 50-hour check ride with apparent ease:

*On my fifty-hour check F/O Vincent, the assistant Supervising Officer here, told me to do a snap half roll and loop out at 2,000 feet. Evidently wanted to see if I would do it (Aerobatics are generally done at 6,000 feet). Tremendous thrill.*

John is constantly challenged not only while flying but on the ground. It is here that his experience at Rugby holds him in good stead; he knows what he must do in order to perform well on exams:

*I expect Scot over here next week-end, when, incidentally, our final Ground School Exams take place. Rumours are that these will be very tough. Tonight our flight got its first late passes (1 o'clock) since being here. I had planned to go down to see "Gone With The Wind," in St. Kitts[6], but am too tired and think that perhaps it would be wiser to get in a good night's sleep before my test tomorrow. So much hangs in the balance. The thought of it is rather frightening. However, to counteract the fear is its most effective enemy, annoyance, because I am so far behind now, having been once ahead of everybody. Had I not been in the hospital, I should now be worrying about my 50 hour check instead of the 20. But such is luck.[7]*

It is worth noting that Flight Officer Vincent is a "regular" RCAF flying officer, not a civilian instructor such as A.K. Paterson. John's ease at passing his 50-hour check ride speaks highly for the program in general and the instructors in particular.

There are a few breaks in training. In March, John managed to visit family and friends in New York, New Jersey and Connecticut. John relates the events in a letter to his parents and brothers:

*I had half hoped to get home [Washington, D.C.] over the weekend, as we got one at very short notice, due partly to the fact that we were well up in flying hours, and largely to the fact that the field was under water. Indeed we thought the spring thaw had at last set in, but for the last two days a real blizzard has been in evidence which has kept us grounded all the time. I got as far as N.Y. on Friday after much hubble-bubble with the border officials . . . . at Niagara Falls. I had half a mind to go on to Washington but the thing that finally decided me was that I had left the Irving Hotel as my telegraphic address in case the thaw should stop and flying be resumed on Sunday. I am sorry I did not phone from the city as it has suddenly struck me that a letter I wrote to David may have led him — and you — to believe that I would be coming. But my idea was to say nothing about coming until I was sure I could.*

John visited Avon Old Farms School, apparently in the company of "Suzanne" and a couple of boys from Avon (note the photograph in the back of this section showing John in his RCAF uniform at Avon's Diogenes Arch):

*On Saturday Suzanne, self, and two Avon boys drove up there to see the place. I was given a very welcome reception by all and sundry. I think the combination of my modest uniform and the very attractive young lady I was with was enough to create quite an impression on the faces I had time to scrutinize. Poor Dean S—is rather worried, I think, about losing half the "student body" — his favorite phrase — to the RCAF at the end of the year! I only had time to flee in and out of everybody's room yelling salutations. Mr. G was pleased to see me, I think. Back in town to a wonderful dinner at the M's for which we were horribly late despite our hasty departure from Avon. After dinner Larry called up, having charged down from Cornell to see me, so Sue, self, Adala and Willet drove in to his mother's apartment to pick him up and we all went out together for a short while. Then I drove Sue and Adala home for an early night.*

Magee then flew back to Buffalo, the nearest commercial airfield to St. Catharines. Along the way, it appeared that the aircraft really struggled, interrupting John's flirting with the "hostess":

*Next day, I had to fly back to make it in time. Caught the 3:05 p.m. from La Guardia for Buffalo. Flew into some very very dirty weather near Buffalo which must have been the beginning of this virtual hurricane we're submitting to now. I had been talking to the 'hostess' for some time when the storm broke. Immediately people were thrown from their seats, the lights in the cabin went on and off. Women screamed and a baby was sick. A hostess immediately enlisted my aid as being the only person used to that sort of thing — then the old man traveling with the baby added to the child's unhappiness by being sick likewise over it. At that point the lights failed altogether and the 'bumps' were so terrific I really began to wonder if the pilot would ever get the big liner down before the wings crumpled. A woman became hysterical and roared with laughter about it all. I had to be rather rough with her. Finally we got down with the help of flares and R/D/F (Radio-Direction-Finding, the study of which is at last becoming some significance to me when I realize that without it that ship could never have reached Buffalo).*

The rain is so heavy that he was forced to walk from the US/Canadian border at Niagara Falls back to St. Catharines. Ever the story-teller, John relates the rest of the story to his family:

*I got to Niagara in pouring rain only to find all the roads going out, under water, bus services discontinued and no taxi willing to risk the nine-mile trip to the field. I had to be in at eleven so decided to walk it. It took me over four hours to make it and though I was a little late nobody said anything. Have a bit of a cold as a result of my simultaneous drenching and freezing, but beyond that no ill effects.*

John's last flying day at St. Catharines was on March 27th and was a busy one. Four flights with instructor Paterson, including formation and blind flights (flying by instruments only) to/from RCAF Hagersville, about 30 miles from St. Catharines. Magee's last flight was a one-hour solo flight, where he said goodbye and thanks to the marvelous Finch. At this point he has had 42 hours, 45 minutes of dual instruction, 50 hours, 50 minutes of solo time (total time: 93 hours 35 minutes), spread out over 99 flights, all in the Fleet Finch.

Growing from a neophyte airman to a confident pilot in three months' time, John had been given a good start. His love of flying has truly been kindled. In spite of all that had happened, John has remained on the path, with all of its twists and turns. Elementary Flying Training

School was done; it was now time to move to the next level: the Service Flying Training School (SFTS). John was assigned to No. 2 SFTS in Uplands, Ontario.

This assignment meant one thing to John: Fighters!

## St. Catharines to Uplands, Ontario
## No. 2 Service Flying Training School (SFTS)
## April 1941 to July 1941

*The stars... seem to watch me through the long night's*

*vigil, and I am not alone. With all its discomforts, this is the*

*life! The throb of an aeroplane engine is music in my ears*

*now. It has all the power of Beethoven, the grandeur of*

*Wagner, and the eagerness and intensity of Strauss...*

*—JGM*

John traveled the approximately 350 miles from St. Catharines to No. 2 Service Flying Training School (SFTS) in Uplands, Ottawa, to join Course #25. By this time John was well on the track to becoming a fighter pilot, and at Uplands he will fly two single-engine trainers: the Yale and the Harvard. (By contrast, prospective bomber pilots would be sent to schools where they would learn to fly multi-engine aircraft such as the Cessna Crane.)

First up on John's list was an intermediate trainer, the North American Aircraft Company's Yale. Called the NA-64 by North American, the Yale had fixed landing gear, a 400 hp Wright R-975 engine, a maximum speed of 166 mph and a cruise speed of 146 mph. As used by the RCAF, the Yale was designed to assist student pilots in bridging the gap between flying primary trainers such as the 125 hp Fleet Finch and Tiger Moth and flying the much more powerful 600 hp Harvard.

Training at Uplands was administered by RCAF instructors (instead of the civilian instructors that were used at St. Catharines). On April 10th, Magee had his first flight in Yale number 3440 with Flight Officer Knowles. It was a mark of Magee's proficiency as a pilot that he soloed in the Yale on the *very first day he flew it*, after three flights with F/O Knowles.

Moving right along, Magee had four flights on April 12th (three of them solo), and two final flights in the Yale on April 14th (both solo).

Nine days after John started flying at Uplands, he had his first flight in the more powerful Harvard advanced trainer. The Harvard, also built by North American, is radically different from the Finch and the Yale. With 50% more engine power than the Yale and retractable landing gear, the Harvard can be a handful, especially during takeoff and landing. Along with the complexity of the aircraft, Magee was now flying at Uplands, an incredibly busy airfield.

John's first flight in a Harvard was on April 19th, in Harvard Mark II number 2645, with instructor Flight Sergeant Grosswith. After that first flight, John was reunited with F/O Knowles on the 19th, 20th and 22nd. On April 22nd, after a mere six instruction flights (six hours and 15 minutes of instruction), Magee solos in the same Harvard that he flew on his first flight. This was very quick progress.

The ubiquitous North American Aircraft Company T-6 Texan, in various guises, trained more Allied pilots during WWII than any other training aircraft. In the United States, the T-6 was known to the Army Air Corps as the "AT-6" and to the U.S. Navy as the "SNJ". Sent to the Royal Air Force and the Royal Canadian Air Force, the T-6 was christened the "Harvard."[8]

The Harvard boasted a Pratt & Whitney R-1340 Wasp radial engine, generating 600 hp. This powerplant resulted in a maximum speed of over 200 mph, and a cruise speed of 145 mph.

Still in "total immersion" mode, John flew the Harvard often, sometimes three or four flights a day. He is still pushing it, walking the thin line between obeying orders and finding his own way. Every pilot takes a different path on the way to becoming proficient. Two students, each following the same curriculum at the same time and having the same instructor, will wind up becoming different pilots. John, being a natural stick-and-rudder pilot, continued to prove that he had all the diverse elements that make a good fighter pilot.

But even with a natural pilot, there is still much to learn. Every type of airplane has its general characteristics which one must learn. And, like pilots, any two aircraft rolling off the assembly line one after the other will behave differently in the air. The student pilot learns to *listen* to his craft as he flies, listen to the story the plane is telling him. Listen well, and the plane will let you know that there is trouble somewhere, long before there is any indication on the instruments. An unknown tremor, a different sound, a sudden or subtle feeling on the controls; all these things inform the pilot who takes the time and effort to be aware of them.

The students at No. 2 SFTS knew that flying the Harvard was the last step in their training. After that, they would (if they continued) graduate to "real" fighter aircraft. There was now a more earnest element in the training: pay attention, for you will most likely need all this information and more when you have the enemy shooting at you with deadly intent.

John continued to write many letters even during this intensive training. He was extremely verbose and descriptive. He described good and bad incidents with equal enthusiasm. It is through these letters that we gain an understanding of what Magee was going through at the time.

In a letter to his family dated April 21ˢᵗ John describes his training up to that point. He had about 10 hours solo in the Yale, and was starting training in the Harvard. He started the letter by describing the Harvard:

> *You have no idea how fast, noisy, and generally terrifying those Harvards are. What thrills me is that planes of this type were actually used by the French against the Germans at Dunquerque. They have between eighty and ninety instruments as well as bomb-racks and machine guns (2) – though we usually carry camera guns for training purposes. I have not actually soloed in one yet, although I was ready to a week ago – the weather has always interfered. However I have flown about ten hours solo on the Yale, an Intermediate trainer rather like the Harvard but without a retractable undercart and with a 350 instead of 600 horse-power engine.*

Later in the April 21ˢᵗ letter, Magee describes his third flight in a Harvard. Instructor Flight Officer Knowles has John fly them up in the country north of Ottawa, and then proceeds to demonstrate just what the Harvard, in the hands of a good pilot, can do:

> *Yesterday I flew my instructor up into the Gatineau Hills, North of Ottawa, about a hundred miles "into the interior" as non-Canadians love to say to a large lake with rocks and islands sticking up all over its surface, every inch of ground covered with bare trees, - just about the most desolate spot I have ever seen. There he took over the controls and for forty-five minutes gave me the most thrilling low-flying exhibition I have ever dreamed of. Low flying in a Fleet was a thrill but going 180 to 200 in a Harvard six inches off the ground (or water) in this case is really something. You*

*haven't live yet, poor earthbound mortals! He flew between*

*two rocks about ten feet apart (wing span of a Harvard is*

*forty-two feet) like this:*

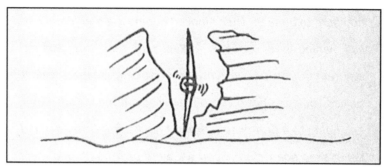

John G. Magee Family Papers, Record Group No. 242,
Special Collections, Yale Divinity School Library

*... and did three slow rolls in succession not more than eighty*

*feet off the surface of the water (the best of fliers expect to*

*lose a hundred feet in a roll). Just to the side of the lake was*

*a big rocky mountain which we climbed in circles, then down*

*went the nose and we flew vertically down a five hundred*

*foot precipice, leveling off once more just over the water. On*

*the way back we ran into a thunderstorm and I came the*

*nearest to being air-sick I have yet in my aeronautical career!*

During this flight, F/O Knowles is implicitly encouraging John to go for it, to stretch himself and his plane. "Learn how to do this properly, and you'll be a long way towards being a fighter pilot." So Magee might be forgiven for some of the adventures he has later on... he has been told, albeit indirectly, that it's okay, even encouraged. And far from scaring John, this particular flight confirmed his desire to fly fighters, and has left him wanting more.

Magee writes another letter on April 30th, describing another experience, this time encountering another advanced fighter:

*I had some fun today. After sitting around in the flight*

*room all afternoon I at last got hold of a boat and started*

*out north to have a look at the mountains in the Gatineau*

*district. After about a quarter of an hour I noticed to my surprise that someone was on my tail. Remembering the elementary lesson I at once went into my Immelman and rolled down out of the loop so as to be on his tail; but he was nowhere to be seen. Then I looked behind me and found him still behind and above me. Realizing that this was no amateur I throttled back until he was alongside me — and it turned out to be a brand new Grumman Gulf-Hawk belonging to a fighter squadron at Rockcliffe, Ottawa. I had never seen one before. Soon we were at it again and must have maneuvered for three-quarters of an hour at least, he of course getting the better of me most of the time. One thing that amazed me was that although he had twice my speed he could still <u>turn inside</u> me, which speaks well for the ship's maneuverability as generally the faster a plane the larger it's turning circuit. And a Harvard is by no means clumsy. From my meager acquaintance with the Gulf-Hawk I prophesy a great future for it. It's just about the most vicious little clipper you ever saw — rather like an overgrown beetle bug in a perpetual temper.*

In some ways, Magee is more at home in Canada than in the United States. His accent and behavior lead some to believe that he is actually from England. John describes one incident in particular:

*Some days ago Colonel and Mrs. O'Connor gave a cocktail party for the Americans here at Uplands – I went along and had great difficulty in persuading people that I either was an American or had ever been in the States! I almost had to show my passport to the gentleman who opened the door!*

The Service Flying Training School lasted just two months; eight short weeks during which the students needed to learn as much as possible. From John's first flight on April 10th through his last flight on his 19th birthday, June 9th, John would be required to learn an incredible amount about all aspects of flight including air-to-air combat, formation flying, and all the other things in the syllabus. As with any proper school, much of what Magee learned was not in the official syllabus, but was nonetheless critical information that he needed to know. Each instructor imparted upon the students their own unique lessons based on personal experience.

There were still misadventures to be had, as well. In the same April 30th letter quoted above, John tells of running out of fuel north of Ottawa:

> On Saturday I got lost and made a forced landing up in the Gatineau Mountains near a tiny village called Notre Dame de la Salette where there wasn't even a telephone. It took me about three hours to hitch-hike back to Ottawa where I was severely reprimanded (a) for getting lost (b) for misjudging my petrol supply so as to have had to make a forced landing and (c) for taking so long to get back. None of these eventualities were exactly preventable and I felt rather unjustly treated. I suppose I might have watched my bearings rather more closely but at best I am no ace navigator.

During the same week, Magee misses a night training flight:

> The next day my alarm clock failed to go off though I had tested it three times to go off at 2:30 AM when I was to report for Night-flying. I woke up at 4:10 and of course it was too late to do anything about it, so I went back to sleep again trying to think of some explanation for the morrow. When I went over to fly in the morning I found I was "on-charge" for missing N-F. This is a significant affair in the Air Force. It's a

*sort of minor version of a court-martial, and if you once get on charge it goes on your records and automatically disqualifies you from getting a commission. I have only been on charge once before which was at Trenton for not shining my buttons on parade! That, however, was struck off my records after six months. But now at this final stage I have another charge on record and I am thoroughly disgusted. I believe I wrote you describing a commission as the one thing I wanted more than anything in the world, but also explaining that I didn't expect to get one. It now comes to light that I was top dog in my class for a commission, with recommendations from the C. O. at St. Kitts of which I hadn't the remotest idea. All of no avail now. You can't imagine how miserable I feel about the whole thing. It seems so petty that something so easy to go wrong on should decide one's future to such an extent, but I suppose they must draw the line somewhere.*

John starts off thinking that, because of his aerial and other mishaps, he will wash out of the program. Then, after he is starting to believe he is going to get his Wings, he is afraid he will not get an officer's commission. Not end-of-the-world if he doesn't, but it will certainly be disappointing.

Toward the end of his training, after surviving everything and still winding up at or near the top of his class, John has one final, horrifying fear: that he has done entirely *too* well, and will be kept in Canada as an instructor-pilot. This would be the absolutely worst thing that could happen to John, that he would be again thwarted in his quest to return to England.

Magee has one event toward the end of his course which could have easily injured or killed him, or gotten him booted out of flight training. During a night flight, Magee misjudges his height above ground while on short final, and puts the Harvard into the ground. Magee related the crash in at least two different letters, one to his friend and another to his family — although the descriptions appear to indicate two separate events, they are in fact the same (John apparently was not above embellishing or completely re-writing the facts in his letters).

John describes what happened to a friend, in an "oh, by the way" manner:

> Which reminds me that, since we last met, I had a lovely crash-up. I stalled too high off the ground at night and spun in from about 30 feet, did a lovely cartwheel, completely demolishing an aircraft. One wing was torn off, the other rumpled up like a concertina. The propeller shattered.
>
> I wasn't even scratched. I think I'd have been happier if I had been but I felt supremely ridiculous sitting in a twisted fuselage without a scratch!  And the undercarriage was wiped out. For all of which I lost my good name as a flier. And so it is, Guy, that my career has been by no means distinguished to date.

To his parents, John varies some of the details. In the letter to his friend, John remains in the aircraft during the crash; in the letter to his parents, dated April 30th, he was "thrown clear":

> Monday night I did something which affected my reputation as a flier, which has been unbelievably good to date, and was my one consolation. I misjudged a night landing and crashed on the runway, totally destroying a $35,000 aircraft but not even scratching myself. I was thrown clear (luckily my safety belt broke off) on the grass just off the runway. I don't think I have ever been so utterly mortified in my life. If I had been hurt myself I might have felt better about it!  Then again it wouldn't have been so bad (a) if it hadn't been my fault and (b) if I hadn't been in the 'dog-

*house' already. But, coming on top of all that, it sort of shattered me.*

In the same letter of April 30th in which John details, 1) running out of fuel causing an off-field landing, 2) missing Night Flying, and 3) the Harvard crash, John includes an amazing amount of detail about these events. Here he goes into more elaborate detail from his perspective on the Harvard crash:

*Since it's all over now I might as well describe what happened. I came in out of the circuit, having been flying one and a half hours and feeling ready for bed. Everything seemed all right until I was approaching the end of the flare-path. Suddenly I began to feel that something was wrong. I glanced at my air-speed indicator which read 85 m.p.h. Rather low, I thought (the Harvard's landing speed is 90 to 95 m.p.h.) and put my nose down a bit to gain the extra speed necessary. Then I couldn't figure out just how high I was. One's idea of elevation is not very good at night. A light looks the same at a hundred feet as it does at ten — at least as far as I can make out. Suddenly I found out that I was practically on the ground and my immediate reaction was to pull the nose up. If I had remembered to hit the throttle I would have been O.K. but in the thrill of the moment I forgot it. The aircraft started up again and stalled about 20 feet off the ground. Immediately I lost control. A wing dropped and I dropped onto the wing-tip. There was a terrific jar, then I was thrown out of my seat as the plane cartwheeled around the wing-tip and dug her nose in, I landing on my face feeling very silly and angry. The plane looked so funny sort of groveling around that I was almost tempted to laugh. Then all was still and I sat and swore silently for about a minute until a car came dashing out with the fire truck and ambulance behind it. It contained my own instructor, Flying Officer K who happened to be Flying Control Officer for that night. He didn't know who it was and when I told him "yes it's Magee" he gave a little laugh and said "I might have known — you've certainly been having yourself a field day, haven't you?" Anyway he was so nice about it that I crawled into the back of the car and cried like a baby. I ought, I suppose, to be grateful for avoiding any black eyes, but I can't help feeling rather mortified that what started out to be such a promising career had to go and spoil itself like that. I think I was very lucky not to be washed out. At least I am still going to get my Wings.*

Here are the facts, insofar as can be gathered from the records: Magee's night crash happened on May 13th in Harvard #2635 at 3:10 in the morning. In Magee's logbook, there is a mark in the Pilot column, an exclamation mark in the Duty column, and a comment by the Officer Commanding: "Aircraft ground looped — assessed as inexperience."

In the "Flying Accident Signal Report" form the damage to the Harvard itself was categorized as "C3." This is defined as:

Category C Damage
The aircraft sustains damage to a major component requiring repair beyond field level resources including those occurrences where:
 **(3) the repair is carried out by a mobile repair party from a depot level or contractor;**

The "Flying Accident Report" (different from the "Flying Accident Signal Report)," has not much more information: "Ground looped on landing causing considerable damage to plain[sic]."

In searching the operational records for RCAF Harvards, there does not seem to be any entry of any incident involving Harvard #2635, other than a Category C accident on December 19th, 1940 at SFTS #2 Uplands (before John had arrived). Also, the Operational Record Book for SFTS #2 does not even mention the ground loop, although it does record many others. There was a visit by VIPs to the Station on that day, which may have distracted the powers-that-be from John's crash.

Even with his record possibly tarnished, there was consolidation in the old aviator adage "Any landing you can walk away from is a good one." But it is certain that John did not feel his night "landing" to be a good one in any way, shape, or form. After Magee walked away from this crash, he had several subsequent instructional and solo night flights (four with an instructor, five by himself) without further incident, so it appears that John learned what he needed to learn about landing at night.

Certainly he had some punishments: John's final remarks in his April 30th letter indicated the punishments ladled out for the week's misfortunes:

> Now for my various offenses I have three days C-B [Confinement to Barracks], seven days R-P (restricted privileges — no canteen, no late passes, and pack drill every day) and eleven days washing planes at the rate of two hours a day. It's a great life! I thought of applying for a week's leave to get rested up but I don't want to impress them too much with the fact that I can't take it! I am passed fit for flying duties now, and am up again for night flying tonight. I should be frightened except for the fact that I've had so much bad luck that the law of averages, if nothing else, demands that I get a good break once in a while!

It seems that John, having suffered a horrible week, was still committed and enthusiastically moving forward. He learned what he could from the events. "This is the life!" he even exclaimed. The last line says it all:

> Meanwhile Excelsior — Onward and Upward!

Magee was able to walk away from his training accidents with a lot of experience. Some of his classmates weren't as fortunate. There were many, many accidents during this intensive training, too many of them fatal. Training accidents, both in Canada and England, account for an appalling number of deaths. Which is not surprising, since you are taking a young man and putting him in charge of high-performance aircraft, expecting him to not only learn to fly but also fight in it, all with a minimum of introduction.

In May John took his various written and flying exams. Every pilot, military and civilian, has to take these tests, and knows how difficult they can be. Especially when events seem to conspire against them. In a letter to his family, John lets them know what happened. All pilots, past, present, and future, can relate:

*The main reason you haven't heard from me these last few days has been our final exams, which are now over. Knowing me to be the mechanized moron I am, I am sure that you will readily agree, with all my Ground School Instructors, that Providence must have had a hand. All the results are not out yet but I got 197/200 in Navigation (phenomenal for me as it is a subject far beyond my innocent comprehension), 98/120 in Engine and Maintenance, and 91/100 in Armament. I came first in Navigation and second in Armament. The other results are not out yet. In my Flying I had a mixture of success and comparative failure. In my Instrument Test (Blind Flying) I started off on the wrong foot and never got right again. My take-off (blind) was all right until I tried to pull the undercart up but it stuck. While endeavoring to get it working I omitted to uncage my directional gyro, which registered 00 degrees ahead when all the time I was turning! That rather shook me up and I stank all the way through. That afternoon it became very hazy — you couldn't see the sun. My only consolation, as I sat in Ground School in the afternoon, was that I wasn't having my Wings Test that day, when all of a sudden a corporal came in and "Magee was wanted for his Wings Test." My heart fell to my boots, because everyone who flies knows that he can fly well one day and not the next. I was panic stricken as*

*I knew it was an "off day" for me — and it was so hazy you couldn't see the ground from a thousand feet. And there was no horizon. However I reported at the Flight room and found, to add to my despair, that I had drawn Flight Lietuenant S— who is accredited with being the toughest marker on the station. It was a very nervous I who climbed into a Harvard for the last time. It just happened that I got the highest standing in my Wings Test of all in our course except Steve B—, who had one mark more (he was at St. Kitts with us — I think I told you about his being dropped from the U.S. Army Air Corps two weeks before graduation).*

*So it all goes to show that you gain on the swings what you lose on the roundabouts. In a way I am rather glad that I didn't do well in Instruments as they are inclined to make bomber pilots of the good instrument fliers. I think I am a cert. for a fighter pilot now but I shall not be getting a commission — at least for a while.*

In a letter written to his family back in May, John had shared some words of warning for his family, and for anybody else who might listen. Perhaps John was speaking more directly to his brothers; they were too young to join at that time but John wanted to make sure that they knew the threat that existed:

*I believe from what I am learning of aerial warfare that if this war is over in two years it will be the wrong way. Furthermore I am convinced that the United States must not make the tragic mistake of France in saying "it can't happen here" — all you have to do is transpose the Atlantic for the Maginot Line and you have what seems to me to be a very similar (almost ominously similar) situation. By all means have your blackout practices. Practice, practice, practice, all* *the time for the worst. It may never happen but <u>nobody</u>*

*<u>knows</u>. Meanwhile if you <u>expect</u> it you are giving yourselves*

*a little free life insurance...*

John's words are very prophetic. Six months later, the illusion of U.S. invulnerability was shattered with the attack on Pearl Harbor. John couldn't have imagined that the attack would come from the west instead of the east, but he was right: *Nobody knows.*

In the quote below, substitute "Atlantic" with "Pacific" and you have a foretelling of the Japanese attack on Hawaii. (John also talked about single bombers carrying massive payloads instead of smaller bombers carrying lighter loads, but he was not far off with the prediction in general. Certainly, after the attack on Pearl Harbor Americans did indeed "rue the day."):

*I have no patience with the Americans who insist that*

*they are safe behind the Atlantic. The fact that bombers are*

*made now which can fly across the Atlantic and back with*

*<u>thirty tons</u> of bombs may not mean anything to them, but*

*they may live to rue the day when they failed to read their*

*newspapers with foresight.*

Then John imparts some hard-won wisdom:

*You can't know too much. In our own case we are*

*learning gradually that it isn't necessarily the most dashing*

*hero who makes the best fighter pilot. It is the man who*

*knows his machine, knows his enemy, and above all who*

*<u>knows himself</u>. It is only by knowing the limitations of all*

*three that he can form any plan of attack.*

## Wings

The last flight Magee took at No. 2 SFTS was on his 19th birthday, June 9th and marked as "Radio Formation" in his logbook (it was most likely a celebratory birthday flight). A week later, despite all of his misadventures and accidents, John finally got his Wings. The Wings Parade for Course #25 was held on Monday, July 16th, 1941, and saw the graduation of 46 RCAF students, five from the RAF, and one lone Australian. John was presented his Wings by Group Captain Curtis, followed by tea for the graduates and guests afterwards in the Drill Hall. Although he did manage to get his Wings, John did not get the officer's commission that he was hoping for, and was, for now, "only" a Sergeant-Pilot.

In the space of time between finishing his training and getting his Wings, John took a trip to the base at Trenton, where he ran into some old comrades:

> The other day I flew a Harvard to Trenton to visit some
>
> of my acquaintances there. (You may remember that that is
>
> where I was so happy doing Guard duty!). I chanced to run
>
> into the C.O. of the Security Guard there. He said to me
>
> "Really, Mr. Magee, don't you feel that all in all you had a
>
> pretty good time here?" You should have seen the look I
>
> gave him — it was one of such ferocity that he turned and
>
> practically trotted away with his tail between his legs.

During the course of his training, John has overcome the initial shock of joining the military, gotten sick several times, survived several crashes, and managed to charm his way out of several incidents which should have seen him either killed or booted out of training. Amazingly enough, he has achieved what he set his sights on. It is a testament to the intelligence, commitment and sheer perseverance of John Magee that he was able to earn his Wings.

Still, one thinks that John wouldn't have been surprised.

## Posting

When entering a military service, bureaucracy is an inevitable force to be dealt with. John called it the "Military Mind" (MM). Most people who have served in any military service are familiar with what John meant — that mindless, faceless machine that determines where you go and what you do while you're under its direction.

After John was awarded his Wings, the MM dispassionately calculated John's fate. Always in need of good instructors, the MM had to have been impressed by John's training record. He could be of great service passing on what he had learned along with his own unique perceptions. This was the fate of many talented new pilots, forced to remain in Canada, with the MM paying no heed to the protestations of the pilot who would rather be flying in combat.

Magee did have an opportunity to express his wishes, though. In his May letter to his family, Magee relates this incident:

> Yesterday "Iron" Bill the C.F.I. (who is the toughest man I have ever run into in my life — and the squarest) asked us all what we wanted to do. I asked for Fighter Reconnaissance (sea), Bomber, and Instructor, in that order. Of all the horrible things that could happen, being kept in Canada to instruct for the rest of the War is the most horrible thing that could happen to any of us. I am only afraid that my lucky high in my Wings Test may lead to my being made an instructor.

According to the caprice of warfare, the MM could decide that the need was greater in England. Combat pilots were *the* critical resource, even more important than aircraft. It was far easier to build a new airplane than create a trained pilot. Either way, the MM most likely had given little or no weight to John Magee's personal desires in the matter.

In short order, the decision was made, and in due course John knew that all of his work, persistence and commitment had paid off, as newly-minted RCAF pilot John Gillespie Magee, Jr., serial number J5823, with brand new Wings, was being sent to war.

## Captains of the Clouds

In one of John's letters to his family, he mentions a movie that he might have played a part in. The movie he was referring to, *Captains of the Clouds* starring Jimmy Cagney, was indeed filmed at Uplands, but several weeks after Magee had left. RCAF Uplands records indicate that filming began during July of 1941, during which time Magee was in the middle of the Atlantic Ocean en route to England. John may have seen some of the preliminary film scout crews, which is likely why he wrote, "This I think is a film made at Uplands in which I took part (formation, etc.)."

## Home for the last time

John received about two weeks of embarkation leave before being sent overseas. He immediately headed home to his family in Washington, D.C.

By all accounts, the two weeks spent with his family was a wonderful time. Mephistopheles, John's ancient Packard, took the family on picnics, sometimes traveling at such speed as to nearly launch the unsuspecting occupants airborne. Years later, John's brother David wrote this about John's last trip home:

*After John received his Wings in June, 1941, he came straight home on leave, and was with us for about ten days before sailing for England. They were ten days full of happiness and interest, and we now love, as a family, to look back upon them. He was so delighted that the desire of his heart was at last accomplished and the Wings were actually on his uniform. During this leave several expeditions were taken in "Mephistopheles," as John had named the big family Packard which had been bought very cheaply on Martha's Vineyard the summer before. The weather was warm during this leave, and on the two Sunday afternoons when he was home, the boys and their mother took out a picnic supper into the country, everyone being glad to cool off and to get away from the hot city streets.*

It appears that while home, John and his brothers hold an event to raise awareness of the threat that most of the United States seemed to be ignoring, and, at the same time, present an option for those who might wish to fight. David's letter also talks of this:

*On the second Sunday the boys hit on the idea of holding a recruiting meeting for the Royal Canadian Air Force, this idea having been inspired by a visit to the "Times Herald" office the day before, in which John had said that he would be glad to answer questions for young men who might be considering R.C.A.F. training. They rang up the different newspapers in town, and even got the news on the air at 4 pm, with the result that that evening from a dozen to eighteen young men (who were total strangers to the family) came in to hear what they would have to do before joining, etc. John put on his uniform and gave the evening to them, telling them all that he could of what would be required of them, and of what would lie ahead should they follow in his steps.*

John's mother Faith recalled this event as well, and told her mother about it in a letter:

*He [John Jr.] has been quite prominent in the newspapers here, chiefly owing to Christopher's efforts. The latter simply loves publicity, and on John's arrival here rang up practically every newspaper in town to arrange interviews. To add to this, young men began inquiring over the phone as to how to get into the RCAF so our boys hit on the idea of holding a recruiting meeting here last Sunday evening. Not only did they ring up endless people in town but they had the following notice broadcast at 4 p.m. from the local station:*

*"Will all young men, 18 to 32 interested in joining the Royal Canadian Air Force, as pilots, observers, mechanics, gunners, radio operators, riggers, etc., come at 8:30 o'clock tonight to 2118 Bancroft Place, where a recruiting meeting is being held. John Magee, Sergeant Pilot, RCAF"*

*As the result of all this, when John Sr. came back from evening service, about 9:30 he found 10 young men here listening to John Junior who was telling them all he could as to how to get into the Service. Some of them were so keen and one of the last to come between ten and eleven p.m. wanted to be a gunner, which as young John told him, is the most dangerous and most heroic job of them all. It was the first time I have seen our boys organize anything completely by themselves and I watched them with the greatest interest.*

It was during this time at home that John unexpectedly received word of his officer's commission, a promotion earnestly desired but not really expected. Back in April, John had written to his family about what he estimated his chances were of getting promoted:

*Commissions are getting scarcer and scarcer. Before the War everyone who got through the flying course automatically got a commission but they are rather expensive for the Government and are therefore getting almost inaccessible. I am gradually resigning myself to going overseas as a sergeant pilot and having to salute all my*

*school friends!*

However, the MM struck again, and this time, the results were wonderful. Notified by telegram, John is, in turns, astonished, ecstatic, and joyful. Faith, John's mother, relates what happened in a letter to her mother:

*I was upstairs when the news arrived and I suddenly*

*heard such an extraordinary noise from the dining room*

*where he and father were having breakfast but I could not*

*decipher whether it mean pain, delight or what. Our maid*

*was scared stiff and hardly dared come into the room but*

*was about to peep around the corner when John came and*

*slapped her on the back so hard that she felt it until evening*

*but as she said, she really did get great kick out of him.*

On July 1st, the day he received the telegram announcing his commission, John took leave of his mother and father. (His brothers were already gone, sent to summer camps.) John apparently felt that, given the raise in pay provided by his commission, he could afford to fly on his way back to Canada for debarkation, in order to save precious time. His parents took him to the brand new Washington National airport (which had just opened two weeks prior, on June 16th [9]).

Faith Magee, in a heartfelt letter written to her mother in England, described what would turn out to be John's last visit home, and the last time she would ever see her son:

*We are sending over to England now, the most*

*precious contribution which we can possibly send in the*

*shape of our eldest son. He has already left us (after a very*

*happy leave of about two weeks) for the Canadian Port from*

*which he will probably sail in a very short time...*

*We had a wonderful evening with him the night before*

*he left when we all three talked frankly about many things*

*and I am sure no one of us will ever forget it.*

Faith went on to describe going to the airport and seeing her son leave:

*The airport is a marvelous place, quite new and air-*

*conditioned and as we stepped into the cool and quiet halls*

*one could hardly realize that one was in a place of travel*

*excepting for the loudspeakers every now and then which*

*announced the arrival and departure of planes. It was like*

*going out into a greenhouse when we went to see him board*

*his plane and we watched it until it was a tiny little speck in*

*the clouds.*

With a heart full of gratitude for being able to see her son before he left into an unknown future, Faith seemed to be certain that John had found his place in the world:

*This leave has been one of the happiest we have ever*

*had with him, and though he is still immature in many ways,*

*yet we feel that his life in the army has done a great deal for*

*him.*

From never having been in an aircraft to having learned how to fly a high-performance airplane in combat, Magee has undergone a near miraculous transformation in nine months. Not all the changes are visible, however, and are more sensed than seen by his family.

Truly, it seems that John has found his place in the sun in becoming a pilot. However, there is a downside to all of this, the reason why a large amount of money has been invested in him to learn how to fly combat aircraft. And the bill, the return on investment, is about to come due.

## Halifax, Nova Scotia, Canada to London, England
## In Transit
## July 1941

On Tuesday, July 1st, John flew from the brand-new Washington National Airport to Boston, where he met with a friend for a couple of hours, then took the night train to Montreal. There he purchased his officer's uniform, and got saluted for the first time:

*I ordered my uniform this morning and it is to be ready*

*at noon. I already have the hat and am wearing it. I was*

*saluted this morning for the first time by an Army Corporal.*

*He was rather taken aback when I rushed up and grabbed*

*him by the hand and congratulated him on being the first*

*man ever to salute my undistinguished self...*

John reminds his family of his new status, writing "P/O John Magee" at the top of his letter.

A long and strange journey has brought John Magee to the brink of achieving his dream of returning to England. Pilot Officer Magee reported to Halifax to embark with an eastbound convoy.

While John was waiting for departure, he belatedly filled out his application to become an RCAF Officer, the "Officer's Application and Record Sheet." John records his flight times as follows:

St. Kits — Fleet Finch — 93 hours, 35 minutes
Uplands — Yale & Harvard — 94 hours
Pittsburgh, Pa. — Stinson SMA — 2 hours
(Total flight time: 189 hours, 35 minutes)

The last entry regarding the Stinson undoubtedly happened with his cousin, Alan Magee Scaife, while visiting Pittsburgh. Alan owned a Stinson 105 "Voyager" in which he must have taken John (and much later, John's brother David) flying.

Sports played are listed as fencing, swimming, sailing, and "all other forms common to school." John lists French, Latin, Greek, as well as "Chinese (moderately)." The application is witnessed by John's friend Terk Bayly, and dated July 4th, 1941.

Prior to leaving home, John and his family arranged code words so that John could let his family know when he was leaving. David Magee recalls the details:

> It had been arranged before he left that when the date of sailing was known he would send us a post card, on which a reference would be made to the weather on a certain day. Two days before he left, he phoned from Canada asking for some money and saying (during the course of the conversation) "Tell Mother that it will be raining tomorrow."

John's final letter from Canada was written before his convoy departed, but was not delivered until a month later:

> We are leaving much sooner than expected (then follows a sentence which was taken out by the censor)....
>
> I was sorry to have to wire for money, but there have been unexpected expenses and we can't get a sou until we got on the boat, when we are to get ten pounds sterling. It will, however, be made up to you as we are going to be paid in England according to R.A.F. rates of pay (less than R.C.A.F.) and the residue has to stay on this side. I have signed this ($87 Canadian per month) over to you, and want you to deduct whatever I owe you from it and then start to invest it in something reliable — I suggest Aircraft.

John's journey back to England was nearly complete. He was poised to return to his adopted homeland, albeit by the hard way.

No. 1 Manning Depot, Toronto
aka the Canadian National Exhibition (CNE).

All photographs on the page are courtesy of the
New Westminster Public Library[10]

Aircraftsman AC2 J.G. Magee, Trenton.

John G. Magee Family Papers, Record Group No. 242,
Special Collections, Yale Divinity School Library

Magee took his 50-hour test in this aircraft,
Fleet Finch #4725,on March 5th, 1941.[11]

Photo courtesy of Canadian Museum of Flight,
Langley, British Columbia.

John (at right) at St. Catharines with (from left to right)
Fred Heather, Tom Gain and Duncan Fowler.

John G. Magee Family Papers, Record Group No. 242,
Special Collections, Yale Divinity School Library

John in Fleet Finch #4673 (which he flew for the first time on
March 21st, 1941... after the date of this picture (March 18th, 1941).
Possibly a posed picture for those at home!

John G. Magee Family Papers, Record Group No. 242,
Special Collections, Yale Divinity School Library

John, at the far left, at No. 2 SFTS, Uplands.

John posing by a North American Harvard aircraft.

John visits Avon Old Farms School in RCAF uniform and
poses in front of Diogenes Arch, March 16, 1941.

John G. Magee Family Papers, Record Group No. 242,
Special Collections, Yale Divinity School Library

From the motion picture "Captains of the Clouds" which started filming at Uplands the month after Magee departed.

Picture taken during production of the motion picture "Captains of the Clouds."

Promotional poster for "Captains of the Clouds,"
the movie filmed at Uplands a few weeks after Magee left Canada.

Getting his Wings from Group Captain Curtis, July 16, 1941.

John G. Magee Family Papers, Record Group No. 242,
Special Collections, Yale Divinity School Library

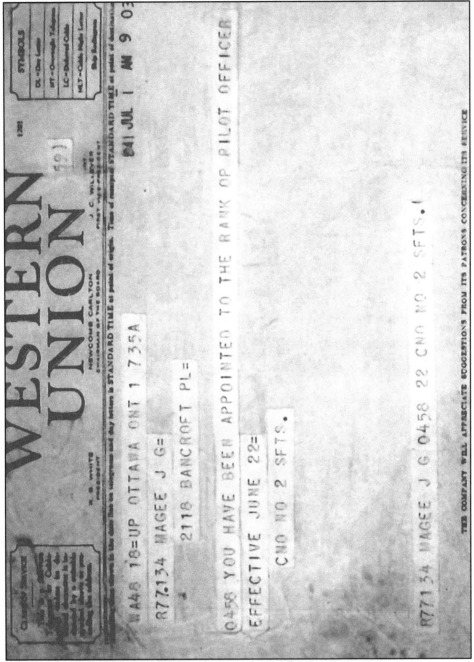

**"YOU HAVE BEEN APPOINTED TO THE RANK OF PILOT OFFICER
EFFECTIVE JUNE 22"**
Telegram informing Magee of his promotion to Pilot Officer.

John G. Magee Family Papers, Record Group No. 242,
Special Collections, Yale Divinity School Library

[1] St. John's Episcopal Church is known as "Church of the Presidents." Every sitting President of the United States starting with James Madison in 1809 has attended services at St. John's at least once. There is a pew at St. John's that is permanently designated for the President.

[2] Sunward I've Climbed, page 93.

[3] Letter from Geoffrey Sergeant to John Magee, dated October 12th, 1939.

[4] Letter from John to his family, dated 12/28/40.

[5] Letter from John to his family, dated 1/15/41.

[6] *Gone With The Wind* was released in Vancouver, BC, Canada, on Feb. 16, 1940. http://www.imdb.com/title/tt0031381/releaseinfo—accessed 2/15/14.

[7] Letter from John to his family dated 2/22/41.

[8] In 1940, the United States could not directly sell arms to Canada. The training aircraft manufactured in the United States by the North American Aircraft Company could not be flown directly to Canada, so they were flown to spots just south of the U.S./Canadian border. There they were towed across the border, sometimes by horses, and then flown to their individual destinations.

[9] http://www.mwaa.com/reagan/1277.htm —accessed 2/16/2014. John Magee departed from National Airport (now Ronald Reagan Washington National Airport). Terminal "A", which was the only terminal in use when the airport opened, is still there today.

[10] http://archives.newwestcity.ca/Photos//IHP9000/IHP9562-005.jpg—accessed 5/12/14

[11] Aircraft is currently located at Canadian Museum of Flight, Langley, British Columbia.

# England—1941

## Trans-Atlantic Journey
## Halifax, Canada to Bournemouth, England
## July 1941

John's convoy back to the United Kingdom departed from Pier 21[1] at Halifax, Nova Scotia, on or around July 6, 1941. He traveled onboard the Armed Merchant Cruiser HMS *California*[2], a ship which served as one of the escorts of high-speed convoy HX.136[3] [4] [5].

During training, John had made some good friends. Several of them were crossing to England about the same time as John, including Jack Coleman (with John on the *HMS California*), and Terk Bayly (on the *HMS Circassai*, an escort ship with convoy HX.137).

The crossing itself could be somewhat hazardous, given the continuing presence of Nazi U-boats in the area, though recently improved submarine hunting and anti-aircraft techniques by the Americans and British had reduced the score of the German wolf packs.

Convoy HX.136 is recorded as leaving Halifax on June 30th, and arriving Liverpool around July 18th. The departure dates don't match the rest of the information on when Magee departed Canada, however, the escort ships may have left Halifax after the convoy departed. Notes on the convoy indicate that the escorts joined the rest of the HX.136 convoy on July 13th.

Having made several ocean crossings in his life, Magee was no stranger to being out at sea. This particular voyage, however, was unlike anything he had ever experienced. The accommodations were very spartan, and he was sharing them with many others. On top of these cramped conditions, there was the looming threat that parts of the large convoy could be attacked without warning at almost any point along their route. The ship he had been on was an escort, and would have had to respond to any attack on the convoy. The area was very active, with the German battleship *Bismark* having been sunk southeast of Iceland in just the previous month.[6]

The *California* let John and Jack Coleman off in Reykjavik, Iceland and returned to Canada to escort the next convoy. HX.136 proceeded to Liverpool with other escort ships. Fellow trainee and friend Terk Bayly joined them, and they spent a week or so exploring Iceland awaiting a ride to the United Kingdom.

It is not certain which convoy ultimately took John and his compatriots from Iceland to Scotland, but it appears that it was SD.7

(departed Iceland July 26th, and arrived Scotland on the 28th). There were five ships in this convoy: *HMS Royal Ulsterman, Royal Scotsman, St. Mary's, Ulster Monarch, and Wells.* This convoy sailed up the River Clyde in Scotland, and disembarked its passengers in Greenock[7].

From Scotland, John took a long train ride southward (nearly 500 miles) to Bournemouth, near London, to find out his next assignment at the RCAF Pilot Reception Centre. Upon his arrival, he was met by long-time Rugby friend Dermott Magill, who, though enormously glad to see his friend, was undoubtedly wondering what in the world John Magee was doing back in war-time England. Years later, Magill recalled:

> When faced with all the amenities and comforts of a country at peace, he chose the harder, grimmer and more dangerous course, because he knew, as only the courageous do know, that peace is all very well but peace is no good if in your own heart you know there is something bad which must be stamped out if any peace is to last. When I went down to see him at Bournemouth the day after he arrived from Canada, I asked him why he had come over into the hell of war, and he replied in his very modest way, "I just felt I ought to." If everyone was like him this war, which now surrounds us both, would soon be over.[8]

John summed up the trip in the first letter he wrote to his family after arriving in England:

> I am afraid my letter-writing has not been any too good since sailing, but, to tell you the truth, we have had absolutely no time off, leave, or opportunities for getting organized at all. Our trip was very tedious, very uncomfortable, and we went all over the place on the way. Naturally, I can't say anything at all about it other than it took about a (censored word) to get over. I hope you got my cable.[9]

Another letter written to his cousin Alan and wife Sarah says much the same thing:

> I promised to write again when I arrived, so here is what little more news there is. It took about a month to get over, and we came by a most roundabout route. There is, I find, some truth in the saying: "Join the army and see the world" – (though, as I write, I can't help remembering a similar exhortation to "Join the Air Force and see the next!").[10]

Against all odds, John Magee was finally back in England.

## Bournemouth, England to Llandow, Wales
## No. 53 Operational Training Unit (OTU)
## July 1941 to September 1941

At Bournemouth, the final decision was made as to the fate of new pilots. The next step in the career of any new pilot in England was the Operational Training Unit (OTU). The RAF established the OTUs to complete the training that its pilots received in other programs, and to prepare pilots to fly combat operations. While at the OTU, the pilots would fly the very aircraft that they would eventually fight in. In Magee's case, having done so well in his training on single-seat aircraft, he was selected to fly the Supermarine Spitfire. This time the Military Mind seems to have gotten it right once more. John was sent to No. 53 OTU in Llandow, South Wales, for his final training.

No. 53 OTU was formed on February 18th, 1941[11]. Specifically formed to train pilots on Spitfires, this OTU moved to Llandow, Wales from Heston, England in June and July, just before Magee arrived.[12] Spitfires from No. 53 OTU were marked with squadron identifier "MV." If the Nazis invaded England, No. 53 OTU would instantly become an operational combat squadron, becoming No. 553 and No. 554 Squadrons, operating from Church Fenton.[13]

Aircraft that were once front-line were eventually replaced with newer models and then sent to the OTUs. When Magee arrived at No. 53 OTU, pilots were training on the Spitfire Mark I, most of which were used in the summer of 1940 during the Battle of Britain.

No. 53 OTU, Course No. 7 commenced on August 4th, 1941, consisting of P/O John Magee along with 12 other Pilot Officers and 29 Sergeant Pilots.

Magee updated his family, finding ways to avoid the censors and still let his family know what he was doing:

> *I am very happy here, though our living conditions*
>
> *aren't particularly luxurious. We sleep in one hut, walk half*
>
> *a mile to the bath hut, then on farther to the Mess, then a*
>
> *mile or so more to the flights. At any rate we shall be getting*
>
> *some exercise for a change. Only three of our whole bunch*
>
> *managed to get on fighters. Jack Coleman and Hugh Russell,*
>
> *both of whom I know very well, are here with me.*

The censors allowed John to give a fairly explicit description of where he was located. However, any enemy reading this would, in all likelihood, not come away any wiser:

> *Dad, do you remember a lady of Welsh origin telling us*
>
> *in the Parish House one day of a marvelous aerodrome with*
>
> *some curious features? Oddly enough that is where I am.*
>
> *You might tell her! This comes with all my love and good*
>
> *wishes. Give my love to the boys and make them <u>write</u>.*
>
> *P.S. I am not allowed to give you my address but I am*
>
> *not far from the place where Uncle E—was an Air Raid*
>
> *Warden.*

In his August 17th letter to his family, John indicated that he was trying to get in touch with Elinor, but seemed to be a bit nervous:

> *It's E—'s [Elinor's] birthday today. [August 17, 1921] I*
>
> *wrote her a letter yesterday, but fear that it won't reach her*
>
> *until tomorrow. Possibly I shall give her a ring tonight, that*
>
> *is if I can think of anything to say!*

Magee's first flight at No. 53 OTU was on August 6th in a Miles Master I. This initial flight was to get Magee back into flying mode after the long trip to the front; Magee's last flight prior to that had been in Canada on June 3rd, more than two months prior. During this flight, the instructor familiarized Magee with local area flying, and they engaged in some "circuits and bumps," flying for an hour and 20 minutes.

The next day, August 7th, had to have been a hallmark day in Magee's life. He was to be pilot-in-command of a Supermarine Spitfire. This was the culmination of so many months of training, effort and resolve, and now he was about to take flight in one of the world's preeminent fighter aircraft. In a coded message, he tells his family that he has achieved his dream of flying the Spitfire:

> *I am now training for operations on the one aeroplane*
>
> *I have always dreamed of flying. I think you know what that*

*is. Ask David. I expect to be here about five or six weeks*

*before joining my squadron...*

John started that day with a 20 minute flight in another Master I with Flight Lieutenant (F/L) Inness, which was logged as a "Spitfire Test." It was important to impart as much information as possible to a pilot who was going to fly a Spitfire, since the vast majority of Spitfires were built as single-seat fighters. The Finches, Yales and Harvards that Magee had previously flown were all two-seaters, giving instructors a chance to check out a student pilot's readiness to fly before allowing the student to fly solo. In the case of the single-seat fighter, the first flight was a solo flight, which had to be at least somewhat nerve-wracking for both instructor and student.

Flight Lieutenant Inness was probably a veteran of the Battle of Britain, which had been fought the year before. He had risen through the ranks from Pilot Officer, through Flight Officer, and on to Flight Lieutenant. At times, pilots who had flown a considerable amount of combat were sent to the OTUs, partially to rest them as well as to allow them to pass on to new pilots their experience in actual operations.

On this August day, F/L Inness had to attempt the near impossible: to distill all of his experience flying one of the world's most advanced fighter aircraft and impart that wealth of knowledge to a student.

The aircraft chosen for Magee's first flight was a Spitfire MKIA, serial number R6602. This particular aircraft had served with 65 Squadron during the Battle of Britain. In it, Pilot Officer Lawrence Pyman claimed to have shot down an ME-109 on August 14th, 1940. This aircraft also served with 238 Squadron before being retired from front-line service and sent to No. 53 OTU to train prospective Spitfire pilots.

Even though John had been briefed about flying the Spitfire, undoubtedly he received last-minute reminders. "Be careful when you retract the landing gear. You have to switch hands to do it." One can almost always tell a beginner Spitfire pilot by the way the plane wobbles after takeoff as the pilot grabs the stick with his left hand, and then moves his right hand to the gear selector.

John goes through the pre-takeoff checklist. Mixture to rich, propeller to coarse, magnetos off, throttle a quarter inch forward. Push one button and hold, then press the other button. The prop turns, slowly at first, then the engine catches and the prop starts turning in earnest. The sound, particular to the Rolls Royce Merlin engine, fills his ears; it is the sound of some wild wounded beast ready to take on anything.

Taxiing to the end of the runway, lining up into the wind, power is applied smoothly. The Spitfire accelerates quickly; much, much faster than the Harvard. Nearly full right rudder is applied to counteract the tremendous torque generated by 1,000+ horsepower engine turning the three-bladed prop.

In a letter to his cousin Alan Magee and wife Sarah, John recounts the feeling of taking off (in John's handwritten letter, he must have written "Spitfire" which was removed by censors):

> I could rhapsodize for pages about the [censored]. It is
>
> a thrilling and at the same time terrifying aircraft. It takes
>
> off so quickly that before you have recovered from that you
>
> are sitting pretty at 5,000 feet![14]

It wasn't long before this flight that John had flown in Pittsburgh with Alan in his Stinson 105 "Voyager," with all of 75 horsepower on tap. Alan had to have been thrilled and more than somewhat envious with John's description of flying one of the world's premier fighter aircraft. By all accounts, the Spitfire is an enormously responsive aircraft to fly; think "turn left" and the plane just seems to read your mind and turns to the left.

After an hour and 15 minutes, Magee reluctantly returned to his airfield, did the circuit, and landed. This momentous flight gets a single line in his logbook: "1st solo on type."

Continuing his familiarization flights in the Spitfire, Magee outstrips his classmates and gets grounded for a most peculiar reason:

> Today I have been grounded as I have too many hours
>
> ahead of the rest of my flight. Every time I go up I can't bear
>
> to come down while I have any gas left. Consequently I am
>
> way ahead of anyone else in "A" flight, to which I am
>
> attached...

In another letter John bemoans this same situation:

> Today the sun is shining for the first time since we got
>
> here. And I can't fly because I am too far ahead of the rest of
>
> the others. The irony of life!

In a pattern which started during flight training and would continue on to his next duty station, John seems to be having the time of his life:

> We are having a wonderful time here. The officer's mess is about the loudest, gayest place I have ever hit. Whenever anybody so much as scratches a plane he has to buy drinks all round. If he is in hospital or the mortuary it goes on his Mess Bill, which he'll never have to pay anyway.[15]

"Hit and run" combat operations are allowed during training, just not air-to-air combat. John eagerly awaits a chance to start inflicting damage on the enemy. In a letter to his family written on August 17th, 1941, John describes his desire to begin the fight:

> If we get a nice day (that is with cloud cover) a bunch of us are going to run across the French Coast and back in the hopes of finding something small and badly armoured to initiate ourselves on! Of course there is no telling what we will make of ourselves in this great game we have gotten into. Few of us, I imagine, have any ideas as to what may lie ahead. Personally, though I feel a certain inexpressible thrill and ecstasy at the prospect of operations. I also have that feeling which I call "dentist's tummy" — my mouth goes dry, hands clammy, and my knees feel as if they are about to give way. Then it passes and once again I am looking forward to it.

Two weeks before the conclusion of the course, on August 30th, John writes a letter to his family updating them on what's been happening, and showing that the reckless, daring John Magee has not altogether disappeared:

> I have been here almost a month now. The flying is as marvelous as the weather is atrocious. The Welsh hills bring

*rain every day. The other day I was lucky enough to get a Spit without any squadron markings on it so I could fly as low as I liked and not get turned in. First of all I beat up the Lyons for about three-quarters of an hour, almost touching the grass on the tennis court several times. After that I shot off to Reading and beat up Dermott for a while, then down to Mortehoe to have a look at Granny. Unfortunately at the top of the hill I misjudged a pull-out and left some elevator fabric on a bramble bush. Must have given her quite a thrill but it took some explaining back here.*

In an event eerily prescient of a future tragedy, John describes leading a flight down through clouds:

*Yesterday also I led a flight formation up through clouds (quite hard) — we stayed up for about an hour and then came down through a hole in the clouds, but when we arrived back here we found cloud right down to the deck. We were lucky all to get in without mishap.*

Evidently Magee is doing well in his training. Taking advantage not only of his instruction, he also seems to benefit from his several "unauthorized" dogfights in Canada. John recounts the results of practice attacks which utilize the gun cameras built into the wings of the Spitfire:

*We did some camera-gun attacks the other day, the results of which encouraged me very much, as I was the only person in the whole course who had the 'enemy' plane on the film for more than half the length. It was not particularly steady, but the aim and range were good. I am going to concentrate like mad on my shooting, as this is obviously what counts.*

John is more than ready to get to operations. He has already found out where he is likely to go first:

> I shall be joining a squadron just about the time you
> get this, I imagine. I am trying to get into a good Canadian
> squadron "resting up" in the North Country. This is the best
> time to join a squadron as they have had a chance to mold
> you into the scheme of things and you have a chance to
> practice, practice, practice so that when the squadron moves
> south again you are (theoretically) red hot...

In a country at war, the food is not the best. John attempts to compensate:

> Incidentally I ordered some vitamin pills especially
> constructed to compensate for rationing of eggs, milk, etc.,
> from the Medical Arts Building, Montreal, and am planning
> to have them regularly.

In a marked contrast to the low speeds and altitudes John was used to flying in the Finch and Harvard while in Canada, he is going much, much higher and faster:

> I have spent the whole day [practice] dogfighting, and
> feel most exhausted. Most of it was at 20,000 feet, where
> oxygen is needed. I felt like Icarus about to singe his wings.
> Incidentally I have been as high as 33,000 feet. Higher than
> the top of Mt. Everest!
> I have about thirty hours on Spitfires now, and expect
> to be through this course is a week, if the rain keeps off.

The reference to his flight to 33,000 feet was the flight he made on August 18th that served as the catalyst to writing *High Flight*.

Magee would fly from Llandow for the next month, getting two more hours of dual instruction in the Miles Master, and nearly 44 hours in

14 different Spitfires. All told, Magee had 30 different flights, three in the Master, and 27 in the Spitfire.

John's last flight at the OTU was on September 13th, 1941, in Spitfire MKIA #9817. He was rated "Average" for the course.

No. 53 OTU Course No. 7 is "posted out" on September 14th, 1941.

All preparations had been completed. John Magee was deemed ready to engage the enemy in single-combat, with Reginald Mitchell's[16] incomparable Supermarine Spitfire as his weapon.

# The Writing of *High Flight* — August 1941

Of all the flights John Magee made while at No. 53 OTU, one of them was very different.

By John's own account, *High Flight* "started at 30,000 feet, and was finished soon after I landed." The letter to his parents containing *High Flight* was dated September 3rd. According to his logbook, Magee made a "Climb to 33,000 ft." on August 18th, in a Spitfire MKI, serial number R6976. Thus, Magee must have written his sonnet sometime during the 17 days between August 18th and September 3rd. (Of course, he may have gotten the idea for the poem earlier than August 18th, with the flight to 33,000 feet bringing the nascent poem into focus.) John also made ten more Spitfire flights during this time period, including one on September 3rd, the date of the letter.

Exactly why John wrote *High Flight* in the first place is open to conjecture. It seems that he had not written any poetry since Avon; at least, there is no poetry in the archives written between Avon and August 18th. Perhaps it was a combination of events: discovering his passion for flying, returning to the land where he felt most at home, and, not least of all, being reunited with Elinor. Not to be underestimated as a source of inspiration was flying the Supermarine Spitfire, by all accounts an amazing aircraft for all pilots who flew her.

All of these elements were present on August 18th, and it could be that his flying Spitfire MKI R6976 to over six miles into the air brought them all together. The perspective is incredible from that high, and John was all alone with his thoughts, experiences, emotion and passion. Maybe for once he could not wait to get back to earth, capture that lightning in a bottle, and put it down on paper.

And certainly one cannot rule out divine inspiration. *High Flight* can be viewed as a tremendously spiritual sonnet.

Anecdotal stories abound regarding the first person to read *High Flight*. In one story, this person was Michael Le Bas[17], who was going through No. 53 OTU at the same time as Magee. Here is how the account about Le Bas starts:

*"The first person to read this poem later that day was*

*almost certainly Air Vice-Marshall M.H. Le Bas, with whom*

*Magee had trained, in the officers` mess."*[18]

Le Bas then gives his account:

> During our acquaintanceship, he had always maintained that his first love was poetry, although he had discovered that flying was not far behind. He was thus able to imbue his flying with a sense of lyricism.
>
> I happened to run into him shortly after his first flight in a Spitfire about which he was waxing lyrical. I urged him, though not very seriously, that since he had always wanted to be a poet he should put his feelings down in words.
>
> He thereupon sat down in the mess and composed, in a very short time, the first draft of High Flight written, literally, "on the back of an envelope".
>
> I must have been the first person to read it, but cannot claim that I foresaw its eventual fame. It was some years later that I heard of Magee's fate.[19]

It can be confirmed that Le Bas was in the same course as Magee; a picture of Class No. 7 at No. 53 OTU shows them both in the same row.

John appeared not to be tremendously forthcoming to his compatriots about his poetry-writing during his career in the RCAF. John's good friend from 412 Squadron, Rod Smith, indicated that he had no idea that Magee wrote poetry:

> I cannot remember John ever quoting poetry or even hinting that he liked it, let alone wrote it. I can only assume he thought barbarians like the rest of us might think him sissified.

John's instructors in Canada were similarly ignorant of John Magee the poet.

It does appear, though, that John did share his poetic efforts with some people. Alistair A. Smith went through No. 53 OTU with Magee, and in a letter written to the USAF Museum in 1975[20], Smith recalls:

*... We were stationed at Llandow Royal Air Force Base,*

*No. 53 Operational Training Unit. John and several others,*

*including myself, had the exhilarating experience of flying a*

*Spitfire for the first time. This experience, for John, inspired*

*him to compose "High Flight." A small number of us who*

*shared a wing of an officers' block were aware of it.*

*We were posted away to different squadrons and I did*

*not see John again.*

Dwayne Linton of 412 Squadron, who was witness to Magee's final flight, believes that the first version of *High Flight* was written on a brown paper bag, but this has not been able to be confirmed.

Exactly how *High Flight* was written will probably never be sufficiently verified. What is clear, however, is that John enclosed a copy of *High Flight* in a letter he wrote to his parents. This letter is dated September 3rd, 1941 (John, in the style of the day, writes "3-IX-41" in the letter). It was written on thin, light blue "airmail" paper, so some of the writing on one side can be seen from the other. On the other side of the page containing *High Flight*, John wrote:

*I am enclosing a verse I wrote the other day. It started*

*at 30,000 feet, and was finished soon after I landed. I*

*thought it might interest you.*

At the bottom of the letter John finished:

*I have no more news so will stop now. P.T.O. for Ditty.*

*With much love for all, from John*

"Please Turn Over for Ditty." The "Ditty," of course, is *High Flight*.

The first publication of *High Flight* seems to be in the November 12th 1941 edition of the Pittsburgh Post-Gazette. The submission likely originated from his Uncle Jim or Aunt Mary, as part of the article reads: "Pilot Officer Magee is a nephew of James M. Magee and Mrs. J. Verner Scaife of this city." Curiously, the article quotes the line, "Up, up, the long, delirious burning blue" as "Oh, oh, the long delirious burning blue..." Looking at the original manuscript, it would be easy to mistake John's capital "U" for a capital "O."

John's Aunt Mary had offered to represent John with any future writings. However, John turned down this offer, saying that he didn't feel he was going to be writing any more. It seems that John wrote just one more poem, *Per Ardua*, a tribute to those pilots who flew the year before during the Battle of Britain. That last poem, in a letter dated December 3rd 1941, was sent to John's parents.

Below are two images of the original letter containing *High Flight*:

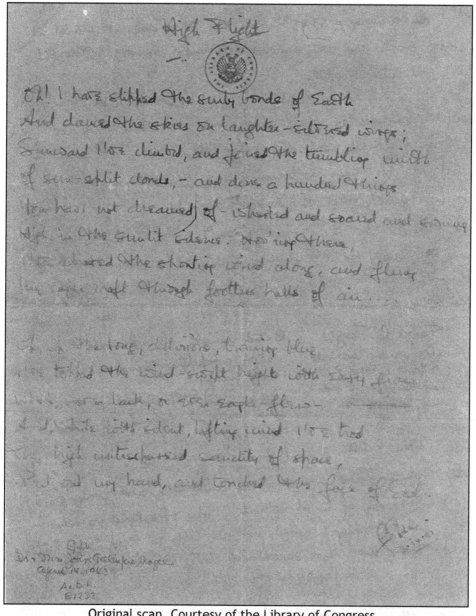

Original scan, Courtesy of the Library of Congress.

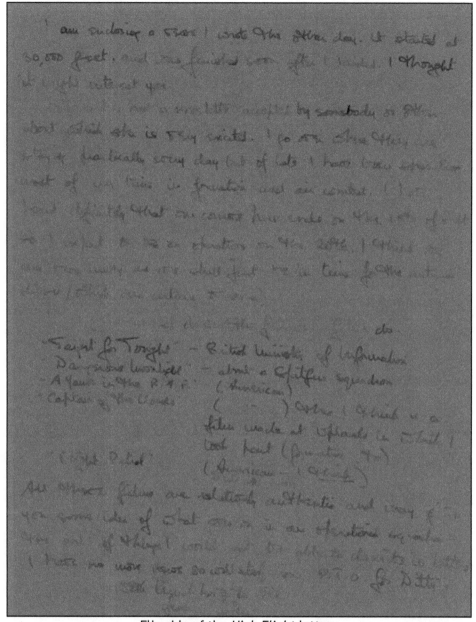

Flip side of the *High Flight* letter.
Note the "I am enclosing a verse I wrote the other day" note at the top, and
the "P.T.O. for Ditty" note in the lower right corner.

Courtesy of the Library of Congress.

## Operations — September 1941 to December 1941

*An aeroplane is to us not a weapon of war, but a flash*

*of silver slanting in the skies; the hum of a deep-voiced*

*motor; a feeling of dizziness; it is speed and ecstasy.*

—JGM

### Llandow, Wales to Digby, England
### 412 Squadron (RCAF)
### September 1941 to October 1941

On September 23rd, 1941, just under a year after John Magee enlisted in the Royal Canadian Air Force, he was finally considered ready to fly and fight. He had trained in Fleet Finches, North American Yales and Harvards, Magister Masters and, lastly, in the Supermarine Spitfire. John had accumulated 230 hours of flight time, learning every aspect of aerial combat. It was now time for him to put all this training and experience to use, and become a front-line fighter pilot.

As usual, John puts it all down in words in a letter (dated September 25th 1941) to his family:

*Since you last heard from me I have finished my course*

*in O.T.U. and spent seven days leave in celebrating the*

*transition from "Pilot, Under Training" to "Pilot, Fully*

*Operational" — and I assure you the change is most*

*satisfying.*

During his leave between OTU and arriving at his operational squadron, John sets out to visit friends and family, and is disappointed to have missed Elinor:

*To begin with, I finished O.T.U. in September — and*

*went straight to London with the boys as I wanted to get*

*fitted for uniform as quickly as possible. (I have been existing*

*to date on one uniform, worn daily since leaving Montreal!).*

*I spent a couple of pretty cheerful days in town before going with Jack Coleman (who is now in 411 Squadron, also stationed here, and with whom I have trained since October '40) to stay with the Magills for a couple of days. Then back via London to Rugby where I stayed with Eric Reynolds (now a Major) and was disappointed to find Elinor away. However I saw the rest of the family and many old friends.*

It seems that John wasted no time integrating in his new squadron. Home at last, it seems:

*I came on "here" [412 Squadron] on the 23rd. My squadron contains surely the grandest bunch of people that ever lived. I am sure I am going to be very happy here. I was rather apprehensive on first coming here, lest they should not turn out to be good fellows, as these, I realized, would be the chaps I shall be living, eating, laughing, and fighting with for the duration. It is an all-Canadian squadron, recently formed. I am glad it is a young Squadron as the newcomer immediately becomes "one of the boys" instead of having to serve a term of virtual apprenticeship. For the first few weeks here I shall not be doing an awful lot. If I am lucky enough to go on an operational flight in the near future, I shall probably fly "in the box" – that is, boxed in by the older boys.*

The weather prevents flying much of the time. Probably much to his surprise, John discovers he needs activities other than flying to keep him occupied:

*The weather has been bad since my arrival, consequently I have not flown yet. Luckily I brought a good many books with me from Rugby (where I found to my immense pleasure that I had some credit left at a book shop – remains of the Poem Prize) and I also brought some model aeroplane kits at Hamleys[21] which make a good pastime.*

*One of the essential things in a squadron is to keep occupied.*

*Some of the boys do the most amazing things. Can you*

*imagine a fighter pilot knitting!!!*

Parties and drinking are frequent events. John gets started right away:

*Last night there was a minor party to celebrate my*

*arrival. It was most warming (actually not so much of a*

*compliment as I thought, as any excuse for a party is good*

*enough)... They are a magnificent bunch (we all retired*

*feeling no pain at all).*

When Magee arrived at 412 Squadron, the commanding officer was Squadron Leader (S/L) C.W. Trevana, a Canadian from Regina, Saskatchewan, and a veteran of the Battle of Britain. Magee is immediately impressed with him:

*The S/L is a peach, quiet but efficient and thoughtful.*

*His name is Travena. He is taking half the squadron south*

*next week to go on sweeps for a few days. I wish I were going*

*but of course I am only small fry as yet!*

While the official "Battle of Britain" had ended a year previously, Britain's survival is still at stake, and the country was very much still at war. After resisting the initial German aerial incursions, England had begun to take the offensive. Despite the great aerial battle's end, there was still a horrific toll being taken on the ranks of pilots, many of whom were brand new, just like John Magee. It is a situation not terribly different from the First World War, where new pilots were immediately thrown into the fray, sometimes being killed in combat on their first day with a squadron, not even having had time to unpack.

412 Squadron (RCAF) was a relatively new squadron, being formed on June 30, 1941, just after John celebrated his 19th birthday and got his Wings. The decision had been made to allow the creation of all-Canadian squadrons that remained part of the Royal Air Force and yet still were a

distinctly Canadian fighting force. The squadron was formed at RAF Digby, about 100 miles north of London. Joining 412 Squadron at Digby were several other Canadian squadrons: 401, 402, 403 and 411, jointly forming the "Canadian Digby Wing," part of RAF 12 Group.

RAF Digby still exists as of 2014, home to both Royal Air Force and U.S. Air Force units. A Spitfire still stands guard outside the gates, and the Digby Sector Operations Museum displays a Sector Operations Room as it was in 1939.

The squadron was originally equipped with the Supermarine Spitfire MKII, and was flying them from Digby when John reported for duty. Fresh from No. 53 OTU where he had been flying the Spitfire MKI, it was a small step to flying the MKIIs that were utilized by 412 Squadron at that time.

Most of the pilots at the newly-formed 412 Squadron were directly out of flight school, with only a few having had any kind of combat experience. Being relatively new, the squadron had to undergo what were called "work-ups" before being ready for full operations. These work-ups were meant as a kind of operational training for an entire squadron, getting pilots familiar flying their aircraft and working as a unit. When John Magee arrived at 412 Squadron, the rest of the squadron had just gone to operational status, so John missed some of these exercises and had to sit out the first couple of operations. Which might have been just as well:

> Last time our squadron went, they ran into a hive of
>
> activity in which 700 Spitfires, Hurrybirds [Hawker
>
> Hurricanes] and 109s were involved.

On the 28th and 29th, Magee flew as passenger on two twin-engine bombers, a Page-Handley Harrow and a Vickers Wellington ("fell asleep" on the 2nd flight in a Wellington, according to John's logbook). He did manage to get 30 minutes of dual instruction in the Wellington.

One of John's close friends at 412 Squadron was P/O Rod Smith, a Canadian from British Columbia. In his biography, "The Spitfire Smiths," Rod recalls his first meeting with John:

> I remember that when he was introduced to me in
>
> front of the fireplace in the officer's mess ante room, his eyes
>
> somehow conveyed a fine spirit.[22]

Smith recounts other impressions of John:

> John was a skillful pilot. His formation flying was tight
> and his practice dogfighting was gutsy, which I have always
> thought were the two early signs of the right stuff.

Of course, John being John does not escape Smith's notice. Rod recounts a couple of John's misadventures (the first account disagrees with John's own account of what happened on the day that the Duke came to visit):

> John was inclined to be impractical at times, however.
> One day when the wind was strong he took off downwind
> towards the hangers at Digby at the very moment that the
> Duke of Kent arrived to visit us. John provided a memorable
> diversion by barely clearing the hangers. He also once forgot
> to connect his oxygen tube to the aircraft's supply tube and
> passed out at 22,000 feet. He came to in a high speed dive,
> just in time to pull out.

Regarding the second event, John's logbook does have an entry in it, dated December 9th, a night flight in Spitfire VZ-D. For that flight, he notes: "Learned effect of no oxygen."
The account by Smith continues:

> He once allowed a wing to drop on landing, damaging
> it, and was so distraught he taxied into a parked aircraft,
> hitting one of its wingtips with one of his own. His flight
> commander, then Kit Bushell, was not amused.

This second event occurred on November 5th. The cover of this book shows John Magee with Spitfire VZ-B, which he named "Brunhilde." On November 5th, an entry in John's logbook shows a flight in VZ-B; comments are: "Climb to 36,000 - Crashed" and "Poor Brunhilde." The official "Report on Flying Accident" includes Magee's statement:

"At 11.30 hours on the 5.11.41 I made a bad landing in Spitfire VB AD-329 resulting in a high bounce, and owing to coarse rudder control and my failure to open the throttle, the left wing tip hit the ground causing damage to the mainplane."

However, the report's summary is actually complimentary to Magee:

This pilot has shown above average flying ability up to the time of this accident. It is felt that this accident should eradicate any tendencies towards carelessness which he may have had.

Overall, Magee quickly integrates into the squadron, making a generally good impression on all with his demeanor and flying qualities.

## From Digby, England to Wellingore, England
## October 1941

In mid-October, 412 Squadron traded their older Spitfire MKIIs for the newer and more capable Spitfire MKVB. Along with the new aircraft came a new location: RAF Wellingore, located about five miles southwest of RAF Digby. Though still part of the all-Canadian Digby Wing, 412 Squadron would have RAF Wellingore all to themselves.

RAF Wellingore had been around for quite a while. In WWI, the field was known as Wellingore Heath, and was a naval landing site for the Royal Navy Air Service (RNAS). There was a concrete perimeter road, but the runways were grass (which turned rather muddy when it rained, which it often did during that fall).[23]

The officers stayed in Wellingore Grange and all others stayed at Wellingore Hall[24]. The RAF, like most military organizations, has a clearly defined caste structure. Generally, officers and non-officers did not "fraternize" except as duty dictated. They slept and ate in different locations. In the air, these ranks became less notable, with a variety of ranks in the same mission.

For John Magee, life at 412 Squadron was varied and exciting. He flew often, sometimes taking passengers up in the Miles Magister for hops around the airfield. He flew Spitfires on convoy escorts; not the most exciting flying, but still it was, after all, flying. Hopping across the Channel, skimming the tops of the waves, attacking ground targets in France and then scooting back home gave some satisfaction, but what John was mostly interested in, what he had trained for, was aerial combat.

In yet another indication that Magee was thoroughly enjoying himself, P/O Rod Smith, years later wrote this about his friend John Magee:

> He [John] loved squadron life, and had many happy times at Wellingore. His casual arrival in the mess or our dispersal hut always gave a lift to us because his company was so pleasing. He was remarkably articulate, precocious and interesting; he had great integrity and high personal standards. He spoke with an accent which owed something to England, New England, and Canada.

Rod and John became fast friends, although it seems that John befriended the entire squadron:

> *When the evenings drew in at Wellingore we often*
> *went into Lincoln to see a movie, in Hart Massey's car, a four*
> *seater MG which could hold five in a pinch. When we got*
> *there we would first have a drink in the Saracen's Head, a*
> *large and far from cozy pub near the southern gate in the*
> *wall surrounding the hill which the cathedral sat on.*

Evidence that Magee enjoyed going to the movies can be found in several different places. Magee's friend Rod Smith mentions it (while in England, Rod and John went to see Charlie Chaplin in *The Great Dictator*), and John himself lists several movies in a letter to his parents:

> *If you get a chance to see the following films, do.*

> *Target for Tonight — British Ministery of Information*
> *Dangerous Moonlight — about a Spitfire squadron*
> *A Yank in the RAF — (American)*[25]
> *Captains of the Clouds — ( " ) This I think is a film made*
>     *at Uplands in which I took part (formation, etc.)*
> *Flight Patrol — (American, I think)*

> *All these films are relatively authentic and may give*
> *you some idea of what goes on in an operational squadron*
> *— the sort of things I would not be able to describe in letters.*

After the Battle of Britain, fought during the summer of 1940, the RAF gradually changed from a defensive posture to one of offense. RAF bombers started crossing the Channel in increasing numbers. "Circus" operations were designed to use bombers to lure Luftwaffe fighters into the air, where they would be engaged by large numbers of escort fighters and destroyed... at least in theory. Due to losses incurred during the Battle of Britain, the German fighters would not go aloft just to engage other fighters, but only softer and less risky targets such as bomber formations.

On October 13th, 412 Squadron engaged in operation Circus 108A along with 266 and 411 Squadrons. It was during this operation that 412 Squadron scored its first victory, a ME-109E shot down by Sergeant Edward N. Macdonnell. Macdonnell was flying "VZ-E," a Spitfire MKIIA. Magee did not join in on this operation, since he had just recently joined the squadron and was considered not quite ready for combat. Magee stayed at Wellingore that day, flying the Miles Magister.

John sent an update to his family via a letter dated October 17th:

> Not much has occurred since last I wrote. I have been on several operations against the enemy already but I think I had better not say much about these. Eddie M- [Macdonell], a sergeant-pilot in 412, got his, and the squadron's first, confirmed victory on an offensive sweep the other day. It was a Me.109E. It of course called for a tremendous party which in no way improved our sensory faculties for the following day's operations.

In what appears to be a formation-flying exercise, John flies with the entire squadron over the Channel:

> Another rather exciting operation in involved low flying just over the top of the water practically all the way to Holland. The whole squadron was in formation and it must have looked pretty formidable to any who might have been watching from some of the naval ships we passed over.

Hart Massey, the son of Vincent Massey (the High Commissioner to the United Kingdom for His Majesty's Government in Canada) is posted to 412 Squadron. Hart Massey's uncle was the actor Raymond Massey.

> Our I.O. (Intelligence Officer – P/O Barnett, an awfully good type) has been posted, and his successor is really a peach. He is Vincent Massey's son (Flight Lieutenant Hart

*Massey). He is quite brilliant and very charming. He and I get*

*along like a house on fire which is good because he has a*

*magnificent car of which I get the use of sometimes.*

Massey was of rather short stature, and according to legend, was one of the few people who was able to fly in a single-seat Spitfire by virtue of sitting on the pilot's lap! (Melodie Massey, Hart's widow, lately confirmed with the author that the event actually happened, and it was P/O Rod Smith's lap that Hart sat on.)

And although John is now part of a real fighter squadron during wartime, there is still evidence of the old John, having fun and doing a bit of low flying:

*We also have a new doc – also a Flight Lieutenant –*

*who is loads of fun. Also a new adjutant whom I took for a*

*ride in the Miles Magister (a wee open runabout) the other*

*day – we have one in the squadron for weekends, odd jobs,*

*etc. He looked quite green when we came down, a*

*phenomenon possibly due to the fact that we had bean-*

*stalks in our undercart when we landed!*

When he could find the time, John intensified his pursuit of Elinor Lyon, seemingly making some progress. A letter to his family dated October 26th gives great detail of a week-long leave, much of it spent with Elinor and Dermott Magill:

*I am now in the middle of seven days leave. I came*

*away from my present abode in Wellingore on Wednesday*

*afternoon (the 22nd) and after one night in London went on*

*to Oxford the next day in time to have supper with Dermott*

*and Elinor. I stayed that night and Friday night in Oriel*

*College where Dermott now is.*

John puts on a disguise in order to attend a lecture with Dermott:

> *On Friday morning I attended a lecture with Dermott*
> *and his roommate, suitably attired in a sportscoat, <u>very</u> loud*
> *canary jersey and gown! It was a lecture on Goethe and I*
> *was terrified that the man would ask me a question.*
> *However he didn't.*

Elinor has invited John and Dermott to her room at Lady Margaret Hall for tea. John has a bit of an adventure getting there:

> *I eventually found her room after butting in on all sorts*
> *of other young ladies. I had been so excited to receive the*
> *invitation on the previous evening that I had completely*
> *forgotten what number she said. Dermott assured me that it*
> *was T 23; I was equally certain that it was H 58; actually it*
> *was D31! Tea went off very well. I think I am making a bit of*
> *headway but of course it may be the uniform.*

After tea, John, Elinor and a few others head off to see a play. It seems that John might indeed be making more of a connection with Elinor. However, he is not really certain:

> *After [the play] Dermott, Robert Wigram (his*
> *roommate) and I invited Elinor and two of her friends to see*
> *a play called "The Blue Goose" which, as I remember it, was*
> *rather poor, but I was not paying much attention as Elinor*
> *and I were conversing most of the time. Then we had supper*
> *at a restaurant and walked the girls back to L.M.H. (they had*
> *to be in at 11:15). On the way one of the other girls walked*
> *with me, but Elinor rather skillfully edged her out by*
> *stumbling more or less between us. I would give my eyes to*
> *know if that stumble was really an accident!*

The next day John heads to Mortehoe via train to see his relatives. He takes some time by himself to visit the same cliffs that he and Geoffrey Sergeant had climbed not so long ago, trying to make sense of the previous day's activities with Elinor. John is confused by the mixed signals he seems to be getting from her.

> ... [I] walked out to Morte Point optimistically carrying a pencil and paper but found my muse absolutely sterile. So I took to watching gulls but they all seemed to be crying, "Elinor!, Elinor!", and her face was everywhere, so in the end I got fed up and came back to tea, on the way running into Auntie Nora and stopping to have a word with her on the cliffs...

There are times when he does seem to believe that he will survive the war. While at Mortehoe John ponders what to do after it's all over. And having had just the slightest bit of seeming encouragement, he seems to envisage a future with Elinor:

> ... I think that if I go to college in America my life will be in that country, whereas my heart is still here! And the fact that that young lady is showing just the very faintest signs of relenting does not encourage me to leave it!
>
> Now that I have a motorbike I ought to be able to get down to see Elinor more often. She has really turned out to be the most inspiring girl. I enjoy her company now more than ever before . . . Really I think she must be the girl for me. But I foresee years of hard work before I win her heart! (Any advice will be gratefully received).

During this trip, John acquired an ancient motorbike, which he plans to primarily use to see Elinor. If the bike continues working, that is. John describes his plans to return to Wellingore:

*I am making an early start back to Oxford tomorrow,*
*catching the 8:27 from Mortehoe. I hope to arrive in time to*
*have tea with Elinor and Dermott. Then we will probably go*
*to the other theater, which is Oxford's chief preoccupation*
*at the moment as it is boasting Vivian Leigh. Then probably*
*dinner and sad farewells as I shall push off early on Tuesday*
*(I think) to Cirencenster on my newly acquired vehicle, (for*
*which I am paying rather unwisely by installments!) to see*
*the Hitchcocks. I foresee, however, not being able to get*
*there as the M-B is very old, I have no idea how to work one*
*(though I was issued with a license in Oxford), have no idea*
*where they live except it is somewhere near Cirencenster,*
*and have to be flying the following afternoon.*

John does manage to return to Wellingore, not certain whether he should be encouraged or discouraged concerning his relationship with Elinor.

There were many lighter moments in squadron life. Rod Smith gives the following example of squadron teamwork in rescuing a lost soul:

*One night in early November, when we were lounging*
*around our bar in the Grange, one of our pilots mentioned*
*that during his walk that afternoon he had seen a sheep*
*stuck in the edge of a pond about a mile away. It was a cold*
*foggy night and the thought of it made us feel*
*uncomfortable. We began to look at each other and then Kitt*
*said, "Let's try to get it out." We put on our flying jackets*
*and went off.*

The rescue party spends some time finding the wayward sheep:

*Though the fog was thickening we found the poor*
*animal, which bleated as we came near. I was tallest so Kitt,*

*John and one or two others gripped the bottom edge of my flying jacket and held me suspended over the sheep like the arm of a crane. I put my arms under the water and around its chest, and they pulled hard. The sheep gave a loud bleat as it came loose and onto the bank. It loped stiffly but happily away in the dark.*

Apparently Magee will seize any opportunity to fly. In the October 17th letter to his family, John describes a couple of flights that nearly did him in:

*Recently I have been acting as Test Pilot for the squadron. We have one old kite that is in the last stages of decrepitude which nobody likes to fly. It had a thorough overhaul but they didn't manage to get the wheels quite right so in a rash moment I volunteered to air-test it. Everything went all right until I came in for a landing, and then the wheels wouldn't come down. The only thing you can do in such a case is to go through a series of short dives and violent pull-outs which is pretty hard on the pilot and very hard on the wings!*

John is nothing if not persistent:

*I went round and round the aerodrome very low doing this until I thought the wings would come off but still they wouldn't come down. I was almost ready to crash-land it with the wheels retracted when I decided to have one more go. I got up to about 2,000 feet (I couldn't get it to climb properly as the engine was not running at all properly), rolled onto my back and chopped vertically onto the aerodrome. I held it as long as I dared – and a little longer, then hauled the stick back into my stomach as hard as I could. All I remember before blacking out is a very violent jerk and shudder which I mentally noted as the disappearance of the wings (a most essential part of any aeroplane!) but when I came to again my impressions were chronologically as follows:*

1. *The wings are here*
2. *The wheels are down*
3. *I am about to hit a hanger*

Unbeknownst to John, he has an audience. A Royal audience:

*However I finally got down safely. On taxiing up to the flight I found – you'll never guess – the Duke of Kent inspecting the squadron. My Flight Commander introduced me and said 'Nice work' which I took as an enormous compliment as he is not exactly given to flattery. The Duke had watched the whole procedure and seemed duly impressed.*

The offending aircraft was a Spitfire MKII, serial number D6612. This test flight was taken on October 14th, with John noting in his logbook:

A/C Test. (U/C trouble + cowlings blew loose)

End of the story? Not quite. Having found himself in possession of a plane without any squadron markings on it, he proceeds to take advantage of this situation during the second test flight:

*Today I tested the same aircraft again. The mechanics had been onto it and guaranteed that it would work, so I took off gaily in the direction of my old school which I duly found, and, the plane having no markings on it (it had just been repainted) proceeded to give the old place a really good 'beating up.' I had fleeting impressions of boys pouring out*

*of class-rooms; Barbara Lyon waving a blue handkerchief;*
*Eric Reynolds standing aghast by his bicycle; and that*
*hideous monstrosity, the school chapel.*

The old John is still around, this time heeding a previously learned lesson on not getting caught, as this time there are no identifying marks on the plane. However, perhaps things might be too good to be true, and the good luck couldn't last:

*Having arrived back at the aerodrome I found once*
*more that the wheels stuck. So mouthing words at the flight*
*mechanics, I started to go through the same maneuvers as*
*before. This time I had a little more height and could afford*
*to be more violent. After 45 minutes I got them down at the*
*expense of two engine cowlings, the hood, and several bolts*
*out of the wing-roots which all shook off in the process. I*
*have just told the engineering officer that next time I'm*
*going to bail out and let it fall into the sea!*

This second flight occurred on October 17th, with a very similar logbook notation:

A/C Test — En. Panel blew out, cowlings loose + U/C
trouble

Still, John is very much enjoying himself. He concludes his October 17th letter:

*P.S. I have decided to be a flying instructor after the*
*war. If it looks like ending suddenly please get me a job at*
*once!*
*P.P.S. (I like flying.)*

Military life is always full of rumors and stories. John writes about one apocryphal story which may or may not have actually happened, but John appears to have seen the actual report:

*One fellow, flying 'in the box' on this, his first engagement with the enemy, got separated from the squadron when they positioned for attack and later found himself flying, as he thought West, but actually East, as his compass needle was stuck. After a while, two other 'Spitfires' joined him and flew in very close formation on him. For a few minutes he took a look at them and, in his own words:*

*"... the only thing I remember thinking was how beautiful they looked in their dazzling new camouflage, and I was just wondering what squadron they belonged to when I felt my body freeze completely. They weren't Spitfires at all, but Messerschmitt 109s. There was no room for either of us to get our guns to bear, and anyway I think the pilots must have had a sense of humor, as they both took off their oxygen masks and grinned at me... one thumbed his nose. Just then it occurred to me that I was flying into Germany and had only about 20 gallons of gas left, and I suddenly feared that this might be some sort of trap, so I half rolled and dove away from between those 109s..."*

*Actually, to cut a long story short, he ran out of gas halfway over the Channel but managed to stay in his plane until he had glided within reach of the English Coast, then baled out from 1,000 feet (this is very low) and landed on the edge of the cliffs about three and a half miles south of Foxburrow.*

*Everybody says the same thing about the Messerschmitts – they are so beautiful that quite frequently it never occurs to the fledgling to fire his guns at them!*

One of the tasks that 412 and others squadrons are given is to practice working with and against ground units, something that the squadron puts to good effect later on in the war (with 412 Squadron's Charley Fox [26] credited with shooting up German General Erwin Rommel's[27] staff car in 1944). John relates the operation in a letter to his Aunt Mary:

> *This operation consisted almost exclusively of beating up tanks, gunposts, artillery, troops, etc. in low level attacks during a big army manoeuvre. Of course it was all pretense but gave us some good experience and, besides, it was wonderful fun and we had a bellyful of thrills.*

Of course, after the operation was concluded, a party was called for:

> *The Winco (Wing-Commander) thought we ought to have a party to celebrate our efforts for the Army. Accordingly, tunics were thrown off, collars loosened, and the Officer's Mess started to disintegrate. The poor W.A.A.F.S. – Women's Auxiliary Air Force Service – who serve at the bar, never had a moment's peace, because, when a whole Canadian Wing (3 squadrons) decides to have a party, you know all about it!*
>
> *At four in the morning we were playing some rough-house game where people were literally being hurled through the air and caught the other side of the room. The proceedings ended when I inadvertently pushed my Squadron Leader into the fireplace and the Station Adjutant landed on his head on the floor, having been missed by the 412th Sqdn. Intelligence Officer, who was supposed to catch him! We (all 50 of us) carried him up to bed in a coma and then retired ourselves. Dawn patrol the next day was an awe-inspiring exhibition. Certainly we flew the straggliest*

*formation that has ever been seen hereabouts, and one of*

*our Flight Lieuts. landed in a tree.*

All fun aside, 412 Squadron is still an operational squadron, and is tapped for a large upcoming operation. This time, Magee is deemed ready, and is selected to go. One unfortunate fact of life with a squadron engaged in active combat with the enemy had yet to be learned by 412 Squadron. Sometimes, it's not good to become too close to others. This inevitable and sobering lesson was about to be taught.

## Circus 110—November 8th, 1941

On November 8th, 1941, Circus 110 operation was launched. In terms of individual fighter capability, the matchup was mostly on par. 412 had been the first squadron to have its Spitfire MKVBs equipped with a negative "G" carburetor (before this fix was installed, early Mark Spitfire engines were subject to cutting out when experiencing negative G forces, which happened when the nose of the aircraft was pushed over instead of being pulled up). German fighter engines didn't have this difficulty, having used fuel injected carburetors from the start. Performance-wise, the Spitfire MKVB compared favorably to the BF-109E. (In this discussion, references are made to the "ME-109" and to the "BF-109." The designations are synonymous.[28])

What was apparently not known to the RAF at that time was that the Luftwaffe was in the process of introducing the much more capable radial-engine Focke-Wulf FW-190 into combat. This wild card fighter figured into the deadly mess that Circus 110 was to become.

Circus 110 was put in motion with 12 RAF Blenheim bombers from 21 and 82 Squadrons as the lure, and nine Spitfire squadrons as the trap (302, 308, 315, 316, 317, 411, 412, 452, and 616 Squadrons). Roughly 12 Spitfires per squadron meant that approximately 120 fighters accompanied a dozen bombers. The nominal task of the escort Spitfires during Circus 110 was to escort the Blenheims on the way to and from their target (Lille in occupied France) and to engage Luftwaffe fighters as they rose to confront the bombers.

412 Squadron put up 12 Spitfire MBVB aircraft for this operation. Magee was flying as Red 2 in Spitfire AD291, with markings of VZ-H. He was acting as wingman to his C.O., Squadron Leader "Kitt" Bushell (Red 1). This was Bushell's first day as acting Squadron Leader, replacing C.W. Trevena who was vacationing on the way to another posting. As an illustration of the dire need for experienced officers at that time in England, it is telling that Bushell was only 27 years old at the time of this mission, and considered old for a fighter pilot.

Being in command of a fighter squadron was the culmination of a considerable amount of work on Kitt Bushell's part. Bushell had joined the RCAF in 1939, at the beginning of WWII. He had been a part of 412 Squadron for months, and had been "acting as" the Commanding Officer after S/L Travena had been posted to another command. In a letter to his parents written the week before November 8th, Bushell had talked about how excited he was to finally get command of a fighter wing. Sadly, his appointment was not to last long. (Another injustice happened when Bushell was not given credit for being Squadron Leader even for one day.

Official histories of 412 Squadron don't list Bushell among the 412 Squadron Leaders, due to S/L Travena still being on leave during this incident, and thus still "officially" being 412's Squadron Leader).

A combination of events seemed to doom Circus 110 from the outset. Three of the Squadrons (412, 411, and 616) were part of the Canadian Digby Wing, and were led on this mission by Wing Commander Douglas Reginald Scott[29] from 616 Squadron. W/C Scott was flying a Spitfire MKIIB[30] on this operation, hardly a match for the ME-109 fighters that were expected, and certainly not for the new FW-190 fighters that were actually among those encountered on that day. Scott had never led a squadron into combat, let alone an entire wing. In aerial combat against a talented and experienced foe, there is little room for error or miscalculation: Scott would be shot down and killed by an FW-190 during this operation. Pilots involved in this operation heard a radio transmission that has been attributed to Scott: "I guess I'm too old for this, boys."

Another major factor that was going to prove disastrous to the Spitfires on that November day was their opponents: The legendary Jagdgeschwader 26 (JG 26, known as the "Abbeville Boys," named after their home base in Abbeville, France).

JG 26 was one of the Luftwaffe's crack fighter outfits. Even though much of JG 26 had been sent to Russia (Germany's eastern front), many of their fighters had stayed in the west for the defense of the homeland and occupied western areas. The Luftwaffe pilots had been flying combat missions for several years now, some as far back as the 1938 Spanish civil war. They were talented and experienced and flew very capable fighters. On this day, several famous Luftwaffe pilots were airborne and would soon add to their scores. These pilots included Hauptmann Josef Priller[31], Oberstleutnant Adolf Galland[32] and Hauptmann Joachim Müncheberg[33].

12 Spitfires from 412 Squadron, including John Magee in VZ-H, took off from Wellingore at 0845 and flew to the airfield at West Malling to refuel and rendezvous with the other Spitfire squadrons. Around 1115 that morning, the Wing took off towards the southeast: 412 Squadron was the "high squadron" at 23,000 feet, 411 Squadron at 21,000 feet, and 616 Squadron at 20,000 feet. The Wing's assignment was to cover the returning bombers back to England.

The Channel between southwest England and France was covered with fog near the surface on that day, but clear above, giving the waiting Luftwaffe pilots a clear view of Spitfires against a white background.

Arriving at the rendezvous spot (NE of Dunkirk) seven minutes early, W/C Scott attempted to have the Wing perform a sharp turn to the left so that they could wait for the bombers. However, turning 36 high-performance fighters flying in formation is not easy; along with the accurate flak they were encountering, it didn't take long for the Wing to dissolve into pairs and singles over the French coast.

High above, the Abbeville Boys were waiting. They knew about the Circus operations, had seen the RAF Blenheim bombers inbound to their targets, and knew that many Spitfires would be coming to escort the bombers. Knowing what was going to happen and where enabled JG 26 to takeoff and climb well above the Circus and wait. Hauptmann Müncheberg's group, equipped with the new FW-190, started attacking the high squadron: 412's territory.

P/O Rod Smith, Magee's friend, saw a Spitfire (which Smith was sure belonged to his C.O. Kitt Bushell) being attacked. The 109 scored hits on the Spitfire and it burst into flames. Smith was relieved to see the Spitfire pilot bail out, but his relief turned to horror as he saw the parachute "streaming" (not opening).

Sergeant Pickell was another victim of the guns and cannons of JG 26. His last transmission was heard by several: "Have used up all my ammunition. Am going home. Have got one." Sgt. Pickell never made it back home.

It is not certain what exactly happened to P/O Denkman, except for the fact that he did not return from Circus 110.

Amidst this confusion, P/O John Magee not only maintained his composure, but survived and managed to shoot at one of the attacking Messerschmitts. Running low on fuel, Magee joined up with the returning bombers and other Spitfires, returned to Hawkinge and refueled. John flew back to the area as part of a search party, looking for any survivors who might have bailed out and wound up in the ocean.

It was a somber group that flew back to Wellingore. Circus 110 was one of the costliest Circus operations the RAF had ever mounted in terms of fighters lost. 412 Squadron suffered the most, losing Bushell, Denkman and Pickell. Magee's entry in his logbook was succinct: "Shot at ME-109. 'Kitt', 'Denk' and 'Pickell' missing."

Here is a transcript of Magee's portion of the official after-action report that was filed on November 8th:

Red 2, (P/O Magee, J.G. Canadian) in company with Red 1 (S/Ldr Bushell, C. Canadian) and Black section reports that both sections had turned left along patrol line when he saw a cluster of Me. 109's upsun flying S.W. These however did not turn to attack. Both sections were at this time turning vertically because of four ME-109's which were diving to attack from the North. Both sections turned to attack but heavy Flak had been getting close behind and due to the fact that Red 2 had been weaving continuously he had dropped behind and lost Red 1 on the turn. At this moment Red 2 saw a ME-109E attacking a Spitfire and another Spitfire attacking this E/A all in line astern. Red 2 fell in behind and weaved. He thought that the attacking Spitfire was Red 1 and the other Black 1 or 2. (Red 1 and Black 1 are missing). Just then a ME-109E came across Red 2's sights. Red 2 turned to follow, but the E/A turned on its back and dived down. Red 2 followed him down and fired a 4-second burst but he does not think the E/A was hit. E/A was soon out of range going straight down. Red 2 was now several miles inland and at this point saw a Spitfire diving straight past him emitting white puffs of smoke, and he lost sight of it. As he started to climb, a ME-109 dived on Red 2 in a quarter attack, who turned right and lost the E/A. Red 2 was now 1,000 feet over the returning bombers and a number of Spitfires were seen above them. Flak was intense but behind the bombers. Red 2 joined up with these Spitfires and landed at Hawkinge at 1245 hours. No claim.

When John described that day in his letters to family and friends, he had to be somewhat circumspect; he could not give any real details that would cause the censors to react. Nonetheless, he manages to make the reader understand that he had been involved in a genuine aerial brawl:

> *I have at last been in action. November 8th I shall never*
>
> *forget. I can't tell you much about it, but it took place in*
>
> *enemy territory. I was flying in the leading section of four as*
>
> *the C.O.'s wing man. We were jumped and I was the only one*
>
> *to avoid getting hit. The C.O., who used to be my Flight*
>
> *Commander, a Pilot Officer, and our best sergeant were all*
>
> *shot down. I arrived back in England with a couple of Poles*
>
> *at a town about 15 miles south of our home, which, by the*
>
> *way, seemed O.K. from the air.*

In the letter quoted above, "Home" refers to the home of his mother's family. The Backhouse family home "Foxborrow" is located in Kingsdown, Kent.

> I had a crack at a Jerry but didn't see any results, so am not claiming it. The mess has an air of forced cheerfulness just now. Our losses (the first we have sustained) were pretty hard to take, but we needed some waking up. Everyone is determined to get something next time.
>
> ... The rest is a long story and must keep until I get home. I was completely terrified throughout but hope not to be so next time.

It is rather remarkable that John, having experienced what had to have been one of the worst days of his life, could write with such incredible detail about this operation.

In another letter to a friend, John gives a few more details:

> The 109's came down in swarms out of the sun. I was terrified at first but, after a while, felt a bit better and had a squirt at one, but another was firing at me so I didn't see whether I hit him or not. Kitt B—, who used to be "A" Flight Commander, had been made a Squadron Leader and took over T—'s place. He had only had his stripes up for one day when he led the Squadron, and was shot down. I was the last man to see him alive, as, just before we took off, he was giving me a little fatherly advice, as it was my first action and I was a little uneasy. I flew as his wing man.

It is interesting to note the differences in the two letters. In the first one Magee was "terrified throughout," but in the second letter he was, "terrified at first but, after a while, felt a bit better..." John continues his account:

*We were jumped by four 109's who picked one of us each. We all turned into them immediately, but I turned so violently that I spun down a good many thousand feet and got away. The other three were all shot down. I saw D — go straight into the sea. P—- tried to bail out, but his parachute didn't open. Nobody saw what happened to Kitt, but we all think and hope he is a prisoner of war. He was one of the grandest men I have ever known.*

Magee clearly describes his attempt to "make a score" by shooting down an enemy aircraft, stopping only when he himself starting getting shot at:

*It was when I was way below the others that I got my squirt. A 109 was following somebody down, firing intermittently, and all I had to do was turn in behind and fire at him, but another one pulled the same trick on me, and, when I saw tracers going by, it was time to forget about my bird, who, I think, must have got it as he was a sitting target for me. However, I couldn't claim him, as I didn't see him go in.*

P/O Rod Smith, Magee's friend, was also on this operation. He recounts the aftermath[34]:

*Our surviving pilots gathered the next morning in an upper room in Wellingore Hall with Hart Massey, our intelligence officer, for interrogation. John Magee had not only survived what had been his first operational flight, he had actually fired at an enemy aircraft, though he saw no results. He told us that when he mentioned to a pilot at Hawkinge that he had fired his guns but seen no damage, the fellow had disgusted him by saying, "Oh, put in a claim,*

*put in a claim!"*

*He made a combat report which, though making no*

*claim, did contain the line: "Foolishly I dived to the attack." I*

*don't know whether Hart let it stay in, or even filed it.*

According to the Combat Report, it does not look like Massey included the statement.

"Kitt" (Squadron Leader Christopher "Kitt" Bushell) didn't make it home. Neither did "D—" (Pilot Officer Ken Raymond Ernest Denkman) or "P—" (Sergeant Owen Fraser Pickell). In John's letters, he could not include actual names, so they were abbreviated "D—" and "P—".

Circus 110 resulted in many casualties in other squadrons, including Wing Commander Scott of 616 Squadron. Altogether, the nine Spitfire squadrons sent up on that day lost 11 Spitfires and eight pilots on this one operation, causing the RAF to bring a halt to the Circus operations until the spring of 1942.[35]

After Circus 110, the journey of John Magee from pacifist to fighter pilot was complete. Not that John was no longer conflicted in some ways: "I'm afraid, if I don't hate him, that his bullets will get me before mine get him," but in other ways he now was truly a fighter pilot: "Gee, I really want to get a score," he told Rod Smith, meaning that he was intent on shooting down and possibly killing his fellow man. Compared with John the pacifist of 1938, this was a dramatic turnabout.

To his Avon friend Larry Viles, Johns writes:

*Really, you have no idea how terrifying – and yet how*

*marvelous – it all is. I am determined to get a "confirmed" –*

*an enemy airplane whose loss is confirmed before Christmas.*

John writes to his Avon friend Robert Dawson, trying to describe the reality the situation that John finds himself in:

*Our squadron has lost rather heavily of late, and we*

*have had three squadron leaders in the last month. I have*

*been in it only three and a half months and, as it is, I am one of its oldest members. Kitt Bushell, who was our best C.O., was shot down with three other fellow.*

*It is indeed a weird and chilly thing to see someone you know and live with go down in smoke. You can see all of the "Dawn Patrols" and "Hells Angels" you like but it isn't the same thing. And, too, it gets you kind of mad.*

In spite of everything, Magee appears to be actually enjoying himself, even after the loss of three of his squadron-mates. John finishes one of his letters in a manner which demonstrates just how much he has changed:

*I have described what happened in one sweep. We shall be doing more and more of these in the future. Once you get over your fear at the 109's you get to love it. We are also doing low flying cannon attacks on aerodromes, power plants, and other such targets. They're great fun but the anti-aircraft fire is a little disconcerting at first...*

*Really, I am loving the whole thing...*

```
                            ┌─────────────┐        ┌──────────┐
                            │   ADQ.      │        │ FORM "F" │
                            │ NO. 12 GROUP R.A.F    │  Form 1151│
                            │   1 2 NOV   │        │  25A     │
                            │ Ref. No.....│        └──────────┘
                            └─────────────┘
```

INTELLIGENCE     **COMBAT REPORT.**

103

Sector Serial No. ........................................................ (A) ......... WC/INT

Serial No. of Order detailing Flight or Squadron to
   Patrol ........................................................ (B)

Date ........................................................ (C) ......... 8/11/41

Flight, Squadron ........................................ (D) Flight : B ..... Sqdn. : 412(RCAF)

Number of Enemy Aircraft ........................ (E) ..... One Me-109E.

Type of Enemy Aircraft ............................ (F) ..... Me.109E.

Time Attack was delivered ...................... (G) ..... approx 1210 hours.

Place Attack was delivered ..................... (H) ..... Approx 10 miles N.W. of Dunkirk.

Height of Enemy ........................................ (J) ..... Sea Level.

Enemy Casualties ..................................... (K) One Me.109E, damaged, shot

Our Casualties ...................... Aircraft ..... (L) (F/Lt Cantrill, C.T. Canadian).
                                                     Three. Category3.

                           Personnel ..... S/Ldr Bushell, G.  P/O Denkman, K.R.E.
                                                     Three missing.

SEARCHLIGHTS
GENERAL REPORT                              (N1) N/A
                                            (R)

A.A. Guns                                   (N2) Heavy barrage AA off Dunkirk.
                                                     Accurate for height.

Aircraft fire: Range and length of bursts (P) 3 second burst at 300 yds
                                                     and another short burst at approx
General Report                              (R) 500 yards.


No.412(R.C.A.F.)Squadron was ordered from W.G. 1 to WEST MALLING on 8/11/41 to take
part in Circus Operation No 110 over the French Coast.  12 Spitfire Vb's took off from Un
W.C.1. at 0845 hours, and landed at WEST MALLING at 0935 hours.  No.412 Squadron took
off from WEST MALLING at 1117 hours in company with No 616 Squadron and 411 (R.C.A.F)
Squadron, the wing being led by WING COMMANDER SCOTT.  The wing came over MANSTON at
approx. 1135 hours at 18,000 feet, and gained height over the Channel with the Squadron
stepped down into the sun at intervals as follows: 412 Squadron in section of four
flying in Vic formation at 23,000 feet, 411 Squadron at 21,000 feet and 616 Squadron
at 20,000 feet.  The wing reached the French coast N.E. of Dunkirk in this formation
at approx. 1145 hours but in view of the fact that this was earlier than the ordered
time of 1152 hours, the Wing carried out a sharp left-hand orbit, and proceeded to
patrol the coastline N.E. of Dunkirk where an heavy and accurate barrage of A.A. was
encountered which split up the wing formation.  The wing did not reach the patrol line
East of Dunkirk.  After approx 20 minutes from the time the wing arrived over the coast
Blue 1 412 Squadron (F/Lt Cantrill) became separated from the wing and finding himself
alone went down to sea level and turned for the English coast.  When 10 miles N.W. of
Dunkirk he saw a Me. 109E at about 200 feet a quarter of a mile away to the North.
                                    Signature

                   O.C.    ┌ Section
                           │ Flight
                           └ Squadron          Squadron No.
```

After-action combat report for 412 Squadron, November 8, 1941.

Courtesy of National Archives of England.
```

Blue 1 turned to attack but enemy Aircraft apparently saw him and turned to meet him. Both aircraft chased each other in tight circles attempting to get inside the other, but after one minute the E/A broke off and returned back towards the French coast having apparently seen another Spitfire closing to attack. Blue 1 immediately opened fire with a 3-second burst at approximately 300 yards range from dead astern and noticed black smoke coming from the engine of the E/A. Both Spitfires then chased the E/A back towards the French coast and was seen to be slightly waggling its wings as if the pilot had been hit. The pilot of the E/A attempted no evasive action. Blue 1 fired another short burst at about 500 yards but with no visible effects. On reaching the French coast both Spitfires turned back towards the English coast, Blue 1 landing at Manston at 1300 hours.

Red 2, (P/O Magee, J.G. Canadian) in company with Red 1 (S/Ldr Bushall, C. Canadian) and black section reports that both sections had turned left along patrol line when he saw a cluster of Me. 109's upsun flying S.W. These however did not turn to attack. Both sections were at this time turning vertically because of four Me 109's which were diving to attack from the North. Both sections turned to attack but heavy Flak had been getting close behind and due to the fact that Red 2 had been weaving continuously he had dropped behind and lost Red 1 on the turn. At this moment Red 2 saw a Me 109E attacking a Spitfire and another Spitfire attacking this E/A all in line astern. Red 2 fell in behind and weaved. He thought that the attacking Spitfire was Red 1 and the other Black 1 or 2. (Red 1 and Black 1 are missing). Just then a Me 109E came across Red 2's sights. Red 2 turned to follow, but the E/A turned on its back and dived down. Red 2 followed him down and fired a 4-second burst but he does not think E/A was hit. E/A was soon out of range going straight down. Red 2 was now several miles inland and at this point saw a Spitfire diving straight past him emitting white puffs of smoke, and the lost sight of it. As he started to climb, a Me 109 dived on Red 2 in a quarter attack, who turned right and lost the E/A. Red 2 was now 1,000 feet over the returning bombers and a number of Spitfires were seen above them. Flak was intense but behind the bombers. Red 2 joined up with these Spitfires and landed at Hawkinge at 1245 hours. No claim.

Top part of 2nd page of after-action combat report for
412 Squadron, November 8, 1941.
The 2nd paragraph details John Magee's (Red 2) actions.

Courtesy of National Archives of England.

Sgt Ellis, White 2, after patrolling near Dunkirk for about 15 minutes saw a Me 109 diving across him above and behind. White 2 gave the E/A a burst of 3 seconds at a range of 350 yards. No hits were observed on the E/A which straightened out for a moment and then went into a dive again. Continuing to patrol again White 2 saw a half opened parachute as if the pilot had just baled out and another parachute which was apparently not attached to anyone. Positions not known. White 2 landed at Hornchurch at 1305 hours. No claim.

P/O Smith, Yellow 1, patrolling near Dunkirk saw a Spitfire being attacked and shot down by a Me. 109F. The pilot bailed out but his parachute wass seen only to be half-opened. The Spitfire was seen to crash into the sea.

Sgt Macdonell, White 1, states that he heard Sgt Pickell, Black 1, report over the R/T "Have used up all my ammunition". "Am going home.. Have got one" (Black 1 is missing).

Sgt Powell, Green 1, states that he saw a E/A attacking P/O Denkman, Blue 2 from dead astern. Blue 2 was seen to go into a steep dive. (This pilot is missing).

Weather was fine with good visibility and no cloud. However there was considerable ground haze against which aircraft could be silhouetted from above.

A report from Sgt Smith, Black 2, who it is believed has a claim, will be forwarded when he returns to W.C.1.

Blue 1 (P/O C.T. Cantrill) rounds fired: 20mm 36 .303 144. No stoppages. Cine Gun fitted but not used. Reflector satisfactory.
Red 2 (P/O J.G. Magee) Rounds fired: 20mm Nil .303 160. No stoppages. Cine Gun fitted but not used. Reflector sight satisfactory.
White 2 (Sgt. Ellis) Rounds fired: 20mm 14 .303 56. No stoppages. Cine Gun not fitted. Reflector sight satisfactory.

*H Massey* F/L
Flight Lieutenant, Intelligence Officer,
No. 412 (R.C.A.F.) Squadron, Wellingore.

Bottom part of 2nd page of after-action combat report for
412 Squadron, November 8, 1941.
Signed by Flight Lieutenant Hart Massey, 412's Intelligence Officer.

Courtesy of National Archives of England.

## November — December, 1941

November 6th saw the crash of Spitfire VZ-B, Brunhilde, described earlier in this book. On November 13th, a few short days after Circus 110, 412 Squadron was honored by a visit from His Majesty King George VI. Accompanying the King were Air Marshal Sir W. Sholto Douglas (C-in-C Fighter Command), Air Vice-Marshal R.E. Saul (A.O.C. No. 12 Group), Air Commodore L.F. Stevenson (A.O.C. RCAF in Great Britain), Colonel Lascelles (Equerry), Group Captain P. Campbell (O.C. RAF Digby), and Wing Commander Fielding A.D.C., Captain King's Flight).

The King, himself a RAF officer, spent time with nearly all the personnel of 412 Squadron. He performed a formal inspection followed by tea in the Dispersal hut.

Dwayne Linton recalls the King's visit on that day:

> I was there when a "gaggle of geese" crossed the entrance road and stopped the royal procession. Someone whispered, "The geese have the right of way" ...
>
> One other interesting point of conversation was when we were having tea and crumpets in the dispersal hut. He [the King] came over to me and almost whispered, "Don't you wish this was a hot dog and a Coke... me and the Queen enjoyed them so much when we were in the United States... can't say too much under present circumstances... it's our secret."[36]

Rod Smith also recalled the royal visit:

> A day or two after Jack Morrison became CO the King came to our aerodrome at Wellingore. He had tea with the officers and the sergeant pilots in our dispersal hut, the interior of which we had never thought would see a king-emperor.

On November 28th, Magee and Flight Lieutenant R.B. Edwards proceeded to Farnborough on a high-altitude flying course. There are no entries in John's logbook until Dec. 1st, when he returned to Wellingore.

December of 1941 was a typical cloudy and cold month in England. Due to the bad weather, the Luftwaffe did not come calling as much and the 412 Squadron took the opportunity to lick their wounds from the previous month's losses, along with resting and training.

John's last letter to his parents was sent on December 3rd. In this letter John included his last poem, *Per Ardua*. Also in this letter he describes the historic visit from the King and includes a picture.

John did not fly a tremendous amount in December; he was on Convoy Patrol on the 1st in Spitfire VZ-H, followed by a flight to Duxford and back (the outbound flight to Duxford has a comment about a "50 FT CEILING!"). On the 5th Magee logged time as a passenger in a twin-engined Whitley medium bomber.

There were no flights on December 7th, the day that Japan attacked U.S. naval forces at Pearl Harbor, Hawaii. It would have been about 5 p.m. in England when the attacks took place; there was likely some delay in getting the news out. On one level, even though the British were as horrified as Americans were with the surprise attack, British people must have breathed a collective sigh of relief; the Americans *had* to join the fight now, even if only against Japan. As proclamations of war soon went out from Germany following the attack, England would no longer be on its own in Europe, as it had been for the past three years.

With this new international development, Magee would eventually have had the option of transferring to the U.S. Army Air Corps (precursor to the U.S. Air Force). Many Americans who trained with the RCAF took that option, though many more stayed.

John made two flights on December 8th in a Magister; the first one shows Flight Lieutenant Hart Massey[37] as a passenger. Another flight on December 8th was in Spitfire VZ-H and was logged as a "SQUADRON FORMATION (PRACTISE SWEEP)".

According to his logbook, John must have had an interesting day on December 9th. Flying Spitfire VZ-D, he logs: "'PIPSQUEAK INTERCEPTION' AND HIGH ALTITUDE DOGFIGHT". John writes a comment: "LEARNED EFFECT OF NO OXYGEN". Not to be dissuaded, Magee flies again that night. Flying again in VZ-D, Magee logs "NIGHT FLYING" and in the comments he notes, "AIRSPEED INDICATOR U/S — BROUGHT IN (FORMATION) BY P/O SMITH". "U/S" stands for "Unserviceable," aka not working. Airspeed, especially at night, is extremely critical. It appears that Magee's friend, Pilot Officer Rod Smith, went up in another aircraft, formed up with John's Spitfire, and flew with him all the way to landing. A tricky procedure even in daytime.

Magee flew twice on December 10th in Spitfires VZ-E and VZ-A. These pair of flights were probably related. The first one John logs: "SEARCHLIGHT EXPERIMENT + CO-OP"; the second flight was logged as: "A/C TEST (FORMATION — BEAUFIGHTER + HUDSON)"[38].

Even though he was having the time of his life, some part of John Magee knew that it all could come to a quick end. In one of his last letters, John wrote to his friend Larry Viles:

*The squadron contains a hell of a good bunch of fellows. Our mess at the moment is an old country cottage in a village about five miles from the aerodrome – the sort of place where you bump your head everywhere you go. I have never had so much fun in my life. Frankly, however, I do not expect it to last. It's not a very sensible thing to talk about, on the whole, but you've got to take chances and you can't win all the time. Anyway, I'd rather be good. The ordinary world seems a long way away and unbearably dull and I can't say that I have a lot of ambition to go back to it under the same circumstances.*

John sums up his feelings by a simple statement:

*So it is that I expect to end my days here in England, and it suits me down to the ground.*

It seems that for years, John had not expected to live long. And it also seems that he was at peace with the thought. In a poem he included in his book *Poems*, John, perhaps thinking of Elinor, wrote the following:

## A PRAYER

SOME evening, when I'm sitting out alone
  Watching, perhaps, a cloud across the sky,
I'll feel as if a strange cool wind has blown,
—And suddenly I'll know that I'm to die;

Then I'll remember how we stood together,
And laughed, and kissed the lovely sun to bed;
And how we talked of Death among the heather,
And wondered gaily at the Ancient Dead . . .

When breath comes short, and tears come all in vain,
And in the silence I must realize
That I shall never laugh, nor love again,
May I find, leaning over me, —your eyes.

Page 17 from John's book of poems.

Property of Erl Gould Purnell, used with permission.

## December 11th, 1941

John Magee's life journey was destined to come to an end on December 11th, 1941. There is only one entry in Magee's logbook for that day, filled in by 412 Squadron's Commanding Officer, Squadron Leader Jack Morrison. The entry is brief and to the point:

Date: Dec 11, 1941
Type of Aircraft: Spitfire V
No. of Aircraft: H [VZ-H]
Pilot: P/O MAGEE
Duty: PRACTICE WING FORM
Time: 0:50
Comment: COLLIDED WITH OXFORD

Spitfires from 412 Squadron took off in the morning of December 11th to take part in a wing formation practice. Rod Smith's Spitfire developed engine problems shortly after takeoff and he had to return to the field. The squadron was scheduled to rendezvous with other squadrons from RAF Kirton-in-Lindsey (about 30 miles directly north of Wellingore). The weather was not perfect, but acceptable with a cloud base (the distance between the ground and the bottom of the clouds) of between 1,200 and 2,500 feet. The clouds were about 3,000 feet thick.

Taking off around 10:40 a.m., 412's Spitfires headed north and climbed above the clouds. For about 45 minutes all went well as the squadrons practiced forming a multi-squadron "big" wing. After being released, 412 Squadron headed home to Wellingore.

In 1941 war-time England, navigation aids were at a minimum. There were no instrument approaches in use at that time;[39] aircraft could be "vectored" (directed to a given position) by talking to the air controllers, but if there were clouds present, the pilots were on their own. There were no warnings of other aircraft in the vicinity.

By reference to radio navigation aids and perhaps getting directions from the Sector Controller, 412 Squadron, flying above the clouds, arrived in the area of Wellingore.

There were two other airfields close by to Wellingore: RAF Digby (four miles to the east), and RAF Cranwell[40] (a bit over four miles to the southeast). On this December morning, 18 year old Leading Aircraftsman (LAC) Aubrey Griffin, Royal Air Force, was flying Airspeed Oxford #T1052 from RAF Cranwell. The twin-engined Oxford was built with wood and fabric and was used as a bomber trainer. Griffin was the only person onboard the Oxford. He might have been doing "circuits and bumps," or he might have been heading to an area to do some practice flying.

The leader of 412 Squadron on this mission had a choice of how to get down through the clouds. He could have had the squadron do a "step-down" procedure, where the aircraft carefully descend in a very controlled manner until clear of the clouds. Or, if an acceptable space or hole appeared, he could have the squadron dive down through the clearing and thus get under the clouds. Usually, a squadron was anxious to get back to base since they were generally low on fuel.

On this day, a hole in the clouds presented itself. Split into groups of four, the Spitfires started diving in "line-astern" (one behind the other) formation, about 100 yards apart. The groups started a procedure called "whip-cracking," where the aircraft weave back and forth in order to keep an eye on each other during the high-speed descent, and to avoid building up too much speed.

LAC Griffin, flying the Oxford, had no idea that a group of Spitfires were headed toward him on a direct collision course.

Magee was number three in his group of four. Dwayne Linton was right behind him, and saw the entire horrifying event unfold right in front of him. Linton caught sight of Griffin's Oxford approaching from the right, headed straight for his group. Rapidly keying his radio, Linton yelled a warning to the group to avoid the closing Oxford. Number one pulled up and out of the way with number two right behind.

Number three was not so lucky. Pilot Officer John Magee and Leading Aircraftsman Aubrey Griffin had no chance to avoid a collision.

Slamming into the Oxford's fuselage at around 350 mph produced an immediate explosion and fire. Dwayne Linton, closely following Magee, was lucky to avoid the collision and resulting debris, immediately breaking to the right and down.

A witness on the ground saw the pilot of a Spitfire attempt to and then succeed at bailing out of his damaged plane. But by the time Magee was able to disconnect his radio cord, oxygen supply, seat buckles, open his canopy and bail out, it was too late. There was not enough altitude for his parachute to open, and John was undoubtedly killed instantly when he hit the ground about 100 feet from where Spitfire VZ-H had crashed to earth.

Back at Wellingore, John's friend Rod Smith watched his squadron returning over the airfield in ragged formation. Before the squadron landed, there was a phone call from sector operations control, saying that they had a report of a Spitfire crash between Wellingore and Cranwell. Smith immediately climbed into his Spitfire and took off, even before all the other 412 aircraft had landed. He headed towards Cranwell, and noticed a burning aircraft in a farmer's field. Years later, Smith recalled his initial impression upon seeing the Spitfire in pieces on the ground:

> *I soon spotted a crashed Spitfire burning in a farmer's field. Its wing was broken in half, with one half lying underside-up across the fuselage showing the roundel on its pale blue surface and its classic elliptical shape. It looked like a beautiful broken bird."*

Smith flew back to Wellingore, picked up 412's Intelligence Officer F/L Hart Massey, and drove to the crash site. Rod's account continues:

> *We found the crash, a little bit to the west of the road, and at the same time saw an ambulance heading away from us towards Cranwell.*
>
> *We left the car and walked across the field to within about 80 feet of the wreckage. It was John's Spitfire. We did not go closer because ammunition was exploding in the fire. We stood there for several minutes.*
>
> *... The wreckage of the Oxford was in some trees about half a mile to the east, and we walked over to it. Its pilot was an eighteen-year-old student, who had been killed and his body removed. We went sadly back to Wellingore.*

The report (Form 7650) filed after the accident stated the following:

DIAGNOSIS OF PRIMARY CAUSE OF ACCIDENT OR FORCED LANDING
This aircraft [Magee's] was No. 3 of a section of four which was letting down through a hold in the cloud and returning to base. An Oxford, which was flying just under the cloud base, collided with No. 3, setting it on fire. The pilot of the Spitfire jumped, but was too low to allow his parachute to open. The collision occurred at 1400 feet.

TECHNICAL REPORT

The aircraft was inspected and it was found that the engine had become detached from the airframe, being found 400 yards away. The airframe was completely wrecked and burnt. The port wing was found 700 yards away from the airframe, the wing tip being a further 300 yards away.

412 Squadron pilot Dwayne Linton wrote an account of what he saw. (Recently, his son Doug provided the author with the story as written by his father):

> I'll never forget that cold December day in 1941. We were stringing down in fours, line astern, from 20,000 feet. We were whip cracking. I was flying in the number-four position, directly behind Magee, who was in the number-three position.
>
> It was difficult to hold in close since I was on the swing-out of each turn. We entered a hole in the cloud base at about 2000 feet and lined out just under the clouds at 1500 feet doing 350 mph.
>
> It was hard to see any great distance due to the haze. I caught a glimpse of an Oxford twin-engine bomber-pilot trainer approaching just under the clouds to my right and directly at right angles in front of our section leader. I pushed my radio switch "ON" and yelled at the leader to miss that airplane! He immediately pulled up into a steep climb with his number two right behind him. Number three was so close that there was no possibility of avoiding an air-to-air collision. Pilot Officer Magee crashed right into the middle of the bomber-trainer's fuselage.
>
> There was a momentary explosion of fire and flaming aircraft parts were everywhere. My evasive action was a screaming turn to the right and down. I pulled out into level

*flight less than a hundred feet from the ground. I saw a stringing parachute near the vicinity of the crash. Magee had managed to get out of his aircraft but he was too low for his chute to open and he was killed instantly. The Oxford's crew was also killed.*

John Gillespie Magee, Jr. was laid to rest at the Scopwick Burial Grounds on Saturday, December 13th. Pilots from 412 Squadron attended, as did pilots from nearby squadrons based at Coleby Grange and Digby. RCAF Chaplain Flight Lieutenant S.K. Belton presided over the service.

John's parents were notified of his death via telegraph by the RCAF Casualties Office in Ottawa. Shortly thereafter, John's Commanding Officer, Squadron Leader Jack Morrison, wrote to Magee's parents:

*Before receipt of this letter you will have received notification from the Air Ministry of the sad loss you have sustained in the passing of your son John.*

*It was during local practice manoeuvres that your son met with the accident causing his death, his plane colliding with another machine when emerging from a cloud, both machines crashing.*

*Your son's funeral took place at Scopwick Cemetery, near Digby Aerodrome, at 2:30 p.m. on Saturday, 13th December, 1941, the service being conducted by Flight Lieutenant S. K. Belton, the Canadian padre of this Station. He was accorded full Service Honors, the coffin being carried by pilots of his own Squadron.*

*Wreaths were sent by his brother officers, and airmen of his Squadron, also from the Royal Air Force Station, Digby. His grave will be taken care of by the Imperial War Graves Commission, who will erect a temporary wooden cross pending the provision of a permanent memorial.*

*I would like to express the great sympathy I and all members of 412 Sqn feel with you in the loss of your son. John was a very popular member of our squadron, which as well as being an operational unit, is also a compact family of its own, and can ill afford to lose so valued a member as your son. He was held in very high regard both as a fighter pilot and as a good friend of all with whom he came in contact. His and your unselfish sacrifice in the cause of humanity is a source of admiration and gratitude from all his comrades in the Royal Air Force....*

In a gesture of understanding and compassion, John's father wrote back:

*When my wife and I saw how deeply he felt about the situation in September 1940, we gave our consent and blessing to him as he left to enter the R.C.A.F. We felt as deeply as he did and were proud of his determination and spirit. We knew that such news might come. When his sonnet reached us we felt then that it had a message for American youth but did not know how to get it before them. Now his death has emblazoned it across the entire country. We are thinking that this may have been a greater contribution than anything he may have done in the way of fighting, for surely our American youth must enter this conflict in the spirit of idealism and faith. May we thank the RCAF for all the training and help you have given to our boy. We saw a tremendous change in him when he returned to us from his training, a change that was all for the good. We do not regret that we gave our consent to his going and will be forever proud of him.*

Just over a year after he interviewed an enthusiastic and anxious teenager who was eager to join the air force and become a fighter pilot, Air Marshall Breadner (formerly Air Vice Marshall) now had to write a letter to the boy's father; the type of letter which he undoubtedly had to write many of during the course of the war:

> Dear Mr. Magee:
>
> I have learned with deep regret of the death of your son, Pilot Officer John Gillespie Magee, on Active Service Overseas, on December 11th, and I wish to offer both you and Mrs. Magee my sincere and heartfelt sympathy.
>
> It is so unfortunate that a promising career should thus be terminated and I would like you to know that his loss is greatly deplored by all those with whom your son was serving.
>
> Yours sincerely,
>      /s/ L.S. Breadner
>      Air Marshal,
>      Chief of Air Staff

A double tragedy had claimed the lives of two pilots. John Magee had died, not violently in aerial conflict as he had thought he might, but in an accident. LAC Griffin had just started his flying career. Who knows what would have become of these young men had they lived?

For several years John had a feeling, a premonition that he was not going to live long. He felt that his final resting place would be in England, and happen during the war. His premonition came true.

John Gillespie Magee, Jr. was only 19 years old.

OH ONCE AGAIN

To climb aloft and watch the dawn ascend
Earth's haze-enshrouded rim.  To daily high
And see the morning ghosts forsake their blend
For sundry silhouettes.  To catch the sky
Transformed, its fawn and silv'ry tints now rife
With brilliant hues recast.  To ease my craft
Below as golden darts give birth to life
And set the world astir.  To catch a shaft
Of beaming warmth, and quickened by its touch
Assault its course through hills of airy fleece.
To burst at last above the crests and clutch
The fleeting freedom – endless blue, at peace.

- Ascribed to John Gillespie Magee, Jr.
Date and time written are unknown

Class Picture, Operational Training Unit No. 53, Course No. 7, Llandow, Wales. John is in the 3rd row, 3rd from the left.

John G. Magee Family Papers, Record Group No. 242,
Special Collections, Yale Divinity School Library

# Circus 110 - 412 Squadron Participants

```
                   Call      Spitfire 412
Name               Sign      Serial    ID
S/L Bushell*       Red 1       W3959    VZ-?
     W3959  Vb  2156  HPAM45   FF  30-9-41   38MU
     9-10-41  412S  12-10-41
     Shot down by Bf109 NE of Dunkerque on sweep
     8-11-41 S/Ldr C Bushell killed


P/O Magee          Red 2       AD291    VZ-H


F/L Cantrill       Blue 1      W3949    VZ-O


P/O Denkman*       Blue 2      W3952    VZ-?
     W3952  Vb  2126  HPAM45   FF  24-9-41   8MU
      29-9-41  412S  7-10-41   R-R  22-10-41   mods
     Shot down by Bf109 NE of Dunkerque on sweep 8-11-41
     P/O K R E Denkman killed


P/O Smith          Yellow 1    AA841    VZ-?


SGT Gould          Yellow 2    AD429    VZ-F
     (might have been Green 2)


SGT Macdonnell     White 1     AA843    VZ-E


SGT Ellis          White 2     W3958    VZ-?


SGT Pickell*       Black 1     AD270    VZ-?
     AD270  Vb  CBAFM45  9MU  20-9-41   412S
     6-10-41
     Shot down by Bf109 NE of Dunkerque 8-11-41 Sgt O F
     Pickells killed


SGT Smith          Black 2     AD509    VZ-?


SGT Powell         Green 1     AD226    VZ-?


SGT McCarthy       Green 2     AD349    VZ-?
     (might have been Yellow 2)
```

* Did not return from this mission

Picture from the London Times that John included in letter
to his family, depicting the King's visit to 412 Squadron.
Numbers were written in by John, and are explained below.

At the moment we are listening to Lord Haw Haw who is not well received in this area but we listen regularly for news of those we have lost.

In the enclosed picture:

1 = Chuck Cardell (Acting C.O.) - it was soon after that is sent.

2 = Me!

3 = W.M.

4 = Air Marshal Sir Stella Douglas C in C Fighter Command.

5 = Group Captain Campbell, Station Commander.

Note the HUD!

—J.

Both items are from John G. Magee Family Papers, Record Group No. 242,
Special Collections, Yale Divinity School Library

The "rest" of the story—the picture in the Times
did not show the geese!
Notations by Pilot Officer Rod Smith.

Picture courtesy of Wendy Noble, Rod Smith's sister.

King George VI inspecting 412 Squadron
during his visit in November 1941.

King George VI inside the Dispersal Hut at Wellingore
during his visit in November 1941.

All pictures on this page are courtesy of Barry Needham.

Pilot Officer John Gillespie Magee, Jr.
Posing by Spitfire MKVB, VZ-B, AD329, "Brunhilde."

John with Spitfire named "Czar."

All pictures on this page are courtesy of Robert Bracken.

John, on the right, with Jack Coleman (middle), and an unknown pilot.

John posing at the Wellingore Dispersal Hut.

All photographs courtesy of National Museum of the U.S. Air Force.

John relaxing in front of the Wellingore Dispersal Hut.

John G. Magee Family Papers, Record Group No. 242,
Special Collections, Yale Divinity School Library

412 Squadron (RCAF) MKVB Spitfires taking off.
Artist unknown.

Courtesy of Barry Needham.

Barry Needham in front of a
412 Squadron Spitfire

Rod Smith

412 Squadron Spitfire MKVB, AD305. Magee flew this aircraft six times.

412 Squadron Spitfire MKIX, MH883, VZ-B. Flown by F/L Beurling in 1944.

All pictures on this page are courtesy of Barry Needham.

VZ-L, a Spitfire MKII from 412 Squadron, at Digby in the summer of 1941.

412 Squadron Spitfire MKVB coded VZ-S, making a low pass
over the field at Wellingore.

All pictures on this page are courtesy of Robert Bracken.

A few Spitfires from 412 Squadron that have crashed.

All pictures on this page are courtesy of Barry Needham.

PER ARDUA

(Italics)

(To those who gave their lives to England during the
Battle of Britain and left such a shining example to us
who follow these lines are dedicated.)

They that have climbed the white mists of the morning;
They that have soared, before the world's awake,
To herald up their foemen to them, scorning
The thin dawn's rest their weary folk might take;

Some that left other worlds to tell the story
Of high, blue battle, — quite young limbs that bled;
How they had thundered up the clouds to glory
Or fallen to a field stained red;

Because my faltering feet would fail I find them
Laughing beside me, steadying the hand
That seeks their deadly courage —
                                        yet behind them
The cold light dies in that once brilliant Land...

To these, who half the quickened pulse run slowly,
Whose stern remembered image cools the brow —
Till the far dawn of Victory know only
Night's darkness, and Valhalla's silence now?

(P.S. If anyone should want this please see that
it is accurately copied, capitalized, and punctuated.)

J.G.M.
R.A.F.
1941

John's last poem, *Per Ardua*.


Courtesy of the Library of Congress.

**POEM – WRITTEN IN 1942 BY UNKNOWN GROUND CREW MEMBER 412 SQUADRON**

The sun comes up to greet a day
That's nicely started on its way.
A day that from our point of view
Is beautiful – and peaceful too.

And yet who knows at morning light
What sorrows we may face ere night?

Our work was through an hour ago,
The kites are now all set to go.
It don't take long for things to hum
Here comes the pilots on the run.
We strap them in and wish them luck.
The engines start up one by one
And taxi off towards the sun.
Each one is like a gentle steed
With a mighty roar the Spitfires
Soar into the blue horizon.
And as they rise to meet the skies
We left below are thinking
There's twelve in that formation
Twelve boys on sturdy wings
Flying off to battle
With noble hearts that sing.
We are standing solidly
On Mother nature's soil
While they are in the heavens
Very close to God.
Will they all come back today?
To welcome beds on which they lay
To dream of home so far away.
Or will one or two be missing
Or maybe three or four?
That we don't know till they return
To bring the final score.

Our work is done, the DIs are signed
And everything's OK.
We sit and talk, we read and write
To pass the time away
While from our hearts a silent prayer
Is being raised to Him
That Smitty will come back again
Along with Red and Jim.
And now the sun is setting,
We hear a steady drone
With tight and heavy hearts we rush
Pell Mell onto the drome
And in the sunset's dying glow
We see the specks we love
We scan them as they pass over head
We're looking for our kite,
And the we see there's only ten
The boys were in a fight!
And as they land we look again.

There's A and K and D
There's R and P – where's V and T?
Our chests are growing tight
Well V and T have not returned
Are they Prisoners of War?
No, they have gone to swell the ranks
Of those who pass before.
We check the kites and fix them up
And so the war goes on,
Two new boys come to take the place
Of our chums who have gone;
Passed on but not forgotten
Just as hundreds more have done
And we who follow won't forget
Until the war is won.

If it were not for the ground crews, the pilots would never have gotten airborne. Apparently John was not the only poet in 412 Squadron!

Author unknown.

Courtesy of Barry Needham.

## HEADINGTON YOUTH'S DEATH

The death has taken place of Mr. Aubrey Griffin, of the R.A.F., the 19-year-old son of Mr and Mrs. E. Griffin, of 23, Western-road, Headington.

Mr. Griffin, who was formerly employed in the City Engineer's Department at Oxford, had been in the R.A.F. since June.

The following appreciation is written by Mr. W. Beament:—

"Aubrey Griffin will be mourned by all those people—young and old

**Mr. E. A. Griffin**

—who had the joy of knowing him. His life has been given in the service of his country.

"He was a great worker in the Scout movement and, above all, a loyal and keen member of Lime Walk Methodist Church, of whose congregation he was the first to pay the supreme price for the great cause of freedom.

"We of the Church and Sunday School would wish to pay our tribute to our comrade, whose wholehearted love and enthusiasm for the work of the King of Kings has been reflected in his happy life.

"We rejoice that he has left many fragrant memories which will help to sustain and strengthen the members of his family and the many friends he leaves behind him."

Leading Aircraftsman Aubrey Griffin, Royal Air Force, who was killed along with John after their aircraft collided.

John G. Magee Family Papers, Record Group No. 242, Special Collections, Yale Divinity School Library

Wellingore, Digby, Cranwell, and the crash site.

Image created from Google, used with permission.
Google and the Google logo are registered trademarks of Google Inc.

Map of where John Magee and Aubrey Griffin
came to earth.

Image created from Google, used with permission.
Google and the Google logo are registered trademarks of Google Inc.

After the crash. John's Spitfire MKVB, AD291, VZ-H.
About the only thing recognizable is the wheel on the left side.

Picture courtesy of Robert Bracken.

Photo believed to be from John's funeral, December 13th, 1941,
at Scopwick Burial Grounds.

Picture courtesy of Barry Needham.

Scopwick Burial Grounds during WWII.

Picture courtesy of Barry Needham.

Scopwick, present day.

John's tombstone, present day.

Bottom three photographs courtesy of Catherine Parker.

John's tombstone.

Photograph courtesy of Catherine Parker.

John's "official" RCAF Pilot Officer photograph.

Courtesy of the Library of Congress.

1 http://www.pier21.ca/wp-content/uploads/files/First_75_Years/research_wwii.pdf accessed 12/08/11.

2 http://en.wikipedia.org/wiki/SS_California_(1923) accessed 03/18/12.

3 http://www.convoyweb.org.uk/hx/index.html accessed 12/06/11.

[4] http://www.warsailors.com/convoys/hx136.html accessed 12/06/2011.

[5] The HX[5] series of convoys is comprised of east-bound ships departing from Halifax and with a between 9 and 13 knots. The higher the speed that a convoy could maintain, the less susceptible to submarine attack they would become. As the crossing is somewhat hazardous, given the continuing presence of Nazi U-boats in the area.

[6] http://www.naval-history.net/WW2CampaignsAtlanticBattles.htm accessed 12/06/2011.

[7] Greenock, Scotland, was the principal port of arrival for many Canadian and U.S. soldiers and airmen. Greenock also had the distinction of being the port from where Britain's gold reserves, some seven billion dollars' worth, departed the United Kingdom for safe-keeping in Canada. This was the largest financial transaction in the world up to that time.

[8] Letter from Dermott Magill to Mrs. Magee, dated December 24th, 1941.

[9] Letter from JGM to his family, dated August 1941.

[10] Letter from JGM to Alan and Sarah Scaife, dated August 15, 1941.

[11] http://www.rafweb.org/O.T.U._3.htm accessed on July 11, 2010
1. Data gathered from website: http://www.rafweb.org/O.T.U._3.htm accessed July 11, 2010.

[13] http://www.rafweb.org/OTU_3.htm accessed August 6, 2014.

[14] JGM letter to Alan and Sarah Scaife, dated August 15, 1941.

[15] Letter from JGM to his family, August 15, 1941.

[16] Reginald Mitchell designed the Spitfire, but died before he saw it fly.

[17] http://www.rafweb.org/Biographies/LeBas_MH.htm –accessed May 11, 2013.

[18]http://www.worldlingo.com/ma/enwiki/en/John_Gillespie_Magee,_Jr.

[19] http://homepage.ntlworld.com/peter.fairweather/docs/Magee.htm–accessed 03/12/2012.

[20] Letter from Alistair A. Smith to Mr. Royal D. Frey, Curator, Air Force Museum, dated 31 July 1975.

[21] Hamleys is one of the world's largest toy stores:
   http://en.wikipedia.org/wiki/Hamleys

[22] "The Spitfire Smiths" by RIA Smith with Christopher Shores.

[23] http://www.raf-lincolnshire.info/wellingore/wellingore.htm.

http://www.controltowers.co.uk/W-Z/Wellingore.htm.
[24]

http://www.google.com/imgres?imgurl=http://s0.geograph.org.uk/photos/64/4 0/644043_95f5fb1a.jpg&imgrefurl=http://www.geograph.org.uk/photo/644043 &usg=__v2GYwA8CLxb7eaP4LnXESpUW0bE=&h=427&w=640&sz=64&hl=en&st art=1&zoom=1&um=1&itbs=1&tbnid=0_wYzd1ngKKX9M:&tbnh=91&tbnw=137 &prev=/images%3Fq%3Dwellingore%2Bhall%26um%3D1%26hl%3Den%26sa%3 DN%26rls%3Dcom.microsoft:en-us:IE-SearchBox%26rlz%3D1I7SUNA_en%26tbs%3Disch:1.

[25] In an interesting bit of synchronicity, *A Yank in the RAF* starred Tyrone Power, who later joined the Marine Corps and became a pilot himself. After the war, Power was at a party during which he recited *High Flight* from memory. In attendance was fellow actor Ronald Reagan. Years later, Reagan remembered the poem when speechwriter Peggy Noonan suggested *High Flight* be included in Reagan's speech to the nation after the 1989 space shuttle Challenger disaster. After Tyrone Power's death, it is said that another actor, Laurence Olivier, recited *High Flight* during Power's military funeral.

[26] https://en.wikipedia.org/wiki/Charley_Fox

[27] https://en.wikipedia.org/wiki/Erwin_rommel

[28] http://en.wikipedia.org/wiki/Messerschmitt_Bf_109 accessed 2014_01_15.

[29] http://www.bbm.org.uk/ScottDR.htm accessed 2012_12_20.

[30] http://www.spitfires.ukf.net/p008.htm accessed 2012_12_20.

P8701 IIb CBAF MXII 39MU 22-6-41 303S 4-7-41 65S 18-9-41 616S 6-10-41 Shot
                down by Fw190 mid-day 18-11-41 FH81.50 W/C D R Scott
                AFC killed

[31] Josef Priller would later become famous as one of the few Luftwaffe pilots to perform ground attacks on the D-Day landing force. The movie, "The Longest Day" portrays Priller and his flight.

[32] On this day Adolf Galland would record his 94th and 95th victories. He would shoot down one more Spitfire before being forbidden to engage in combat missions (Galland had been promoted to command all of Germany's air forces). Galland managed to shoot down another nine Allied aircraft before the end of the war, for a grand total of 104 victories.

[33] Joachim Müncheberg recorded 135 victories, of which 46 were Spitfires. On November 8th, Müncheberg would shoot down three Spitfires.

[34] From "The Spitfire Smiths" by Squadron Leader RAI Smith DFC & Bar, with Christopher Shores.

[35] 'Jagdgeschwader 2: "Richthofen"' by John Weal.

[36] Letter provided by Dwayne Linton's son Doug Linton.

[37] F/L Hart Massey was 412 Squadron's Intelligence Officer. Massey was related to actor Raymond Massey; curiously enough, Magee's father had suggested that John see Raymond Massey's portrayal of Abraham.

[38] It is not known for sure, but there was an experiment going on at the time involving Lockheed Hudson aircraft using searchlights mounted in the nose of their aircraft. The Hudson, in its night-fighter role, would find enemy bombers at night with its radar. Accompanied by Hurricanes (or, apparently in this case, Spitfires), the Hudson would close with enemy bombers and then illuminate them with the searchlight. The fighters, who were not equipped with radar, would then attack.

[39] (GCA, or Ground Controlled Approach, was a couple of years away from being implemented).

[40] Cranwell was in use primarily as a training field, but there were other uses as well (Sir Frank Whittle had test-flown England's first jet aircraft at Cranwell the previous May). At the start of WWII, Cranwell had been converted to No. 17 Service Flying Training School (SFTS).

## Aftermath

"DEEPLY REGRET TO INFORM YOU..."

A parent's worst nightmare during wartime involves a telegram being delivered, saying in so many impartial words that the child whom they have brought into the world, raised, nurtured and loved, is gone.

A telegram is delivered. 42 words. No details, no circumstances, nothing except "KILLED ON ACTIVE SERVICE."

Shortly thereafter, another telegram, informing them of an event that none from the family could not possibly attend, since it has already happened. "... THE FUNERAL OF YOUR SON PILOT OFFICER JOHN GILLESPIE MAGEE WILL TAKE PLACE AT SCOPWICH PARISH CHURCH LINCOLNSHIRE AT 230 PM GMT DECEMBER 13TH."

The first telegraph arrived at the Magee home on December 12th, the second in the evening of December 13th.

Washington D.C., along with the rest of the country, was still reeling from the shock generated by the Japanese attack on Pearl Harbor. President Roosevelt had declared war against Japan on December 8th and against Germany on December 11th.

John's brother Christopher, ever the organizer, felt the need to let the press know what happened. Reporter Izetta Winter Robb relates this experience in an article written for the Washington D.C. *Daily News*[1]:

> When a reporter up to now answered a phone it might have been to hear about a fire or a fraternity house. But it's different in war. It was a boy calling.
>
> "I thought — you might be interested," he said. "My older brother joined the Royal Canadian Air Force."
>
> There was a pause. "Yes?" the reporter said.
>
> Well — the telegram just came ... He's been killed in action."
>
> The boy's voice broke. He was only 13.
>
> Later, tho, in the Magee home at 2118 Bancroft St NW, the boy Christopher seemed older. He had had to become a man in a half-hour. He displayed the RCAF telegram....

John Sr. and his wife Faith knew that this event was a possibility. Intellectually, that is. Nothing could have prepared them for the actuality.

In early December, John's mother Faith had written her own mother and sister Ruth, describing recent events in Washington. She included news about John Jr.:

> After being in several Canadian Training Camps, he received his wings in June. He came home full of happiness and enthusiasm as a Sergeant Pilot, but, on the morning his leave ended, to his great delight, he received a wire saying that he had been given a commission as a Pilot Officer. (The equivalent of a 2nd Lt. in the American Army.) He had hardly expected this, and it was a great help to him and to us on the day of parting. He sailed for England a day or two afterwards, and we are now receiving very happy letters from him. His address is: 412 Squadron, R.C.A.F, C/O Overseas Base P.O. England. We think you will like to see one of his recent poems, which we think are very lovely, and which he began at 30,000 ft. and finished on the ground:

A copy of *High Flight* is typed in the letter. And in a sad coincidence, a postscript dated December 11th is included. With no premonition of what is happening with her son in England, Faith includes small details of her family life in the U.S.:

> Hugh [Magee] said the other day – 'Poor old Granny! I wish she wasn't so old, so that she could come over here with us." He really is very fond of England, & of his family & friends there. He told me the other day he was "Kingsdown-" sick (the word home-sick being in his mind!)

Faith also notes the recent loss of two British ships, *HMS Prince of Wales* and *HMS Repulse*, both recently sunk in the Pacific by Japanese forces:

> *We are all feeling very sad over here at the loss of the*
> *'Prince of Wales' & the 'Repulse' – such a tragic loss from*
> *every point of view – for England. Also there was – of course*
> *– great excitement here on Sunday – over the sudden attack*
> *on Manila. Christopher – who loses no opportunity – was out*
> *till very late selling 'extras' & sold most of them among the*
> *crowd which had gathered outside the Japanese Embassy. It*
> *was a tragic thing to happen, but at least it has woken the*
> *country up, & filled the different parties & factions together,*
> *as perhaps nothing less could have done. It will be a sad*
> *Christmas, one which can only really be kept by those who*
> *have the deep meaning of the Christmas message in their*
> *hearts.*

Faith had no idea just how sad the Christmas of 1941 was to be. On December 16th, after learning of her son's death, Faith had to write a very different letter to her mother:

> *By now you will have received our cablegram telling*
> *you about our young John's death. I really hardly like to use*
> *that word because we know he is alive and we have such a*
> *feeling that he is so happy and free now. We cannot make*
> *out whether you will have heard this from other sources in*
> *England, and am hoping soon to have word from you about*
> *it. Of course we knew all along when he went in to the air*
> *force that this might happen, but as he had had several such*
> *marvelous escapes, we began to feel that possibly he was to*
> *be brought through.*

As a result of their strong faith, the Magee family seems to have borne the tragedy relatively well:

*The thing that I found hardest was the time when we received the second telegram about the funeral, but I have come to realize that that was not John himself and that he is alive and I believe wonderfully happy. I have often heard (and I found this true about [Faith's] father) that those who have gone often seem nearer to us than when distance separated on this earth, and I have certainly found this now with our John.*

In these early days since John's death, the Magee family are just now beginning to realize the impact of *High Flight*. Continuing her letter of December 16th, Faith Magee tells her mother about the realization that *High Flight* is very special not only to the Magee family, but to many others:

*We have had so many lovely letters that we have not yet had time to read them all and offers of help from so many people in different ways. The thing that has thrilled us so particularly has been the wonderful reception that is being given to his poem "High Flight" a copy of which I sent you recently. We ourselves think it is beautiful but did not realize that so many others would feel the same way and more about it. We are sending you a set of newspaper clippings and you will see how very beautifully the notice of his going was put in the local papers.*

*High Flight* is the subject of a sermon held at the Washington Cathedral:

*... last Sunday, in the Washington Cathedral, with about 2500 people present, Bishop Freeman centered all he had to say round John's poem, centering particularly on the thought of "touching the face of God".*

David Magee was away at Hotchkiss School. Faith tells her mother about a letter received from David after being informed of his brother's death:

> We were rather concerned as to how David would feel, as we knew how greatly he loved and admired John. And we were so happy to have a very nice letter from him this morning. I think I will give it to you in part: "Mr. Murphy told me the sad news about John last night. I know how you must all feel. We must all take it well and be very very proud of him. The main thing seems to me for us to think about all the other families in England, and now here in the United States. Thousands and thousands have received the same news. I think we must realize that we are not the only ones who have been so grieved. We must all be proud of his courage in undertaking such a grave responsibility and task."

The youngest Magee brother, Hugh, exhibits the same strong faith shared by the entire Magee family, a faith that assures them that John is in a better place:

> Hugh feels that John is in Heaven and is very happy to think that he will see the kittens, two of which died here recently through a special illness. He thinks the kittens have wings and is quite happy to think of them all being there together!

Faith closes this letter in a handwritten postscript dated December 17th:

> ... John would love to have won the DFC, or some other distinction, but instead is has been given to him to win distinction through this beautiful poem, and we are both proud and glad.

> *His poem has been reprinted in papers all over America. So much love to you both in which John [Magee Sr.] joins. Faith*

Magee Sr. had also written to Faith's mother on October 1st, expressing much the same sentiment about *High Flight*:

> *In his last letter he [John Jr.] gave us a poem that he had started at an altitude of 30,000 feet & called it "High Flight." It was really lovely & gave one the joyous feeling of the freedom he felt in the air.*

The Magee family received many letters expressing sadness, shock and dismay at the news of John's death. Some of these letters came from total strangers; many more came from friends and family.

In a letter to John's father, Hugh Lyon expresses his and his family's feelings:

> *Nothing since the war began has given us such deep distress as yesterday's notice in the Times — My wife and two elder girls and I myself feel as if we had lost one of the family... What it must mean to you and your wife and the other boys I just can't imagine — You have our deepest sympathy; you are much in our thoughts and our prayers.[2]*

Hugh Lyon's last recollections of John:

> *He arrived late one night, and, just before he went back the next afternoon, he came and talked a little to me as I was sawing wood in my garage. It was good of him to come round, for he was in a hurry. He spoke a little about my family, a little about the prospects of going abroad, but not much about anything. It wasn't necessary somehow. 'So in all love we parted.' After he had gone, I went on sawing, and*

*thinking of him, and the fine man he was growing up to be.*
3

Elinor Lyon-Wright recounts her reaction upon hearing of John's death:

*I learned of his [John's] death by seeing a very brief announcement in 'The Times.' I think my parents already knew — I expect somebody had given them the news earlier. It was very upsetting, for them as well as for me. I had got into the habit of reading all the Deaths in the paper, as so many of our friends were on active service. I raced upstairs to my room when I read it, and my mother followed and we mourned together — I think she was as fond of him as I was.*
4

Elinor felt that John could not have stood to become much older:

*He liked to live at full speed and danger only made life more thrilling. I don't think he could have borne to grow old. I think he had found out how to live, and loved being alive so much that he could not have been afraid of death.*

Nearly 50 years after John's death, St. Clare's friend Robert Dawson recalls:

*I don't know when I heard about John's accidental death but it was quite a long time after it happened and I remember the sense of loss that even then I felt. Good God, what he might have done and been, that wild and wonderful youth!*

*.... The fact that I was privileged to know John contributes to whatever justification there may be for my existence.*

Frank Wylie, a friend of John's at Avon wrote to the Magee family shortly after John's death, describing his recollections of John:

> At this time of great sorry, I fully realize how fruitless
> are any words of mine; and yet I feel the need, & the duty, of
> forwarding you my deepest regrets…
>
> For a term, or year, at Avon, it was my pleasure to be
> esteemed as a companion by your son. Not once did I ever
> hear a justifiable word against him, nor was there a friend
> for whom he would not do anything. Typical of this, his great
> feeling of responsibility or duty, was his joining the air force.
> I was with him the day he first gave it thought, and could not
> help but admire the courage with which he was always ready
> to face the world, undaunted, courageous & filled with faith.

In letters of condolence, many remarked that John seemed very happy with where he was and what he was doing at the end of his life. It seemed that, at long last, John had truly found a family and a home when he joined the Royal Canadian Air Force and learned to fly.

Hugh Lyon wrote:

> You can be certain that the last few months of his life
> were among his happiest.[5]

Dermott Magill, John's good friend, wrote to John's Aunt Mary, who Dermott had met when John and he had come across from England to the U.S. in 1938. In a letter dated December 27th, 1941, Dermott expresses his sentiment about John's state of mind:

> As you probably know he [John] came and stayed with
> me at Oxford for a long weekend about a month ago. He was
> looking better than I had ever seen him look before. He said
> that this was the happiest time of his life.

Dermott also wrote a letter to John's mother. In this letter, Dermott expresses the esteem in which he held his friend:

> ... he was the greatest friend I have ever had: we had
> grown up together at Rugby and he had a very great
> influence on me in that critical time of life. He always had
> that great quality of being serious and gay, always at the
> right time.[6]

Even decades later, there were many who recalled serving with Magee. Alistair A. Smith went through Operational Training with John at No. 53 OTU in Llandow, Wales. In a letter written in 1975, Smith remembers John:

> Those of us who knew John recognized his talent and
> he was, without question, always the most popular member
> of our group. His tragic death was a great loss to our world.

In April of 1942 John's parents received an interesting letter from a James Hartland. In the letter, Hartland (who was 20 years old when he wrote the letter), explains that he was John's "batman" (otherwise known as an orderly or servant. Commissioned officers had such orderlies who would take care of many of the incidentals of military life, such as maintaining the officer's quarters and uniform, waking them, and performing other errands as requested.)

It seems that John had requested his batman to write a letter to John's parents, letting them know that John was being well taken care of. At the start of the letter, Hartland is not certain that he is writing to the correct people:

> I believe that your son P/O Johnny Magee was serving
> in England with RCAF till the time of his death. Well sir I was
> Johnnys (Batman) and was asked by son to make contact
> with you (to let his people know that he was well looked after
> and made great acquaintances in England).
>
> I do not know your correct address so I am sending this
> letter by chance, and as I have mentioned, I pray that you

*will not be offended and hurt in any manner or form, as I am fulfilling the wish of a great officer and flyer. I feel it is my duty to fulfil his wish as I never served for one so good. We were with 412 squad. at the time, but now I are with an English squadron in Alberta.*

Hartland explains that he is "not a very good writer" but hopes that his letter means something to John's parents. It seems that Magee's parents did indeed get the letter and wrote back to Hartland requesting more details. In a subsequent letter, Hartland writes:

*The first time I met P/O J. Magee I thought to myself what a sissy, what have they given me now, I called him Longfellow Magee so did the other members of the staff. As time went on he changed sir believe me he changed. The R.C.A.F. made a man out of him and if it comes to that so did England. You [John's parents] mentioned was he thoughtful. He was very thoughtful towards me in fact too thoughtful. I could never do anything for him unless he said you need not have bothered it was okay it was okay what do you ask for have a rest take it easy. What are you panicking for.*

*Another thing I was not to call him sir many a time believe me sir that was one of the main things that got me to like J. Magee.*

*The men of 412 liked him sir as much as I did, his ways, his manner, his work, and his cooperation with the men. He was a grand flyer, crazy on flying, plenty of guts and believe me sir he lived up to his nationality. I am sure that he died the way he wished to (flying).*

It was not only pilots, instructors and fellow students that were impressed by John Magee. In a letter written on May 10th, 1942, an airplane mechanic who served with John at Uplands in Canada wrote to John's parents:

>Yesterday I was one of the many yet few privileged to receive a copy of your late son's "High Flight" issued by our Canadian Ministry of Information.
>
>I shall prize it very much as your late son was a student attached to "G" Flight at Uplands where I served as a mechanic. We grew to love him for his many fine ways and gentleman-like ideals.
>
>... His courage he displayed could not keep him down to attain a very high goal, which he alone was able to realize. On this day, Mother's Day, last year, I recall him mentioning your name and no matter where he is, his thoughts are of you and may I express my humble thoughts.
>
>You see, I, too was greatly moved when I read of his fatal accident, but upon reading his poem, I believe he realized his goal and I an inspiration which I shall keep as a guide through me life as a member of the R.C.A.F., whom your late son John so greatly admired.

P/O Rod Smith, who would eventually become a Squadron Leader and win the DFC (Distinguished Flying Cross) later recalls the burial of his friend:

>John's burial service took place in a graveyard that is a nearby continuation of one beside the church at Scopwick, a small village about a mile from Digby. I was an honorary pallbearer and I remember clearly that when the air force ensign was removed from the single oak coffin, the brass plaque on the latter read:

*P/O John Gillespie Magee*
*R.C.A.F.*
*Died December 11, 1941*
*Age 19 years*

*We never saw anyone like John again.*

On a trip back to Wellingore in 1984, Rod and a friend visited the location of the old airfield as well as the graveyard where John was buried:

> *The south side of Wellingore was just the same, quieter if anything. We turned into the leafy lane where the Grange, the church and Wellingore Hall were. All were as serene and beautiful as I remembered them.*
>
> *We drove the short distance south to where the aerodrome had been, and found that it was a farm again. We then drove east towards Digby and came to the graveyard where John was buried. Its general aspect was pleasingly natural as before, in large part because of some aging trees along its southern boundary and a few rustic buildings beyond them. We entered through the lych-gate, on its east side. First are older graves of villagers and then of several RAF pilots from the twenties and thirties. Many graves of wartime RAF and RCAF aircrew lie just beyond, each marked with the simple form of air force tombstone which replace the wartime white wooden cross.*
>
> *John's grave is on the south side, among several other 412 Squadron pilots, all of whom were killed in collisions. I recognized his name first, and noticed that the first and last lines of High Flight were inscribed below it. To my surprise, tears suddenly came to my eyes, and I turned away and pretended to look for other names so that my friend wouldn't notice.*

*On that beautiful morning, as I looked southwards over the churchyard and through the trees to the rustic buildings beyond, it struck me there was no finer place to lie forever.*

In February 1942, John's father received an unexpected letter:

*Dear Sir,*

*I hope you will forgive me writing to you: but I think you will understand when you have finished reading this letter.*

*On Thurs. 5th Feb 1942 I read the "Sonnet" published in the "Daily Express" composed by your son after he had been flying. It also said that he was killed on active service in Britain, on December 11th, 1941.*

*My son, aged 19 years, was flying a twin engine plane just below the clouds near Cranwill, Lincs, when a Spitfire coming out of the clouds collided with his plane and they were both instantly killed.*

This had to have come as a shock to The Reverend Magee. Details about wartime accidents and events were hard to come by, and undoubtedly the Magee family at that time had no idea of the identity of the other pilot involved in the collision.

*... We have been wondering since reading the account of your son's death on Dec. 11th 1941, the same day as my son's, if by any chance it happened to be your son.*

*It is indeed a great blow to us & I think the longing for him to come home grows as time goes by. We expect it is the same with you. You have our deepest sympathy & may God comfort you...*

The letter is signed, "E. Griffin", LAC Griffin's father. Years later, Faith Magee met with the parents of Aubrey Griffin.

At the end of his life, John seems that John fulfilled Tecumseh's admonishment:

> When your time comes to die, be not like those whose hearts are filled with fear of death, so that when their time comes they weep and pray for a little more time to live their lives over again in a different way. Sing your death song, and die like a hero going home.

John Magee had died, not in "violent combat" as he might have thought or even wished for, but in an accident. He died doing what he had come to love doing. He was where he wanted to be, where he felt he belonged. Before he died, he managed to give the world a magnificent gift. His poem *High Flight* lives on; and in that manner, John Magee will live forever.

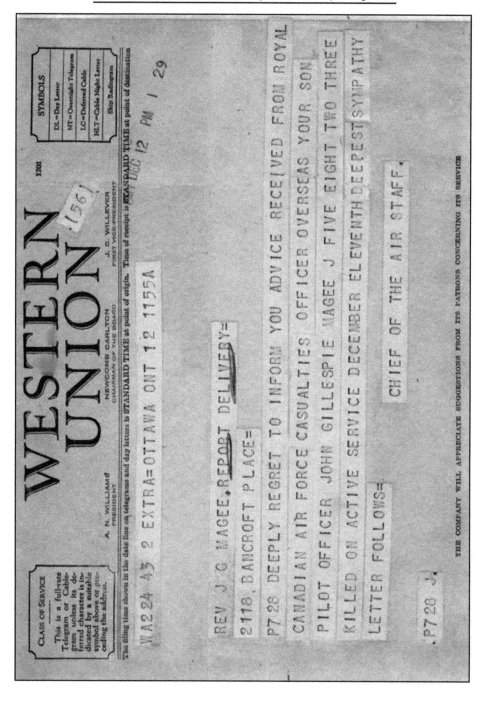

Courtesy of the Museum of the United States Air Force.

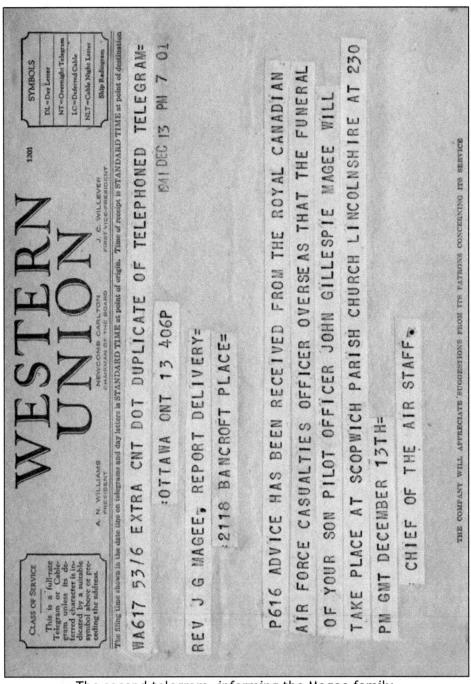

The second telegram, informing the Magee family
of John's funeral.

Courtesy of the Museum of the United States Air Force.

[1] "My Hand Touched the Face of God," The Washington Daily News was published from 1921-1972, and was the news home for famous reporter Ernie Pyle. The reporter in this article did not have to go far to visit the Magee residence; it was less than four miles from the Daily News offices.

[2] Letter from Hugh Lyon to Rev. John Magee, December 23rd, 1941.

[3] Hermann Hagedorn, Sunward I've Climbed, p. 162.

[4] Personal correspondence with Elinor Wright-Lyon, 10/20/2006.

[5] Letter from Hugh Lyon to Rev. John Magee, December 23rd, 1941.

[6] Letter from Dermott Magill to Mrs. Magee, December 24th, 1941.

# PART TWO

## THE STORY OF
## *HIGH FLIGHT*

## How *High Flight* became famous

And what of John's little sonnet, what he called his "ditty?" Just how did that 14-line sonnet go from being included in a letter to Magee's parents to still being talked about over 70 years later? It is quite a story.

In his 1940 application to join the RCAF, John had listed Washington, D.C., as his home town. As a result, notice of his death was first published in the D.C. newspapers: "Pilot Officer John Gillespie Magee, Jr., of Washington, D.C." Erroneous details varied from paper to paper: Magee was shot down in action or over Germany; he was a Lieutenant; his age varied from 19 to 21, and so on.

John's death occurred a mere four days after the Japanese attack on Pearl Harbor and on the day that the United States declared war on Germany, making John one of the first "official" American combat casualties of WWII, which possibly contributed to what was to come with regard to *High Flight*.

In September of 1941, The Reverend Magee was assistant rector at St. John's Church, across from Lafayette Park in Washington, D.C. During Magee Sr.'s tenure at St. John's, he performed several services for President Franklin Delano Roosevelt in the White House (and was also one of the clergy officiating at the funeral services for Roosevelt on April 14th, 1945).

Sometime after John had sent the letter that contained *High Flight* to his parents, his mother had shown the poem at her "Forward in Service" meeting at St. John's Church. After John's death, *High Flight* was printed in the "Leaflet of St. John's Church," along with a brief biography of John. The leaflet also indicated that the poem would be shown at "Poems of Faith and Freedom," an exhibition at the Library of Congress.

## Poems of Faith and Freedom

Archibald MacLeish, Librarian of Congress, was a distinguished poet in his own right. MacLeish may have attended St. John's Church, and may well have known The Reverend Magee. This might have been the way that MacLeish first became aware of *High Flight*, after reading the poem in the church bulletin. He was impressed by the poem, and undoubtedly wished for a way to have *High Flight* read by more people. The combination of war being recently declared and John Magee Jr. becoming one of the first "official" American casualties of the war might have contributed to the gravity of including *High Flight* in an exhibition of poetry. MacLeish did make the statement, recorded in many newspapers, that *High Flight* was to WWII what *In Flanders Fields* was to WWI, and that John Magee was the "first American poet of the present World War."

The "Poems of Faith and Freedom" exhibition at the Library of Congress opened on February 5th, 1942. A press release by the Library dated February 5, 1942 described the exhibition:

> The work of John Gillespie Magee, Jr., the young Washingtonian who lost his life in action with the Royal Canadian Air Force over enemy territory last December, is shown in an exhibition opened today at the Library of Congress, it was announced by Archibald MacLeish, the Librarian.
>
> Featured in the exhibition are two manuscripts, lent by Mr. Magee's parents, The Reverend and Mrs. John G. Magee, Sr., of Washington D.C. One of these is the manuscript of the sonnet, "High Flight", sent to his parents in a letter from the young flyer, and published in many newspapers across this country and in Canada shortly after his death. The other manuscript is a sixteen line poem, probably Magee's last, recently received by his parents in a letter, and as yet unpublished. Its title is "Per Ardua", a phrase taken from the motto of the Royal Canadian Air Force, and it is dedicated to Magee's companions who perished in the Battle of Britain.
>
> Also exhibited, as evidently related in spirit and circumstances, are a Photostat of the first draft of Rupert Brooke's sonnet, "The Soldier", better known by its first line: "If I should die, think only this of me..."; and the first printing, in Punch, of Colonel John McCrae's rondeau, "In Flanders Fields". A little book of poems, written and printed by Magee in 1939, while he was in high school in Avon, Connecticut, is another feature of the exhibition.
>
> The showing forms a part of the group of Poems of Faith and Freedom, including manuscripts by Shelley, Burns, Longfellow and Whitman, on view in the Library for the past month.

This exhibition was covered extensively by the press, and could be considered the critical event that catapulted *High Flight* to worldwide prominence. Newspaper coverage of this exhibition invariably carried John's biography along with the text of *High Flight*.

In today's terms, *High Flight* went "viral."

Magee's mother and father were inundated with letters about their son and *High Flight*. Requests came for pictures, biographical details, and permission to print *High Flight*. The Associated Press requested a picture, which was supplied to them by Magee Sr. with the instructions that the RCAF be contacted for permission to reproduce. In a letter dated February 9th, 1942, Magee Sr. wrote to L.M. McKechnie at the RCAF Public Relations department:

> *Saturday night the Associated Press here asked me for a picture of my son, John G. Magee, Jr.... When I sent the picture I wrote a note to say this again and told the person receiving it to look on the stamp on the back which stated this and also that permission must be gained from the RCAF for its reproduction. In this morning's Washington Post the picture appears with "Associated Press Photo" with nothing said about the RCAF...*
>
> *... If I have embarrassed you in the matter, I am very sorry...*

Magee Sr.'s letter goes on to explain the renewed interest in his son and *High Flight*.

> *The cause of the new wave of publicity — the poem appeared on the front page of the New York Herald Tribune yesterday and in the Washington Post several days before and again this morning — is that recently the Library of Congress here gave out a statement to the papers in which they hailed this sonnet as the equal of some of the finest poems of the last World War.*

The "Saturday Review of Literature" (Executive Editor: Norman Cousins), dedicated their April 25, 1942 issue to "poetry and the cause of poetry." In the issue's introduction, contributing editor William Ross Benet made these comments:

*In time of war we believe that poetry has a great deal to give. We have the honor to publish in this issue the original manuscript of a poem by a young American airman, which came to his parents in a letter after he had been shot down. It illustrates the fact — as did also his former widely-quoted poem "High Flight," written after piloting a Spitfire at 30,000 feet — that poetry plays a part wherever heroism and exaltation are in the air.*

The poem that Benet references is Magee's last poem *Per Ardua*. The article written by Lillian Porter Say in the Saturday Review is entitled, "Young America Singing":

*Young America singing. Singing and giving wings to the world. That was John Gillespie Magee, Jr., nineteen-year-old Pilot officer in the Royal Canadian Air Force. In September, 1941, he was flying, flying 30,000 feet above the earth while in combat training. As he flew, words sang themselves into his heart. When he returned to earth, he scribbled them on the back of a letter to his mother in Washington and called them "High Flight."*

Later in the article she recounts how *High Flight* came to be added to the Poems of Faith and Freedom exhibit:

*"The moment we read 'High Flight'," says Joseph Auslander, head of the Poetry Division of the Library of Congress, "we knew instantly that here was another voice with a certain universal quality, a certain heroic spirit, a gallantry that ranked it with our best known poets of faith and freedom. We immediately asked permission of Magee's parents to add the works of their son to this exhibit.'*

In the Saturday Review article, a brief biography of Magee is presented along with the text of John's poem *Per Ardua*.

## Harold H. Booth, the RCAF and *High Flight*

The Royal Canadian Air Force received so many requests for copies of *High Flight* that an "official" poster was put together to be given out to those who requested it. In early 1942, RCAF Flight Lieutenant/Squadron Leader and artist Harold H. (H.H.) Booth was commissioned to create several renditions of a Spitfire to be used in the poster. A picture of Magee and a short biography were included. The original order called for 1,000 copies to be printed (later revised to 1,500 copies due to the increasing demand) and to be sent to all RCAF training bases and stations.

Squadron Leader Booth was authorized by the RCAF to travel to Washington D.C. in order to present the original poster to John's father. The Canadian Legation in D.C. was notified, and on March 18th, 1942, the poster was presented to John's father in a quiet ceremony.

Booth again communicated in May of 1943 with the Magee family about a reprint of the poster — there were so many request for copies of the poem that the initial print run of 1,500 was quickly exhausted..

By June 1945, Booth must have been released from the RCAF and was working for Luscombe Aircraft Corporation in Trenton, New Jersey. On Luscombe letterhead, Booth wrote to his friend Laurie McKechnie at the RCAF Public Relations Directorate in Ottawa, requesting copies of the poster that he, Booth, had contributed to in 1942:

> *I have had at various times from people in the Army Air*
>
> *Forces down here requests for copies of High Flight. Do you*
>
> *know if there are any more still in stock at D.P.R.?*

McKechnie must have been extremely busy, for a Squadron Leader L.C. Powell replied on his behalf:

> *Laurie, as usual, is up to his neck in paper work and has*
>
> *asked me to reply to your letter requesting additional copies*
>
> *of High Flight.*

*Although we are running short of these I managed to scrounge forty odd copies which I hope will be of some help to you. They are going forward under separate cover.*

A sample of the kind of requests that the RCAF was getting for *High Flight* is contained in a letter written by Allan Bennett, a flying instructor located where Magee started his flying career: No. 9 Elementary Flying School, St. Catharines. Dated May 26th, 1942, the letter is typed on "St. Catharines Flying Training School Limited" stationery:

*Would it be possible to obtain a number of copies of the publication "High Flight".*

*This article was written by Pilot Officer Magee, Jr. He was a student at the Flying Training School, No. 9 E.F.T.S.*

*He was well liked by everyone during his course at this school, and we would like to place copies of this publication in various rooms around the station.*

## Congressional Record

The *PROCEEDINGS AND DEBATES OF THE 77TH CONGRESS, SECOND SESSION*, dated Thursday, February 12th, 1942, has the transcript of a speech made by the Hon. Martin J. Kennedy of New York, in the House of Representatives. The speech was entitled, "Abraham Lincoln" (February 12th is Lincoln's birthday).

*Mr. Speaker, this morning, on my way to the House of Representatives, I visited the Lincoln Memorial, built as the tribute of a grateful people to a famous and beloved President, Abraham Lincoln.*

Mr. Kennedy goes on to talk about President Lincoln, and then starts talking about the Library of Congress exhibition:

*The Library of Congress has an exhibit of poems and works of men who, like Lincoln, were inspired by serious events to great deeds and words. At the exhibit you will find many original documents through which run the spirit of Honest Abe, and, like the masterpieces of Lincoln, are in the handwriting of the authors.*

Quoting Mr. Joseph Auslander, Mr. Kennedy continues:

*"These are the words of the posts of free and proud people. These are the proverbs of their experience of freedom, the songs of the struggle, and 'the long labor of liberty.' These belong to the vigilant and heroic record. These poems have become famous because they were carried alive by passion and truth into the hearts of men. The have become familiar because they stayed there."*

The speech then goes on to quote from several poems, including *The Peacemaker* by Joyce Kilmer, *O Captain, My Captain* by Walt Whitman, *In Flanders Fields* by John McCrae, and *The Soldier* by Rupert Brooke.

About *High Flight*, Mr. Kennedy writes:

*"High Flight," written during this war, should make us realize and appreciate the beauty of soul of the youth in our armed forces. The writer, a young man of 19, John Gillespie Magee, joined the Royal Air Force of Canada and was killed in action. While soaring above the clouds he wrote this poem for his parents, one which I think will live forever in the hearts of millions of grateful Americans.*

*... Mr. Speaker, it is almost unbelievable that a soldier as young as John Magee could be so inspired as to be able to write High Flight. He is typically American...*

The inclusion of *High Flight* (in its entirety) into the Congressional Record is a testament to the extraordinary power of Magee's poem.

## US Air Force *High Flight* Television Sign-off Film

AUTHOR'S STORY

The next major event in the life of *High Flight* happened in the late 1950s and early 1960s. A decision was made to use the resources of the United States Air Force to create a short film based on *High Flight* and distribute it to television stations in the U.S as a recruitment tool.

The producer of the original version of this film called *High Flight* "the poem that television made famous." He was referring to this short film that was shown on TV during the sixties and seventies. Just before TV stations would sign off (remember those days?), they would show this film, followed by a film featuring the National Anthem. I recalled seeing that film many times while growing up in Los Angeles. I was quite captivated by it, seeing as I had always wanted to be an astronaut and this was the closest thing to describing how I felt about flying and going into space.

When I started on the John Magee biography project, I decided to find this film. I went through several Air Force offices, the National Archives, television stations, and so on. Through my webpage I requested information from anybody who knew about the film.

For years there was no response, then I got an email from a gentleman in Florida. This man had worked for a TV station for twenty years; during that time, the station had switched from film to video and was about to throw out all their old film. This gentleman rescued the films from the trash and stored them in his garage for 25+ years.

Somehow he had found my website, read my request, and contacted me. Eureka! The film was sent and I wasted no time in getting it converted from 16mm film to digital. I should not have been surprised when I found out that the film stock had, in the intervening 25 years, turned completely pink. I was able to mostly get rid of the pink via digital video editing software, using a color correction process.

During this whole process, I got to know something about how this film came to be made. I was contacted by Carlton Weber, a retired Lt. Col. (USAF). Mr. Weber claimed to be the producer of the original film featuring *High Flight* that the USAF put together. Unfortunately, before I could get the entire story, Mr. Carlton passed away. But I do have some elements of the story gathered from emails that passed between Mr. Weber and myself.

The original film (featuring the F-104 "Starfighter"), was made around 1962, and was instigated by the Secretary of the Air Force, Office of Information (SAFOI). Here's how Mr. Weber describing some of what happened:

> When I got the Producer/Director assignment, the
> Pentagon gave me carte blanc to do the show. I have to
> thank TAC [Tactical Air Command] for furnishing me with an
> F-104 and a two place F-106, which I used as a flying camera
> platform. The F-104 was perfect (a real hotdog with a 16 foot
> wing span that could maneuver like no other aircraft). All of
> the flying sequences were planned for specific maneuvers,
> for the camera plane. And all turned out as planned.

Out of the blue, another person contacted me regarding the making of this film:

> My name is Dub Pool. My father, Col. Lawrence W.
> Pool, was the pilot of the F-104 that was filmed for the
> original High Flight television spot.
>
> Unfortunately, my father passed away in 1981. He was
> a pilot in WWII and Vietnam. My mother remembers that we
> were stationed at Tyndall AFB in Florida. They came to my
> dad, a major at that point, and filmed him in an F-104.

I contacted Mr. Weber to confirm that Col. Pool had been the pilot of the F-104. He did so, and provided me some more details of the filming:

> The High Flight [movie] was filmed in one take. We had
> pre-planned the shots and the maneuvers which Col. Pool
> had noted on his knee pad of his flight suit. We also had
> communications between him and the camera plane F-106.
> So the photography was rather easily performed by Sgt.

*Graumaldi, using a 35mm Arriflex camera and Eastman ECN*
*color film. Pool had to perform for the camera plane and he*
*was all on the money in his performance with the F-104.*

*The narrator was John Cannivan, a professional voice.*

*The film was distributed to every television station in*
*the United States. I have heard from many people who were*
*inspired to join the Air Force after watching the film.*

Sadly, before I could arrange for an in-depth interview, Carlton Weber, Lt. Colonel USAF (Retired), passed away on October 21st 2006. Mr. Weber was very proud of his accomplishment.

*I guess I'm a little sensitive, but it is a beautiful piece of*
*which I had something to do with. I think the purity of the*
*poem, the flight sequence, music selection, all the*
*production elements came together and were enjoyed by*
*millions of television viewers across the Nation.*

*At one time HIGH FLIGHT was my baby. While I had*
*little acknowledgement for producing the film, I did have the*
*satisfaction that it was well received and seen my millions of*
*viewers for a long time. I'm not a glory seeker. I just know*
*that in my own heart it was inspiring and greatly*
*appreciated.*

In his last email to me, Mr. Weber summed up his feelings: "I'm still very proud of *High Flight*."

In another development, I found part of a Library of Congress Veterans History Project story that shed a bit more light on this TV film. Retired Sergeant Major Richard Burkett had an extraordinary career, part of which including editing the USAF *High Flight* film. He relates it in his verbal interview:

*... fortunately was able to get on as a film cutter for the*
*Air Force at Wright Patterson Air Force Base at Wright Field.*

*And I made—helped make some movies there. And one is still—at least from what I heard, is still in use today. It was a film we did of the poem High Flight which was written by John Gillespie Magee, Jr., who was a pilot, a Sergeant pilot with World Canadian Air Force that was killed during World War II. And it's really a beautiful poem, that I cut the film for that and a number of other films.[1]*

The author of this book hopes to fill in the missing pieces of the USAF *High Flight* TV Sign-Off film, including more information on the narrator, and who composed and performed the music. If you can give more information, please contact me at: info@highflightproductions.com

## Challenger Shuttle Disaster with President Ronald Reagan

In some ways, *High Flight* experienced a revival after the tragic crash of the space shuttle Challenger in 1986. President Reagan, during his speech to the nation directly after the disaster, quoted two lines from *High Flight*.  Here is the end of Reagan's speech:

*The crew of the space shuttle Challenger honored us by the manner in which they lived their lives. We will never forget them, nor the last time we saw them, this morning, as they prepared for the journey and waved goodbye and slipped the surly bonds of earth to touch the face of God.*

In a Feb. 23rd, 2003 Opinion article in the Wall Street Journal, Peggy Noonan, who was President Reagan's speechwriter at the time of the disaster, explained how the quotes from *High Flight* made it into the speech:

*I felt in my heart that Mr. Reagan knew that poem, and that if he did he would want to use it. He did know it. He told me afterward that it was written on a plaque at his daughter Patti's school when she was a kid. He used to go and read it.*

*I was later told that Mr. Reagan had in fact read the poem*

*at the funeral or at a memorial for his friend Tyrone Power,*

*who had been a World War II pilot.[2]*

*So, when struggling to find the right words to calm a*

*traumatized nation, it's not surprising that the Great*

*Communicator borrowed from Magee's poem.*


## Summary

In 1947, John Magee's father responded to a request from Angelica Davidson, who was writing a book: *Twenty Poems of Faith and Freedom*. Magee Sr. gave Mrs. Davidson a complete history of his son and of the creation of the poem *High Flight*. The resulting book has both Spanish and English versions of Magee Jr.'s story and *High Flight*. In Magee Sr.'s letter to Mrs. Davidson, he comments:

> *A book could be written about the amazing influence*
>
> *of "High Flight" that does not appear in the biography*
>
> *[Hermann Hagedorn's Sunward I've Climbed]. Letters from*
>
> *all over the world - & they still come occasionally – have told*
>
> *us many interesting stories.*

Over the past many years, the author of this book has received hundreds of emails and letters, many of which tell of the effect that *High Flight* has had on them. Many have become pilots and/or joined the Air Force due to the poem. Some of the people are not even pilots, yet find *High Flight* to be a very spiritual poem, feeling that they don't really even need an aircraft to "slip the surly bonds of Earth."

It has been over 70 years, as of this writing, since *High Flight* was written. And still it maintains its immense power, and evokes the same feelings in all of those who have read it. Truly, *High Flight* is a classic poem, and will likely be read into the unforeseeable future.

RCAF poster created by Harold Booth, in response to popular demand.
Thousands were printed and distributed, many to every RCAF & RAF airfield.

Courtesy of Library and Archives, Canada

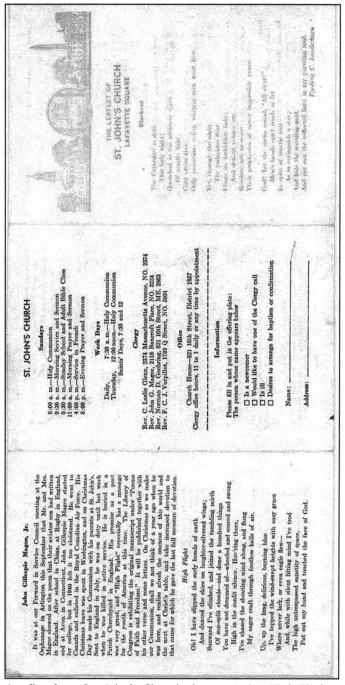

Leaflet from St. John's Church that contains *High Flight*.

Courtesy of National Museum of the United States Air Force.

## CONGRESSIONAL RECORD

In spite of false lights on the shore,
Sail on, nor fear to breast the sea!
Our hearts, our hopes, our prayers, our tears,
Our faith triumphant o'er our fears,
Are all with thee—are all with thee!

Written in 1849—this poem sprang from the national agitation and discord that were to culminate in the Civil War.

Lincoln wept when the poem was recited to him, and, after some minutes of silence, said:

It is a wonderful gift to be able to stir men like that.

### HIGH FLIGHT

(John Gillespie Magee, Jr.)

Oh, I have slipped the surly bonds of earth
And danced the skies on laughter-silvered wings
Sunward I've climbed and joined the tumbling mirth
Of sun-split clouds—and done a hundred things
You have not dreamed of—wheeled and soared and swung
High in the sunlit silence. Hov'ring there
I've chased the shouting wind along and flung
My eager craft through footless halls of air.
Up, up the long delirious, burning blue
I've topped the windswept heights with easy grace
Where never lark, or even eagle flew.
And, while with silent, lifting mind I've trod
The high untrespassed sanctity of space,
Put out my hand, and touched the face of God.

I hope many people will visit the Congressional Library and, as I, be refreshed by reading the beautiful words and sentiments contained in these priceless gems of poetry and literature. "High Flight," written during this war, should make us realize and appreciate the beauty of soul of the youth in our armed forces. The writer, a young man of 444346—21660

19, John Gillespie Magee, joined the Royal Air Force of Canada and was killed in action. While soaring above the clouds he wrote this poem for his parents, one which I think will live forever in the hearts of millions of grateful Americans. His beloved parents are in Washington, and his father is serving as acting rector of St. John's Protestant Episcopal Church.

You will find all these poems of which I speak today possessed of a positive spiritual influence. Courageous men, hardfighting men are these writers, giving their lives for their country, and, although engaged in the dreadful business of war, they have not forgotten their God. Each of these—Joyce Kilmer, John Gillespie Magee, Rupert Brooke, and John McCrae—died in the service of their country and, in addition to giving their lives, they have bequeathed to us their beautiful thoughts. In my opinion, the heart of Lincoln spoke the words of the Gettysburg Address. Down through the years that same love of country and fellowman, expressed by Lincoln on November 19, 1863, may be found in the writings of our contemporary poets.

Mr. Speaker, it is almost unbelievable that a soldier as young as John Magee could be so inspired as to be able to write High Flight. He is typically American and, please God, may his tribe increase.

I am sure, that regardless of how difficult for our beloved land the days ahead may be, with men like Kilmer in the last war and Magee in this war, we must and shall win, because they, the flower of our manhood, represent the true character of our people and the principles of our glorious Nation.

From the Congressional Record, Vol. 88, No. 31, Feb. 12, 1942.

Screen captures of the original USAF TV
*High Flight* Sign-Off Film,
Featuring the F-104 "Starfighter."

Screen captures of the next generation
USAF TV *High Flight* Sign-Off film,
featuring the T-38 "Talon."

1

http://memory.loc.gov/diglib/vhp/story/loc.natlib.afc2001001.00060/transcript?ID=sr0001 – accessed 10/12/13.

2 http://online.wsj.com/article/SB122427328139145395.html#printMode – accessed 2/10/2012.

# The Travels of *High Flight*

John wrote the letter containing *High Flight* between August 18th and September 3rd, 1941, while he was undergoing Spitfire operational training in Llandow, Wales. His parents, in Washington, D.C., must have gotten it within a few weeks

*High Flight* was published in the November 12th, 1941 issue of the Pittsburgh Post-Gazette. This may have been the first publication of *High Flight* outside of the publication in the St. John's church bulletin.

The next major event for *High Flight* was the death of its author on December 11th, 1941. The United States declared war on Germany and Italy on that day, making John Magee, Jr., one of the first "official" American casualties of what was clearly a Second World War. News of John's death, along with *High Flight*, was published in every major newspaper in the United States.

A couple of months later on February 5th, 1942, the Library of Congress decided to include *High Flight* (as well as Magee's last poem, *Per Ardua*, and his book of poems) in the exhibition: "Poems of Faith and Freedom."

In September of 1942, the *High Flight* letter was loaned to the Yale Library in New Haven, Connecticut, and was put on exhibition in the main corridor of the library.

On April 14th, 1943, *High Flight* was then donated by John's mother and father to its current home at the Library of Congress in Washington, D.C., after it was clear that *High Flight* was a poem destined to be a classic.

In 1975, *High Flight* was loaned by the Library of Congress to the U.S. Air Force Museum in Dayton, Ohio, where it was put on display for an unknown period of time. The year before, John's brother David had donated several items to the U.S.A.F. Museum such as John's R.C.A.F. Pilot's Logbook. At some point *High Flight* returned to the Library of Congress, where it resides today.

Over the years, the *High Flight* letter has been copied numerous times. Certainly some of these copies were made by copiers with extremely bright lights. Also, the letter was out in the open and subjected to constant light. These factors contributed to the current faded state of the letter, and the reluctance of the Library of Congress to expose the letter to any more light. The Library wants to keep the letter as intact as possible so that some future technology might be able to restore it to its original state; as a result it is stored in a special archival folder that is stored in an archival box, all stored in a very secure location.

# Tributes to John Magee, Jr. and *High Flight*

In the times following John's death and subsequent widespread publication of his story and *High Flight*, many wrote to John's parents with expressions of condolence and appreciation. It seems that John's mother, father and his Aunt Mary sent *High Flight* to many well-known people, several of whom wrote back. Here are a few of the tributes given to John and to *High Flight*.

## Anna Wood Murray, *The Evening Star*, Washington, D.C.

Miss Murray had written a poem as a tribute to John, called *Return to Base*, published in The Evening Star of Washington, D.C., on December 30th, 1941:

RETURN TO BASE

(To Pilot Officer John G. Magee, Jr., R.C.A.F., killed in action over Britain. December 11, 1941).

You turned your plane into the silvered blue
    Of endless dawn, and as you sped along,
Above the clouds where never eagle flew,
    You heard with bursting heart the crystal song
The morning stars first sang, beheld the glow,
    Of irised light that bade the darkness flee;
You passed each starry outpost, skirted the flow
    Of silent seas of lapis lazuli;
On, on beyond the amethystine peaks
    Before the white shores of the timeless land,
Came in upon the beam that each soul seeks,
    And knelt, and bowed your head beneath His Hand.

In a letter dated January 29th, 1942, Faith Magee wrote back to Miss Murray on behalf of both herself and Magee Sr. They had found a welcome perspective on John's death in Murray's poem:

*We have heard quite recently that our boy's Spitfire collided with another aircraft as they were coming out of the clouds, and that both planes crashed. It has been a temptation, at least to me personally, to let my imagination dwell on the horror of that moment and of all that might have happened. This is where your poem is such a wonderful help and blessing. Instead of thinking of the fall downward, we are helped to picture the glorious flight upward. One of my friends has told me, and she is one who is very often right in her intuitions, that she thinks probably the whole thing happened so suddenly that he was hardly conscious of anything but the marvel of passing over into that "timeless land." The last two lines of the poem will ever be to us both among the very precious thoughts that have been given us in our sorrow.[1]*

## Helen Keller

On July 29th, 1942, a letter was written by Helen Keller to Mr. and Mrs. Magee. It is worth quoting in its entirety:

*The copy of your son's Heaven-radiant poem has just been forwarded to me from "The Prudential Family Hour," and I thank you for the dear privilege of sharing such a unique sacrament with me.*

*Faith assures you, I know, that in the song John Magee left behind his very spirit is still alive, and your grief cannot but turn to holy joy in harmony with his own.*

*There is such exultation in me when I fly that every line of "High Flight" seems an utterance from a kindred spirit — "the surly bonds of earth" broken — the climb up sky billows*

*— the hurtling clouds — Youth keeping a gallant tryst with sun, wind and "the untrespassed sanctity of space," that awful aura of Liberty! I weep in happy sympathy at his last words, "Put out my hand and touched the Face of God." Blessed are they who have courage to look upon His Face at life's Sinai, but O the wondrous peace for those like your son who draw near enough to feel beneath them the Everlasting Arms that shall win mankind's final deliverance.*

The letter is signed with Helen's unique signature.

## Tyrone Power

Actor Tyrone Power wrote a letter to Aunt Mary (or, as typed on the letter, "Mrs. James Verner Scaife"). The letter is dated December 7th, 1942. It is short and to the point:

*"Sunward I've Climbed" [John's 1942 biography by Hermann Hagedorn] has reached me. I want you to know that I consider it a rare privilege to have been singled out to be one of the proud possessors of a copy of this book. It is, indeed, a beautiful tribute to a life well lived. This book seems to put in words the feelings so many young men possessed, as was John Magee, of such incredible courage, fine sentiment and true spirit. I shall always cherish its possession.*

Power knew what he was talking about, having joined the U.S. Marine Corps in August of 1942 and becoming a cargo pilot flying in the Pacific Theater of Operations.

## Winston Churchill

On White House stationery, Sir Anthony Rumbold, a British diplomat accompanying Churchill on a U.S. visit, wrote to John's mother, conveying Winston Churchill's sentiments regarding John and *High Flight*:

> *The Prime Minister has asked me to thank you for your letter of December 26th [1941] which greatly touched him not only by its generous words about himself but, far more, by its evidence of the courage and faith with which you and your husband have accepted the death of your brave and gifted son. His last sonnet is very fine. Mr. Churchill is sincerely grateful to you for bringing it to his attention and asks me to convey to you his deep sympathy in your loss.*

Prime Minister Churchill was in the United States at that time, arriving on December 22nd and spending Christmas with President Roosevelt.

## Kenton Kilmer

The son of poet Joyce Kilmer, Kenton Kilmer worked at the Library of Congress, Office of the Consultant in English Poetry. Kenton worked closely with the Magee family in getting *High Flight*, *Per Ardua* and John's *Poetry* book included in the Library of Congress exhibition "Poems of Faith and Freedom." Many letters were sent by Kilmer to the Magees, but this one stands out:

> *... I like the association of my father [poet Joyce Kilmer] with your son, and am glad to have them represented together in the "Poems of Faith and Freedom". I enclose a copy of my father's sonnet to Rupert Brooke, of which I spoke to you. It might have well been written of your son.*

Included in this letter is Joyce Kilmer's poem, *In Memory of Rupert Brooke*:

In alien earth, across a troubled sea,
   His body lies that was so fair and young.
   His mouth is stopped, with half his songs unsung;
His arm is still, that struck to make men free.
But let no cloud of lamentation be
   Where, on a warrior's grave, a lyre is hung.
   We keep the echoes of his golden tongue.
We keep the vision of his chivalry.

So Israel's joy, the loveliest of kings,
   Smote now his harp, and now the hostile horde.
To-day the starry roof of Heaven rings
   With psalms a soldier made to praise his Lord;
And David rests beneath Eternal wings,
   Song on his lips, and in his hand a sword.

To be compared to his idol Rupert Brooke in a poem... John Magee undoubtedly would have been pleased.

## King George of England

In a letter dated March 12th, 1942, Kenton Kilmer, in one of his letters to Mrs. Magee, included a newspaper clipping. There is nothing indicating which newspaper this clipping came from, or what date. It is rather remarkable:

### King's Tribute Added To Library Exhibit

The original copy of a tribute from King George of England has been added to the John Gillespie Magee exhibition of poetry at the Library of Congress, it was announced yesterday by Archibald MacLeish, Librarian. The consolation message and tribute of the King was sent to the Rev. and Mrs. John G. Magee sr., after their son, John jr., had lost his life in action with the Royal Canadian Air Force last December.

Courtesy of the Library of Congress

The author of this book has been unable to locate any articles detailing the message from the King. It is entirely possible that the King remembered meeting John Magee during his visit to 412 Squadron the previous November. The only other reference to this event is in the papers of famous actress Merle Oberon Korda (see Korda's entry later in this book).

## Stewart Edward White

An American writer, novelist and spiritualist, Stewart Edward White wrote an appreciative letter to the Rev. John G. Magee on October 26th, 1942:

> I hope you will forgive a short note from a total stranger. Gertrude Foster gave me your address and informed me that you are the father of the John Magee who wrote what seems to me the most beautiful poem to have come out of either war. Flanders Field and Rendezvous with Death were the highlights of the last war, but this one of your son's to my mind eclipses them all.
>
> The lines are all magnificent, but the next to the last, to my mind, really hits tops... You are to be not only proud of the boy for what he was and showed himself to be, together with his record in the high adventures, but also that he was enabled to leave this lovely memorial.

## Corey Ford and Alastair MacBain

Corey Ford (later Lt. Col. Corey Ford) was an American humorist, author, outdoorsman, and screenwriter. Ford and writing partner Alastair MacBain (later Major MacBain) wrote several books on WWII (such as *The Last Time I Saw Them*). On November 17th, 1942, Corey Ford along with writing partner wrote to John's mother:

*We are taking the liberty of writing you to express our deep admiration of the very beautiful sonnet written by your son, John Magee, Jr., and to request permission to quote this sonnet as the most appropriate possible frontspiece to a book on the Army Air Forces... The magnificent spirit of the sonnet which your son wrote, it seems to us, is an inspiration to any flier and to the family of any flier...*

## Katharine Hepburn

A letter dated May 18, 1942 was sent from well-known actress Katharine Hepburn to John's Aunt Mary:

*Dear Mrs. Scaife:*

*What a charming poem. It has real feeling and imagination. You were sweet to send it to me and I shall enjoy having it — just for myself if not to read on some fitting occasions.*

## Merle Oberon Korda

In early 1942, the Hollywood Victory Caravan[2] was organized to promote war bonds. The Caravan was emceed by Bob Hope and Cary Grant, and consisted of stars such as Bing Crosby, Desi Arnez, Groucho Marx, Olivia De Havilland, Laurel and Hardy, Charles Boyer, and Pat O'Brien. (There was a picture taken of the entire troupe, including Merle Oberson, on the lawn of the White House, posing with Eleanor Roosevelt.[3])

On May 1st, 1942, Magee Sr. wrote a letter to the Capitol Theater (still there, as the Loew's Capitol Theater). In the letter, Magee Sr. sought to thank whatever organization had given him two tickets to the Washington D.C. appearance of the Hollywood Victory Caravan. Faith Magee was out of town, so son Christopher went in her stead. Magee Sr. wrote:

*We were deeply touched by Miss Oberon's recitation of our son's poem, "High Flight", and want to thank you sincerely for making it possible for us to do so...*

*... The serious note raised in the little playlet about Alsace and Lorraine and the one about Bataan with the recitation of "High Flight" were all the more impressive in the midst of all the good fun.*

The "Miss Oberon" referenced in the above was famed actress Merle Oberon Korda, who was part of the Victory Caravan.

In late 1942 Oberon wrote a response to Magee Sr.'s letter:

*I can't tell you how much pleasure I got from reading John's poems. I think they are beautiful.*

*One very great sorrow to me is that I never knew your son John. What a lovely mind he must have had... apart from his work his sensitive face shows it. I think "Per Ardua" simply beautiful.*

The Margaret Herrick Library at the Academy of Motion Picture Arts & Sciences (AMPAS, home of the Oscars awards) in Los Angeles contains the papers of Merle Oberon. Included in these papers is a handwritten copy of *High Flight* and introductory notes to what was obviously the Washington D.C. performance where Ms. Oberson recited *High Flight*. These handwritten notes contain a short biography about John, and also this somewhat startling statement:

*This is an excerpt of from a letter written by the King of England to his [John's] father. "We pray that the Empire's gratitude for a life so nobly given in its services may bring you some measure of consolation."*

*His father and brother are in the audience tonight. Our hearts go out to them.*

This corresponds with the newspaper clipping about King George which is shown earlier in this book (Kenton Kilmer).

## Orson Welles

Orson Welles recited *High Flight* in 1942, as part of the Radio Reader's Digest radio program. Some of the readers sent letters to the Magee family in care of Mercury Productions/Orson Welles. Here is an excerpt from a cover letter, signed by Orson Welles, sent to the Magee family:

> *The enclosed poem, written in reply to "High Flight,"*
>
> *was recently sent to me by Mrs. Crosby with the request that*
>
> *you get to read it. With it go my best regards, and my great*
>
> *admiration for your son.*

See the section on Erma Mellish Crosby which contains the forwarded letter and poem.

## Bob Considine, "On The Line With Considine", NBC News

In 1968, Bob Considine of NBC News, as part of his "On The Line With Considine" program, broadcast a segment about John Magee:

> *On Memorial Day, I came across a poem I had never*
>
> *read before, the poetry of a young American killed in the*
>
> *Battle of Britain while flying for the Royal Canadian Air*
>
> *Force. It reminded me that once upon a time there was*
>
> *surging, soaring life and laughter in the endless rows of dead*
>
> *we were honoring...*
>
> *One can only dream the eminence John Gillespie*
>
> *Magee, Jr. would have attained if his life had not been*
>
> *snuffed out so early. The year before he joined the RCAF he*
>
> *had won the coveted poetry prize at England's famed Rugby*

*School. He came of age with "High Flight", and never had*

*time for more.*

*There, in microcosm, is the bitter taste of Memorial*

*Day services, the taste that lingers long after the last orator*

*has left, the last wreath placed on a silent grave, the last*

*echo of Taps. What those men might have accomplished had*

*they lived! What their muscle and imagination might have*

*accomplished to make this a better world? What skills, what*

*genius, are prematurely crushed by mankind's insanely*

*endless wars...*

Considine gave a short biography of Magee, and also recited *High Flight* on the air.

### Erma Mellish Crosby

A "Mrs. Crosby" is referenced in the above letter from Orson Welles. There is a letter in the archives from a Mrs. Erma Mellish Crosby of Beverly, Massachusetts, with a poem attached. It is unknown whether this is the same person and poem that Welles forwarded to Mrs. Magee.

Erma Mellish was a published poet, and is listed in the *Women of Maine Anthology of Poetry*.

Here is an excerpt of Crosby's letter to "My dear Mrs. Magee":

*I am a young poetess who at the present time received*

*small remuneration for my efforts. Nevertheless, I write and*

*shall continue to write for the sheer joy of self-expression.*

*In my poem "Forgive Me My Trespasses," I represent*

*the chap who may have directly or indirectly been*

*responsible for John's last flight. Somehow I find no room in*

*my heart for either hate or revenge. Obviously John too, was*

*so filled with beauty and love of God; combat was secondary*

*and purely in the line of duty...*

Here is Erma's poem that was attached to the letter:

FORGIVE ME MY TRESPASSES
(To John G. Magee Jr. killed in action
with the R.C.A.F.)

I too have left my khaki coat behind
And loosed my stubborn wings of angry steel,
Straight up into the naked blue I've climbed
'Till bruised by sun and wind I learned to feel.

I was conceived to toil my shabby land
And so confused by blood and filthy sod;
How long, how far must I stretch out my hand
To touch the face of God?

- Erma Mellish Crosby


## Robert Dawson

John attended school at St. Clare's in Walmer, England, starting at age nine. His best friend at St. Clare's was Robert Dawson, who had also been a family friend in China. Many years later, Dawson writes about the impact that *High Flight* had on him over the years:

> For me, though, his poem HIGH FLIGHT is not only a superlative achievement in itself; it is a superlative expression of what John was.
>
> The thing that impresses me most about it is its ability to communicate the sheer exultation of a nineteen-year-old in control of a supremely powerful, agile, and beautiful machine and flinging it about the sky with heroic, virtually Godlike ease. And it communicates in perfectly accessible language. There is not a word or phrase that is difficult to understand. And even the most vivid phrases are completely and unselfconsciously <u>natural</u>. Not only did John "reach out

*and touch the face of God"; God had already reached down and touched the mind and heart of John Gillespie Magee... It is a "people's" poem with none of the vulgar connotations that Communism has given that word.*

*To my sorrow, I've shown it to countless "teachers of English" in this country [United States]... with the suggestion that it could help them to reach students whose energies are devoted to, for example, the construction of "hot-rod" cars, who are generally disdained by most teachers as being entirely without aesthetic sense. The fact is that they are vibrant with aesthetic sensibilities but they are focused on machines. And here is a poem that classically demonstrates the idea that one can write poetry about machines!*

The letters quoted above are but a small sampling of the letters that were written about John Magee and his masterpiece *High Flight*. They were written by those who knew him quite well and also by those who were complete strangers. These letters represent the millions of people who feel the same way about John and his famous poem.

---

[1] Letter from Faith Magee to Anna Wood Murray, January 29, 1942.

[2] http://en.wikipedia.org/wiki/Hollywood_Victory_Caravan– accessed 10/12/13.

[3]

http://myloc.gov/Exhibitions/hopeforamerica/causesandcontroversies/entertai ningthetroops/ExhibitObjects/HollywoodVictoryCaravan – accessed October 12, 2013.

# Postscript — People

### David Backhouse Magee

John's first brother was David Backhouse Magee, born July 6th, 1925 in Kuling, China. David flew as a bombardier aboard B-25s from 1943 until the end of the war. After the war, David finished his college education at Yale and then worked for the Morgan Guaranty Trust Company for nearly 30 years.

David was an active advocate for both his father and his brother, working hard to make sure that his father got the recognition he deserved after his selfless actions in China. David was equally active in preserving and protecting the memory of his brother John.

David passed away after a short illness in White Plains, NY, on March 11th, 2013.

### Christopher Walford Magee

Christopher Walford Magee, John's second brother, was born in Karuiza, Japan on August 19th, 1928. Christopher served in the U.S. Army and in the Merchant Marine as a 16-year old merchant seaman aboard hazardous-duty oil tankers in the Atlantic and Pacific during WWII. Christopher subsequently had a successful business career, serving at times in Hong Kong and other western Pacific locations, and passed away in Los Angeles, California, on March 19th, 2005.

### Frederick Hugh Magee

Frederick Hugh Magee, the last of John & Faith Magee's sons, was born in England on August 23rd, 1933. Following in his father's footsteps, Hugh became an ordained minister. Hugh has served in both the United Kingdom and the United States, and served as Dean of Wenatchee in the Diocese of Spokane, Washington. Hugh is also the author of *An Upgrader's Guide*, an excellent book based on *A Course in Miracles*. As of this writing (June 2014), The Reverend Canon F. Hugh Magee was living in the United Kingdom.

## Edward Jennings Magee

John's nephew Edward, the son of Uncle Jim, become an air gunnery expert. Edward spent some time with Magee while John was in Pittsburgh on leave, and may well have been inspired to join the Army Air Corps due to John's early service. Nicknamed "Sam" (after the poet Robert Services's poem *The Cremation of Sam Magee*), Edwards Jennings Magee would wind up getting shot down in a B-17 Flying Fortress and spending the rest of the war as a German P.O.W.[1]

## Christopher Lyman Magee

John's cousin, Christopher Lyman Magee, possibly inspired by John, joined the RCAF in mid-1941, around the time that John was leaving for England. Not long after the attack on Pearl Harbor, Christopher transferred to the U.S. Marine Corps and re-commenced his flight training on the AT-6, the U.S. equivalent of the Canadian Harvard. Christopher succeeded in becoming a fighter pilot and left for the South Pacific, where he soon joined up with VMF-214, the famed "Black Sheep" squadron commanded by USMC Major Gregory "Pappy" Boyington. Flying the Chance-Vought F4U Corsair, Christopher became an ace with nine kills and also earned the Navy Cross.

Not one to settle down, Christopher flew for the nascent Israeli air force after WWII[2]. Returning to the U.S., he would begin a new career: bank robber. Caught, Christopher served eight of a 15-year sentence. After being released from prison, Christopher lived a quiet life until his death in 1995.[3]

Christopher Lyman Magee, USMC.

Official USMC photo.

## John Gillespie Magee Sr.

It is hard to know just how many Chinese lives John's father helped save during the time he spent in China; estimates run between 50,000 and 250,000. After sending his own family to safety, John Magee would help in establishing the Nanking Safety Zone just before soldiers of the Japanese Army invaded. Though the most tenuous of agreements, the Japanese generally recognized the Safety Zone, and did not interfere (though there were significant exceptions, some of which John Magee would film). Not soon after returning from China in 1938, John's father would tour the United States speaking about the horrors of what would become known as the Nanking Massacre. The films that John Magee, Sr. took are used to the present day as evidence of a horrific chapter of WWII.

After John Magee, Jr. left to join the RCAF, his father would continue to serve at St. John's Church in Washington, D.C., officiating at the funeral of Franklin Delano Roosevelt in April of 1945. Later he become the Episcopalian Chaplain at Yale, retiring at the age of 68. The Reverend John Gillespie Magee passed away in Pittsburgh on September 11th, 1953.

## Faith Emmeline Magee

Faith Magee, John's mother, would visit China again at least once after taking her sons away in 1938. Faith was active in various ministries for the rest of her life. She would recite her son's poem *High Flight* for the U.S. Air Force Museum in 1975, shortly before passing away in April of that year.

## Elinor Lyon-Wright

A large part of the inspiration for John's poetry (especially the poems written while at Rugby) can be attributed to Elinor Lyon, daughter of Rugby Headmaster Hugh Lyon. It can also be argued that Elinor was the primary reason for John's determination to return to England after he was stranded in the U.S.

Elinor was born on August 17th, 1921, in Guisborough, Yorkshire, England[4], making her nearly a year older than John Magee.

Elinor took her turn at writing poetry starting at a very young age, which was likely part of the attraction that John felt towards her. It was to John that Elinor initially shared her writing, and she was likely one of the first to hear John's poetry.

John became a good friend of the entire Lyon family. However, it could be said that the Lyon family "adopted" all the boys at the school, inviting many of them to accompany the family on holiday outings. And for much of the time that John was at Rugby, Elinor was in Oxford attending school. As a result, Elinor saw John mostly on those Lyon family vacations when the Rugby boys were invited. (According to Elinor, the boys "livened up the vacations quite satisfactorily."[5])

Although Elinor has stated that she was never "in love" with John, she (along with the rest of her family) was very fond of him. Elinor believed that John did love her through the end of his life, though John was too much the gentleman to push the issue. Instead, John resorted to pouring out his feelings in poems and in letters to family and friends. Inadvertently, Elinor gave just enough attention to John to keep his hope alive, and John felt that given enough time and effort, he would be able to win Elinor's love.

What John didn't know is that Elinor had met her future husband Peter Wright in 1940, while John was undergoing RCAF training. Peter was in the Royal Air Force, mostly flying Mosquito bombers. So the kind of relationship John wanted with Elinor was already a lost cause by the time John returned to England in mid-1941.

It was probably just as well that Elinor never had to be firm with John and tell him exactly how she felt. That would have probably broken John's heart. John had come such a long way, overcome so many obstacles, and given up so much to return to England and Elinor. While in America and Canada, John had been involved with several young ladies (even to the point of stating that he was engaged to one of them), but the relationships never amounted to much. Ultimately, Elinor was the person to whom John returned to England for.

After he returned to England, it doesn't appear that John went out with any other women, spending much of his free time with the Lyon family (and Elinor, when he had the chance).

Elinor Lyon-Wright did become a published author, writing several young adult books[6]. She passed away in Wales on May 28th, 2008[7].


## Percy Hugh Beverly Lyon

Elinor Lyon's father was Percy Hugh Beverly Lyon. There could not have been a better suited mentor and stand-in father for young John Magee than Hugh Lyon, Headmaster of Rugby School (and Housemaster of

School House, where John Magee resided). Hugh could probably empathize with John so well since they both followed similar paths from birth: Hugh was born in India (1893), John in China (1922); both came to England when they were nine years old; both attended boarding schools (Hugh at Bilton Grange near Rugby and John at St. Clare's); and finally both attended Rugby.

After Rugby, Hugh attended Oriel College at Oxford as a Classical scholar. However, his time at Oriel was interrupted by the outbreak of the Great War (subsequently known as World War I). Hugh immediately enlisted, and was posted to the Durham Light Infantry. He served in France from April to December of 1915, returning to England after reinjuring his knee, requiring an operation. Back to France in September of 1917, he was taken prisoner in May of the following year, and released in December 1918. While in France, Hugh wrote close on to 70 poems, some of which were published in *Isis*, *The Oxford Magazine*, and *Punch*. Like many young men before and after (including John Magee), some of Hugh's poetry was inspired by a girl he had fallen in love with. In 1930, Lyon also authored a textbook on poetry, titled *The Discovery of Poetry*.

In 1920, Hugh and Nan Richardson were married, the marriage lasting until Nan's death in 1970. They had four children, of which Elinor was first (three daughters: Elinor, Barbara, and Jill, and one son: Christopher. Sadly, Christopher only lived to be 14 years old, dying of a congenital heart disease).

Hugh was remarried in 1973 to Elizabeth Beater, known to all as "Biddy."

Hugh Lyon passed away in January 1986, aged 92, leaving a widow, three daughters, four grandchildren, three grandchildren-in-law, and eight great-grandchildren. In describing Hugh Lyon, a former pupil quoted Thomas Hardy: "He was a good man and did good things."[8]

## Tanya Davis

It appears that sometime after John arrived in Toronto he had gotten met and gotten engaged to a Tanya Davis from Czechoslovakia. It is not clear whether this was done with the prior knowledge and/or consent of his parents. In his October 29th, 1940 letter to Avon teacher Max Stein, John requests a copy of his *Poems* book for his "fiancé":

> *Since our last meeting I am an airman. Fantastic as it*
>
> *seems, they are going to make a fighter pilot out of me. Even*

*more fantastic things are happening. I am going to be married, and am going overseas (I hope with a pair of "Wings" by Spring!*

*What I want to know is, could you possibly send me two copies of the Book (bound or unbound) with all possible dispatch? I want one for my fiancé...*

In November, John writes to his brother David:

*Incidentally, I have a new fever frau, a blonde Czechoslovak actress in Toronto.*

No mention of a fiancé in John's letters to his parents, though he does mention going with a Czech girl to an exhibition:

*This afternoon I am taking a Czechoslovak girl to an art exhibit in aid of British War Relief...[9]*

There does not appear to be any further mention of Tanya in any correspondence from or to John. After John's death, Tanya did write two letters to Hermann Hagedorn, author of the 1942 John Magee biography "Sunward I've Climbed." She describes her relationship with John in this letter dated August 16th, 1942:

*John and I met about three weeks upon his arrival in Toronto. During his stay we saw a great deal of each other. And when he went away to the different stations we corresponded regularly, seeing each other when we could.*

*During the time John was in Toronto he composed and dedicated to me, a poem called "A Prayer." One of the most beautiful things I have, to cherish the rest of my life.*

In his book of poems, John included a poem called *A Prayer*. However, there is another poem Magee wrote with nearly the same name. This poem is called *The Prayer*:

(To Tanya Davis, a beautiful blond young Czechoslovakian who writes poetry and plays and had been an actress in Prague, now living in Toronto)

The Prayer

Be gentle to her, grey-haired Time,
Walk with slow pace;
Beat not with bitter blows
Against her face.

Be generous to her, O Life,
Fill her with laughter
That there be no sad memories
When death comes after.
And thou, sad Death, be chivalrous to her,
Come without pain;
Fall on her tender, smiling brow
Like summer rain.

In July of 1942, Tanya wrote a letter to John's mother:

*Kindly accept my deepest sympathy for the loss of your beloved son John. I had known John during the time he was stationed here in Toronto.*

*I do not know whether or not John has ever mentioned my name to you. But never the less I just had to take this opportunity of writing to you. I have a poem John had dedicated to me. I shall always cherish it as long as I live.*

John's relationship with Tanya Davis appears to have ended with John's return to England and resumption of the pursuit of Elinor.

There is probably an entire unknown chapter in John Magee's life that is out there regarding Tanya Davis, one that we may never know.

# Discussions

Since the author of this book began his research into John Magee and *High Flight* in 1990, there have been several recurring questions and issues that have come up. Below are some of them.

## Different interpretations of the *High Flight* text

Over the years, *High Flight* has been studied and analyzed by many people. There have been some alternate interpretations put forward, most of them having to do with "even" and "ever."

"Where never lark nor *even* eagle flew..."

Magee might have actually written:

"Where never lark nor *ever* eagle flew..."

It is difficult, looking at the original manuscript, to tell which word was the intent of Magee, since his "n" and "r" look very similar.
Another interpretation regards the "Up, up" portion:

"*Up, up* the long delirious burning blue..."

This line might be seen as:

"*Oh, oh* the long delirious burning blue..."

In the publication of *High Flight* in the Pittsburgh Post-Gazette in November of 1941, "Oh, oh" was used. It is not clear is whether Magee's Uncle Jim and Aunt Mary had a copy of the September 3rd letter that was sent to Magee's parents, or if John sent them their own copy which may have, indeed, had the alternate usage.
There are several compelling arguments for "even" and "Up, up" being the correct interpretations. Hermann Hagedorn, author of the Magee biography "Sunward I've Climbed," uses "even" and "Up, up." Hagedorn, having written the biography in 1942, undoubtedly saw the original letter less than a year after it was written. (These days, the copy at the Library of Congress is extremely faded and hard to read, so close examination yields no clearer result.)

The author requested a high-resolution scan from the Library of Congress of Magee's letter to his parents which contained *High Flight*. Indeed, Magee's "n" appears nearly identical to his "r". In the word "never" ("never lark, or even eagle"), both letters are used—and they are very similar. On the flip side of the page containing *High Flight* is an entire page of Magee's handwriting, with plenty of samples of "N" and "R" letters. The author has also read (and transcribed) several dozen letters from John, and has gotten quite familiar with his writing.

Faith Magee, John's mother, made an audio recording of *High Flight* for the U.S. Air Force Museum in Dayton, Ohio, in 1975. In this recording, Faith clearly says "even" and "Up, up." Of all the people who have read Magee's letters, Faith Magee would probably be the one most familiar with his handwriting.

As a result of this evidence, the author of this book is sticking with "even" and "Up, up."

## Source Material for High Flight

There have been claims of plagiarism leveled against John Magee in his most famous poem, *High Flight*. These charges stem from lines in *High Flight* that are also similar to those found in the book, *Icarus: An Anthology of The Poetry of Flight*, compiled by R. de la Bere "and Three Flight Cadets of The Royal Air Force College, Cranwell, Lincolnshire," published by Macmillan & Co, Ltd in 1938. In the acknowledgements, it states that this collection of poems was compiled by "one of the senior instructors at the Royal Air Force College," presumably Mr. la Bere.

This remarkable book contains poetry from Rudyard Kipling, J.W. Goethe, John Milton, Aristophanes, Homer, William Butler Yeats, and even a short poem by Rupert Brooke.

It is entirely possible that Magee was able to obtain this book in the short time that he was in England prior to writing *High Flight* (John arrived in England near the end of July, and started writing *High Flight* on August 18th). John had some money left over from his winning the Poetry Prize at Rugby, and it seems that he used some of that money to purchase books. Certainly, a book on the poetry of flight would have caught his eye.

*Icarus* is composed of some 110 poems spread across 190 pages. There are three poems which contain lines that are identical or very close to the lines in *High Flight*. Below, I show the lines which appear in *Icarus*, along with the similar lines in *High Flight*.

In the poem *New World* by G.W.M. Dunn on page 143, there are lines similar to those in *High Flight* (NW indicates *New World*, HF shows the comparable line from *High Flight*):

> **NW:** "With zest we soar on laughter-silvered wings"
> **HF:** "And danced the skies on laughter-silvered wings"

> **NW:** "Only the hushed limbs and the lifting mind"
> **HF:** "And, while with silent, lifting mind I've trod"

> **NW:** "With powered laughter and shouting of the air"
> **HF:** "I've chased the shouting wind along, and flung"

In the same book, poet C.A.F.B., in the poem *Dominion over Air* (on page 128, marked below with DA), writes the following lines:

> **DA:** "Across the unpierced sanctity of space,"
> **HF:** "The high untrespassed sanctity of space,"

Lastly, the poem *The Blind Man Flies* (BMF) by Cuthbert Hicks (page 100) contains the same identical line as in *High Flight*. The line concludes both poems:

> **BMF:** "And touched the face of God."
> **HF:** "and touched the face of God."

If John Magee read this poem, it probably made a great impact on him. To put the single line "And touched the face of God" into context, here is the entire poem by Cuthbert Hicks:

**The Blind Man Flies**

I am blind: I have never seen
Sun gold nor silver moon,
Not the fairy faces of flowers,
Nor the radiant noon.

They speak of the dawn and the dusk,
And the smile of a child,
Of the deep red heart of a rose,
As of God, undefiled.

But I learnt from the air to-day
(On a bird's wings I flew)
That the earth could never contain
All of the God I knew.

I felt the blue mantle of space,
And kissed the cloud's white hem,
I heard the stars' majestic choir,
And sang my praise with them.

Now joy is mine through my long night,
I do not feel the rod,
For I have danced the streets of heaven,
And touched the face of God.


**By Cuthbert Hicks**

The following is the opinion of the author of this book, who is admittedly not an expert in poetry or plagiarism. It can be difficult to know whether any poet has consciously or unconsciously used material from another source. In this case, even if John Magee deliberately used some of the lines that were in other works, the common lines are used in a new way, and the work itself is not substantially copied. In essence, Magee has created a brand-new work. If you were to read *High Flight* and then immediately read *The Blind Man Flies*, you would never confuse the two, although there are some similarities. You would notice that the last line of each poem is the same, but they are in different contexts.

The same could be said of all the other common lines. Yes, they are borrowed, but they are put into a completely new structure.

What author and poet T.S. Eliot had to say about "borrowing" is applicable in this case (bolding is by author of book):

> *One of the surest tests [of the superiority or inferiority of a poet] is the way in which a poet borrows. Immature poets imitate; mature poets steal; bad poets deface what they take, and* **good poets make it into something better, or at least something different**. *The good poet welds his theft into a whole of feeling which is unique, utterly different than that from which it is torn; the bad poet throws it into something which has no cohesion.*
>
> *—T.S. Eliot (1888—1965). The Sacred Wood: Essays on Poetry and Criticism. 1922.*[10]

Certainly what John Magee created with *High Flight* is something very different. What is borrowed is put into a context which is "utterly different from that from which it is torn."

One other factor to consider is what John's intention was in writing *High Flight*. John had written a letter to his parents in which he talked about several things: movies he had seen, what Elinor (Lyon) was up to, and so on. On the other side was *High Flight*, included almost in passing.

From all this it seems clear that Magee did not really intend *High Flight* to be published and that it was written for his family. It is not clear if John's parents sent a copy to Aunt Mary in Pittsburgh or if John himself sent it, but it resulted in *High Flight* being published in the November 12th issue of the *Pittsburgh Post-Gazette*.

John's Aunt Mary had recognized the possible commercial value of John's writings, and offered to be his agent. John responds:

> *You offer kindly in your letter to act as my agent for*
>
> *anything else I might write. It is very kind of you, but I assure*
>
> *you that there will not be any more!*

Commercial publication or not, John still wanted to make sure that if his poems are used in any way, that they are accurately copied. In connection with his last poem *Per Ardua*, John Magee requested that, "If anyone should want this, please see that it is accurately copied, capitalized, and punctuated."

It could be speculated that John did not advertise the existence of *High Flight* because John knew that he had "borrowed" several phrases. Probably acceptable if *High Flight* was written as a gift to his family, perhaps less so if it was written for publication.

As a matter of fact, very few in 412 Squadron knew that John wrote poetry. Even Rod Smith, a good friend of Magee's, did not know of the existence of *High Flight* until years later.

So in view of all of this, perhaps John Magee might be forgiven for using a few phrases in a poem that he had no intention of ever having published.

## Copyright of High Flight

The sonnet *High Flight* by John Gillespie Magee, Jr., is considered in the Public Domain, meaning that no permission is required to reproduce it. This has been verified via various letters to and from John's parents regarding this specific issue.

John's father apparently attempted to get *High Flight* copyrighted very soon after it was received. A letter dated November 7th, 1941, from C.L. Bouve, Register of Copyrights at the Library of Congress, was sent to Rev. John G. Magee in Washington, D.C.:

*The Librarian of Congress has referred to this Office for attention your letter of Oct. 28 in regard to securing copyright on a poem by your son entitled "High Flight," a manuscript of which you enclose.*

After a quite detailed explanation of what it would take to secure a copyright, Mr. Bouve indicates that *High Flight* is not eligible to be copyrighted:

*According to your letter, the poem in question was published in the Parish Bulletin of St. John's Episcopal Church. If it bore the required notice of copyright when first published in this form, registration of copyright may be made upon deposit of two copies of the bulletin with an application on Form A-1 and the fee of $2.00. If, on the other hand, the work was published without the required notice of copyright, no entry of copyright would be in order. By publishing a work without the copyright notice the copyright privilege is lost.*

Thus, as far back as November of 1941, *High Flight* was considered in the Public Domain.

Since that time, the copyright laws have undergone considerable change. At the present time, a work is copyrighted as soon as it is created, with no need to put a notice of copyright on the work.

There is also mention of the question of copyright in a letter that Mrs. Magee wrote to the RCAF on June 2nd, 1943. In this letter John's mother is replying to a request by the New York Herald Tribune asking permission to copyright *High Flight*. Mrs. Magee writes:

*I had already written to Mr. Miller, telling him that High Flight was not copyrighted and that Thomas Nelson would be free to use it in their textbooks as they pleased.*

Later in the same letter Mrs. Magee explains further:

> *When we first received the poem from our son in England, it was printed in our Church leaflet here in Washington. A little later on, when we took up the matter of copyrighting it with the authorities at the Library, they informed us that this could not now be done as it had already been in print. We were at first disappointed and felt we had made a mistake, but when our son was killed we were glad that a copyright had not been taken out, as it was possible for it to be printed widely throughout the country without permission being obtained from us.*

Another letter emphasizes that *High Flight* does not require permission to be copied. In a letter dated November 14th, 1941, she wrote to her mother:

> *I don't think we've sent you a copy of this poem of young John's. We think it is the best thing he has written; it was printed in the St John's bulletin, and met with very warm appreciation. We wanted to get it copy-righted, but apparently ruined our chances of doing this by having put it in the bulletin. It is going to be printed in "Forth," our Mission magazine. I think you will also like to see the other poem about England which was printed in the "Churchman" ...*
>
> —Faith Magee, letter to her mother, November 14th, 1941

The "other poem" is a reference to John's last poem, *Per Ardua*.

[1] *Mud, Wings, and Wire: A Memoir* by Harry X. Ford  by John R. Ford

[2] Ironically, one of the aircraft that Chris Magee flew with the early Israeli Air Force was the German BF-109.

[3] Lost Black Sheep: The Search for WWII Ace Chris Magee  by Robert T. Reed

[4] http://en.wikipedia.org/wiki/Elinor_Lyon accessed November 28, 2010

[5] Author's correspondence with Elinor Wright (Lyon), 2006

[6] Elinor's publisher:  http://www.fidrabooks.com/publishing/lyon.shtml–accessed 2/21/14

[7] http://www.telegraph.co.uk/news/obituaries/2446416/Elinor-Lyon.html–accessed 2/21/14

[8] Information on Hugh Lyon obtained from the book, *Hugh Lyon, 1893-1986, A Memoir*, compiled by Elinor Wright and Barbara Lyon. Used by permission from Elinor Wright, 2006.

[9] Letter from John to his family, dated 3/30/41.

[10] Eliot, T.S., "Philip Massinger," The Sacred Wood, New York: Bartleby.com, 2000.
http://www.bartleby.com/200/sw11.html–accessed 2012_08_01

# Uses of *High Flight*

Since immediately after it was written, *High Flight* has been put to many uses. Starting with being posted in every RCAF installation around the world, and going on to being used at the memorial services for many pilots, *High Flight* continues to stir the imagination, pulling us skyward, both physically and spiritually.

The following is just a small sampling of some of the notable uses and mentions of *High Flight*:

## Magazines

- *Reader's Digest*, August 1942 issue
- *Canada at War*, March 1942 issue
- *Flying Magazine*, 1942 issue
- *Airmen*, January 1978
- *Wings of Gold*, Spring 2005

## Books

- *If We Had Wings: The Enduring Dream of Flight* by Rinker Buck.
- *God is my Co-Pilot* by Col. Robert Scott.
- *Samurai* by Japanese Ace Saburo Sakai and Martin Caidan.
- *Carrying the Fire* by Astronaut Michael Collins.
- *Airport* by Arthur Hailey.
- *Return with Honor* and *Basher Five-Two* by Scott O'Grady
- *Twenty Poems of Faith and Freedom*, compiled, translated and commented by Angelica B. de Davidson.
- *The Last Man on the Moon* by Eugene Cernan and Donald A. Davis. Cernan mentions *High Flight* in this book:

> It was not by accident that we three veteran spacemen had John Magee's *"High Flight"* poem aboard *Apollo 10*, for there were indeed moments when I honestly felt that I could reach out my hand, just as he said, and touch the face of God.

# Movies

### *For the Moment* with Russell Crowe

Russell Crowe did a wonderful recitation of *High Flight* from the 1994 movie, *For the Moment*. Crowe portrayed an Australian who travels to Canada to join the RCAF during the early part of WWII. Crowe's character pursues a young woman whose weakness is poetry. Knowing this, the young pilot does a performance recitation of *High Flight*. The young lady, however, knows the poem, and even gives credit to "John Gillespie Magee, Jr." Nice touch by the filmmakers.

### *Man Without A Face* with Nick Stahl and Mel Gibson

This movie contains a very touching reading by actor Nick Stahl. Even though the filmmakers decided to leave out the entire center portion of *High Flight*, it is still effective.

### *Snow Walker* with James Cromwell

James Cromwell's character recites *High Flight* at the memorial service for a missing pilot who is believed dead.

### *Slipstream* with Mark Hamill

This little-known film, starring Mark Hamill of Star Wars fame, made frequent use of *High Flight*.

# Music

*High Flight* was almost immediately put to music after it was written. One newspaper records that Mrs. John Magee attended one of the public performances. Songs with the words to *High Flight* were recorded, some by very well-known performers (Ronald Colman, Eddy Nelson, John Denver, and so on). The musical score that accompanies the USAF *High Flight* Sign-Off film was very effective in underscoring Jack Cannivan's recitation of the poem.

Continuing to the present day, the words to *High Flight* have been and are being adapted to all kinds of music from choral to country western. Here are some of the adaptations:

### *Flight (The Higher We Fly)* by John Denver

John Denver's song *Flight (The Higher We Fly)* is on his 1983 *It's About Time* album. This song featured the words to *High Flight*, along with a chorus. John sung this this song on the *Bob Hope TV Show* (the episode, *N.A.S.A: 25 Years of Reaching for the Stars*, aired September 19, 1983). Denver was an avid pilot for many years.

### High Flight by Dwayne O'Brien
*High Flight* forms part of O'Brien's wonderful *Song Pilot* album, which includes many other flying-related songs.

### Radio Reader's Digest by Orson Welles
Orson Welles recited *High Flight* in 1942, as part of the *Radio Reader's Digest* radio program.

### 25th Anniversary of Air Force Song
### by Brigadier General James Stewart
In 1964, an album celebrating the 25th anniversary of the Air Force Song was released. Former USAF Brigadier General and actor Jimmy Stewart recites *High Flight*, followed by a vocal rendering by the Singing Sergeants.

### Everything for the Boys with Ronald Colman
A popular radio program during WWII, *Everything for the Boys* featured a singing of *High Flight* by host and singer Ronald Colman during its February 15, 1944 performance.

### The Kraft Music Hall starring Nelson Eddy
This radio program with host and singer Nelson Eddy featured a musical version of *High Flight* by Eddy. The program aired on September 16th, 1948.


## Television

### Hawaiian Son
Actor Richard Chamberlain quotes *High Flight*.

### The West Wing
Actor Martin Sheen, as President Josiah Bartlet, recites part of *High Flight* during season one, episode five (*The Crackpots and These Women*) of *The West Wing*.

### Battlestar Galactica
Lines from *High Flight* are quoted during the "Daybreak" episode.

## Mad Men

Season Two, Episode 6 ("Maidenform") uses the USAF *High Flight* "Sign-Off" film playing on a TV in the background of a scene, presumably to establish the lateness of the hour (the "Sign-Off" film was shown during the early 1960s just before TV stations would go off the air).

## Time Team

During episode three, season seven of this British documentary series, *High Flight* is recited.

# Art

There have been a number of pieces of art created featuring *High Flight* as the theme. Here are a few of them:

### On Laughter-Silvered Wings by Keith Ferris

Famed aviation artist Keith Ferris created a wonderful painting which shows a Spitfire with markings of VZ-H, Magee's favorite plane.

### A Tribute to High Flight by Edward Ash

Created to commemorate the 65th anniversary (2006) of the death of John Magee.

### High Flight by Graham Wragg

A nice rendition of a Spitfire flying among the clouds.

### Battlefields of Britain by C.R.W. Nevinson

Nevinson was a pilot in WWI. After reading *High Flight*, he is inspired to create a painting of fighter planes flying over England. Under the title is this inscription: "Where never lark, nor even eagle flew – Pilot Officer John Magee." The painting was given to Winston Churchill as a gift.

# Other notable recitations and significant mentions of *High Flight*

### Alan Shepherd's Memorial Service with John Glenn

During the NASA memorial service for astronaut Alan Shepherd, John Glenn gives a very eloquent reading of *High Flight*. During the reading, Glenn put special emphasis on the line, "And done a hundred things you have not dreamed of…"

### Patty Wagstaff

Champion aerobatic pilot Patty Wagstaff recites *High Flight* during an interview her during her visit to the Rose Festival Airshow at Hillsboro Airport in Oregon.

### *National Aviation Hall of Fame* with Cliff Robertson

Actor Cliff Robertson recited *High Flight* during the National Aviation Hall of Fame's induction ceremony.

### President Ronald Reagan

In January of 1986, President Ronald Reagan used two lines from *High Flight* during his speech to the nation regarding the space shuttle *Challenger* disaster ("slipped the surly bonds of earth," and "put out their hand to touch the face of God").

Several months later, on March 18th, 1986, the President mentioned Magee and *High Flight* during a toast at a State Dinner at the White House for Canadian Prime Minister Brian Mulroney[1]. Though during the *Challenger* speech Reagan was not able to give Magee credit, during this toast he not only gives credit, but tells the story:

> … and freedom is what America — Canada and the
>
> United States — is all about.
>
> A story that reflects this love of freedom concerns a
>
> young man, John Magee, whose father was rector of St.
>
> John's Church, which is right across the Lafayette Square
>
> from the White House here. In 1940, in the dark days of the
>
> Second World War — the United States was still not in the
>
> fight — Canada, responding to the pull of ancient loyalties,
>
> had joined the struggle the year before. So, like thousands of
>
> others, John Magee crossed the border to join up. He became
>
> Pilot Officer Magee of the Royal Canadian Air Force. In 1941
>
> his squadron was sent to fight in the Battle of Britain. A few
>
> days after his arrival in England, he sent a letter back home.
>
> "I am enclosing," he said, "a verse I wrote the other day. It

*started at 30,000 feet and was finished soon after I landed."*
*But on December 11, 1941, Pilot Officer Magee was killed at*
*age 19. He had lived just long enough to see his own join the*
*struggle at the side of his foster land.*

*Well, that verse he sent back is called "High Flight."*
*And the day we lost the valiant seven of the space shuttle*
*Challenger, it came instantly to mind: "Oh, how I have*
*slipped the surly bonds of Earth, put out my hand, and*
*touched the face of God." "High Flight" was a beloved*
*favorite of the Royal Canadian Air Force, whose motto was*
*"Through Perseverance We Reach The Stars." As a matter of*
*fact, it was adopted by our own Air Force, and it was — I*
*don't believe that there's an Air Force installation in the*
*country that did not have someplace — displayed his poem.*
*It resonates in the hearts of all who cherish the twin values*
*of faith and freedom. And it resonates in the hearts of North*
*Americans. And so, we remember Pilot Officer John Magee*
*— American poet, Canadian pilot, North American hero.*

The entire text of *High* Flight was apparently in Ronald Reagan's collection of "notes," and is included in the book, *The Notes: Ronald Reagan's Private Collection of Stories and Wisdom*.

### Marilyn vos Savant
According to the 1985 Guinness Book of World Records, Marilyn vos Savant holds the record for the "Highest IQ (Women)." Marilyn has stated that her favorite poem is *High Flight*.[2]

### Dr. Katharine Jefferts Schori
In 2006, Dr. Katharine Jefferts Schori was elected as the Episcopalian Church's 26th presiding bishop. In an interview with CBS News shortly after her election, Schori revealed that she was a private pilot (Schori is an instrument-rated and a third-generation pilot. In addition, her daughter Katharine is a Captain and pilot in the US Air Force).

From her CBS News interview with Russ Mitchell in July of 2006[3]:

*Russ Mitchell: What's so special to you about being up in that airplane, in the pilot's seat?*

*Katharine Jefferts Schori: Ahh...there's a wonderful poem that was written in the 2nd World War by a fellow named Magee that's called "High Flight", and he talks about the experience of being aloft as a religious—spiritual encounter. And there is certainly an element of that. It gives one a very different perspective on the world. It gives one a larger view.*

### *A Celebration of the life of Neil Armstrong*
### Washington National Cathedral, Washington, D.C.

During this celebration on September 13th, 2012, fellow astronaut Gene Cernan, the last man to walk the lunar surface, sent a message to Neil Armstrong: "As you soar through the heavens beyond where even eagles dare not go, you can now—finally—'put out your hand and touch the face of God.'"

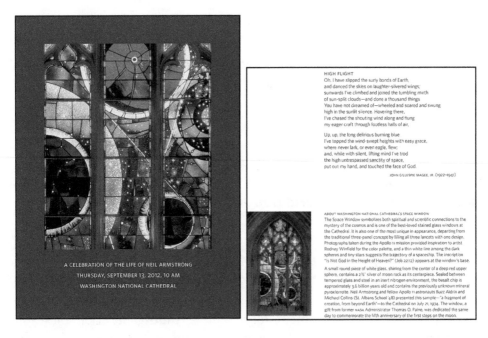

Pages one and two of the program for *"A Celebration of the life of Neil Armstrong." High Flight* is quoted on the second page.

### James Irwin

Astronaut James Irwin apparently carried a copy of *High Flight* during his flight to the moon onboard Apollo 15. After retiring from NASA, Irwin created the High Flight Foundation, which is still in existence to the present day (http://www.highflightfoundation.org).

James Irwin on the moon as part of Apollo 15.

Photo courtesy of NASA

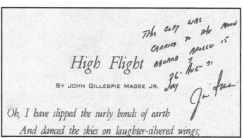

"This copy was carried to the moon aboard Apollo 15."

John G. Magee Family Papers, Record Group No. 242,
Special Collections, Yale Divinity School Library

## RCAF Overseas Headquarters Christmas Card, 1942

A year after Magee died, the RCAF Overseas Headquarters in London, England, sent out a Christmas card which contained *High Flight*.

Front and back of RCAF Overseas Headquarters Christmas card 1942.

Courtesy of Library and Archives Canada

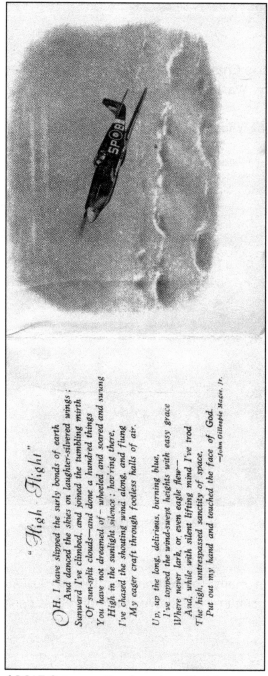

Inside of RCAF Overseas Headquarters Christmas card 1942.

Courtesy of Library and Archives Canada

## Memorials

### The Shuttle Challenger Memorial, Arlington National Cemetery, Washington, D.C.

*High Flight* is inscribed on the one side of the memorial marker.

Public Doman.

There are many tombstones located in the Arlington National Cemetery and in cemeteries all over the world that contain all or part of *High Flight*.

## National Museum of the United States Air Force, Dayton, Ohio

There is a permanent John Magee & *High Flight* exhibit located at this museum. John's brother David donated many of John's personal effects to the museum. For a brief time, the *High Flight* manuscript was on exhibition here.

Photo courtesy of the National Museum of the United States Air Force

## Veteran's Memorial, Experimental Aircraft Association, Wittman Field, Oshkosh, Wisconsin, Warbirds Area

This memorial is located on the grounds of Wittman Field in Oshkosh, Wisconsin, in the Warbirds area.

Photo by the author.

**High Flight**

Oh! I have slipped the surly bonds of Earth
and danced the skies on laughter-silvered wings;

Sunward I've climbed, and joined the tumbling mirth
of sun-split clouds – and done a hundred things

You have not dreamed of – wheeled and soared and
High in the sunlit silence. Hov'ring there,

I've chased the shouting wind along, and flung
My eager craft through footless halls of air...

Up, up the long, delirious burning blue
I've topped the wind-swept heights with easy grace

Where never lark, or even eagle flew–
And, while with silent, lifting mind I've trod

The high untrespassed sanctity of space,
Put out my hand, and touched the face of God.

*John Gillespie Magee, Jr.*

Detail of Veteran's Memorial, Oshkosh, Wisconsin.

Photo by the author.

## Kitty Hawk Memorial to a Century of Flight, Kitty Hawk, North Carolina

Just north of the site of Orville and Wilbur Wright's "first flight," there is a wonderful monument to man's journey from the first flight to landing on the moon within a single century. This is the *Monument to a Century of Flight*, placed by the First Flight Club of Rotary International under the sponsorship of the Bank of Currituck. The *High Flight* granite marker is at the entrance to the monument.

Photo by Kevin W.[4]

## National Air Force Museum of Canada, Trenton, Ontario, Canada

*High Flight* is depicted on a tablet just inside the entrance to this museum, in the Memorial area.

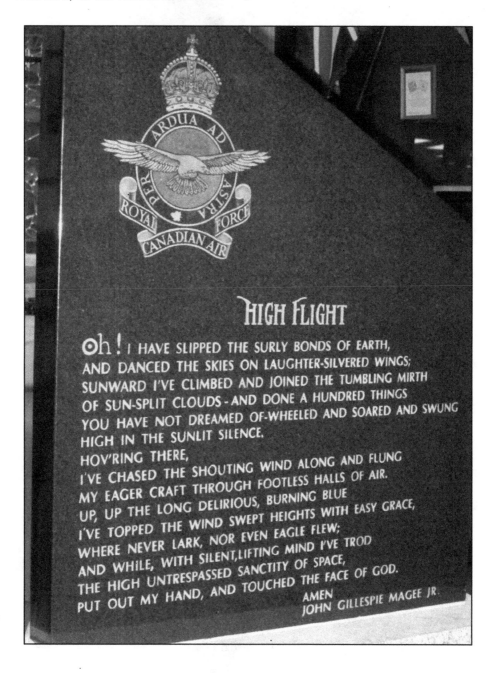

Photo by author.

## St. Paul's Episcopal Church, Jackson, Michigan

An abbreviated version of *High Flight* appears in this stained glass:

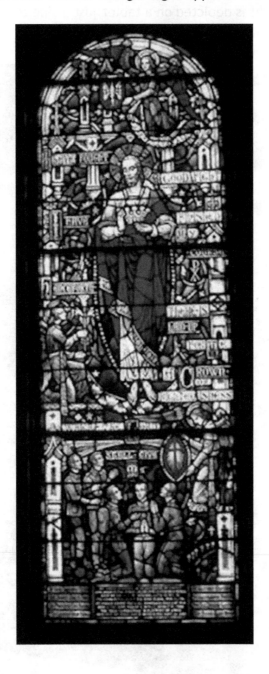

Michiganstainedglass.org[5]

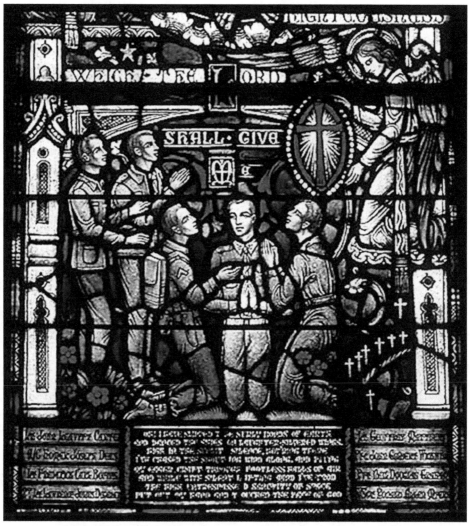

*High Flight* can be barely seen at the bottom center of this
picture of the stained glass.

Michiganstainedglass.org[6]

## Beth's Poetry Trail, Belper, Derbyshire, England

This amazing walking trail contains poems from many authors, such as Spike Milligan, Emily Dickinson, R L Stevenson, Gerard Manley Hopkins and Philip Larkin.

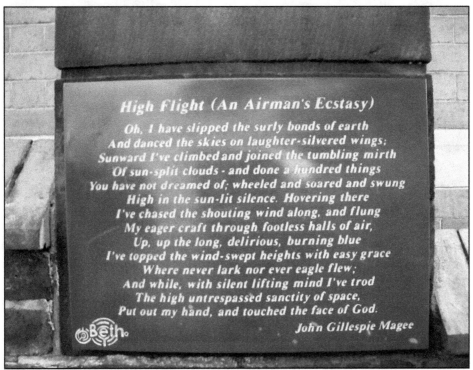

*High Flight (An Airman's Ecstasy)*

Oh, I have slipped the surly bonds of earth
And danced the skies on laughter-silvered wings;
Sunward I've climbed and joined the tumbling mirth
Of sun-split clouds - and done a hundred things
You have not dreamed of; wheeled and soared and swung
High in the sun-lit silence. Hovering there
I've chased the shouting wind along, and flung
My eager craft through footless halls of air,
Up, up the long, delirious, burning blue
I've topped the wind-swept heights with easy grace
Where never lark nor ever eagle flew;
And while, with silent lifting mind I've trod
The high untrespassed sanctity of space,
Put out my hand, and touched the face of God.

John Gillespie Magee

Beth's Poetry Trail, Belper, Derbyshire, England.

Used by permission.[7]

## Bolling Field "Magee Memorial" Triptych, Washington, D.C.

On Sunday, April 28, 1946, John's entire family was present for a sermon at St. John's Church in Washington, D.C. Even though John's father was no longer officially at St. John's (he was Yale's Episcopalian Chaplain at that time), he delivered the sermon. St. John's was dedicating a "triptych" (a picture or relief carving on three panels) in John's memory to the chapel at Bolling Field in southwest Washington D.C. (Bolling Field is located directly across the Potomac River from Reagan National airport.)

The triptych was created by the Citizen's Committee for the Army and Navy, with the cooperation of the Magee family. Sadly, the chapel at Bolling Field burned down in 1950 or 1951, completely destroying everything, including the triptych.

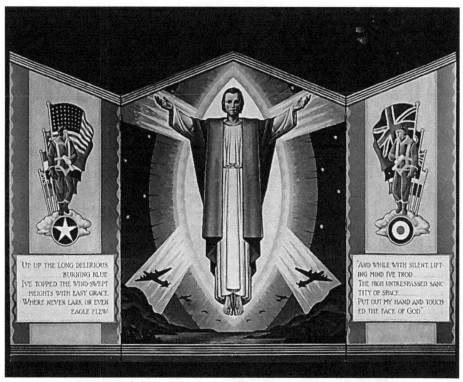

Picture of the triptych that was given to the chapel at
Bolling Field by St. John's Church.

John G. Magee Family Papers, Record Group No. 242,
Special Collections, Yale Divinity School Library

## Monument including John Magee, St. Catharines, Ontario, Canada

This is a monument located outside of the Niagara District Airport, formerly the site of RCAF No. 9 Elementary Flying Training School at St. Catharines. This memorial is dedicated to the flying school located there during WWII. John Magee is mentioned on the plaque.

Plaque located at Niagara District Airport.

John G. Magee Family Papers, Record Group No. 242,
Special Collections, Yale Divinity School Librar

y

## Monument to Ensign Kristopher Krohne, USNR, Coronado, California.

This bench and the stone marker that display *High Flight* are located at the Vista del Barco Park, Coronado, California, near San Diego. They are very close to the North Island Naval Air Station.

The entire park was created as a monument to Ensign Kristopher Krohne, USNR, who was killed in a T-37 plane crash during a solo training flight in 2000 at Vance Air Force Base in Enid, OK.

Pictures courtesy of eCoronado.com,
used with permission from Kay and Ted Krohne.

## Proposed Monument to John Magee, Wellingore, England

This is a proposed monument to John Magee, to be constructed in Wellingore, where John lived in the last few months of his life. At the time of this writing in early 2014, funding had yet to be obtained.

Model of the proposed Magee monument in Wellingore.

Both photographs by Catherine Parker

[1]http://www.reagan.utexas.edu/archives/speeches/1986/31886d.htm–accessed 2/19/2014

[2] Personal correspondence with author.

[3]

http://www.cbsnews.com/stories/2006/07/23/eveningnews/main1826924.shtml  accessed 2013_01_08

[4] http://www.hmdb.org/marker.asp?marker=10126 – accessed 5/12/14.

[5]http://www.michiganstainedglass.org/collections/window.php?id=17-81-43 –accessed 4/1/13.

[6] http://www.michiganstainedglass.org/collections/window.php?id=17-81-43 Accessed 4/1/13.

[7] http://www.bethspoetrytrail.co.uk/memorialgardens.html–Accessed 4/1/13.

# *High Flight*—Parodies

Inevitably, there have been parodies of *High Flight* written. I think John Magee would've appreciated them. Here the ones I could find, in no particular order. (Many of these parodies come from the excellent book *Slipping the Surly Bonds* by David English. Credit is given when it is known.)

## Glider Flight

Oh, I have slipped the surly bonds of rope
A few feet from "The Road".
I whip the Schweitzer 'round so fast
Exceeds the max'mum load.
I've slipped, I've stalled, I've spiral dived,
Spun past the sixth full turn.
"You can't do that!" the new ones say,
They've got a lot to learn.
I find a thermal, turn in it
To try and gain some height.
But I must beat the towplane down
Or this is my last flight!
On 2-3 fly a crooked base
Then crank the plane around.
Or 2-9: pass the hangars then I dive straight for the ground!
But the best is 3-6 final when I know I should be higher,
Put out my hand and touched
The passing telephone wire!

## ATP High Flight

Oh! I have slipped the surly bonds of gate times
And held rigid by impossible air traffic controllers;
Upward I've climbed and joined the congested skies
Of fixes, missed approaches and done hundred things
My passenger did not care for — delays, turbulence, and held
In the holding pattern low on fuel. Waiting there,
I've chased the schedules, and flung
Myself against management and union rules.
Up, up the long ascent in seniority list.
I've topped and gone to the next aircraft
Hoping that I do not get furloughed.
And, while with worried mind I've trod
The difficult sanctity of regulation,
Waiting for the FAA inspector who is God.

> Brian Caver, in honor of Phillip Valente,
> Captain American Eagle Airlines.

## Low Flight (1)

Oh! I've slipped through the swirling clouds of dust,
   a few feet from the dirt,
I've flown the Phantom low enough,
   to make my bottom hurt.
I've TFO'd the deserts, hills,
   valleys and mountains too,
Frolicked in the trees,
   where only flying squirrels flew.
Chased the frightened cows along,
   disturbed the ram and ewe,
And done a hundred other things,
   that you'd not care to do.
I've smacked the tiny sparrow,
   bluebird, robin, all the rest,
I've ingested baby eaglets,
   simply sucked them from their nest!
I've streaked through total darkness,
   just the other guy and me,
And spent the night in terror of
   things I could not see.
I've turned my eyes to heaven,
   as I sweated through the flight,
Put out my hand and touched,
   the master caution light.

## Low Flight (2)

Oh, I've slipped the surly bonds of earth
And hovered out of ground effect on semi-rigid blades;
Earthward I've auto'ed and met the rising brush of
Non-paved terrain;
And done a thousand things you would never care to
Skidded and dropped and flared low in the heat soaked roar.
Confined there, I've chased the earthbound traffic
And lost the race to insignificant Headwinds;
Forward and up a little in ground effect I've topped the
General's hedge with drooping turns
Where never Skyhawk or even Phantom flew.
Shaking and pulling collective, I've lumbered
The low untrespassed halls of victor airways,
Put out my hand and touched a tree.

## Freightdog's Flight

Oh! I have slipped the surly bonds of instructing,
And plowed the skies on ice-laden wings.
Moonward I've climbed and joined the tumbling turbulence
Of lightning split clouds—and done a hundred things
The Feds have not dreamed of—scud run, busted mins,
Flown handheld, homemade approaches. Yawning there,
I've chased the impossible schedule, and flung
My ancient craft through convective sigmets.
Up, up the long over-loaded, over-heating climb,
I've topped the MVAs with red-line power,
Where bats and even owls fly,
And while with hypothermic, fatigued mind I've trod
The complex, congested New York airspace,
  Put out my hand, and touched the de-ice switch.

Name withheld per Freightdog's attorney

## Cruise Flight

Oh, I have slipped the surly bonds of my spouse
And danced the clubs on Kiwi-polished boots;
Moonward I've climbed, and joined the tumbling mirth
Of Moon-split clouds — and done a hundred things
You have not dreamed of — in the Philippines
High in the domelit silence. Holding there,
I've scared the airsick pax, and flung their baggage through
footless halls of air.
Up, up the long, delirious, burning black
I've topped the turbulent heights with little grace
Where never C-130, or even C-5 flew.
And, while with fuzzy, sleep deprived mind I've trod
The high untrespassed sanctity of controlled airspace,
Put out my hand, and touched the face of
The Aircraft Commander, who thinks he is God.

     by Rob Robinette

## *High Flight,* with FAA Supplement

Oh, I have slipped the surly bonds of earth(1),
And danced(2) the skies on laughter silvered wings;
Sunward I've climbed(3) and joined the tumbling mirth(4)
Of sun-split clouds(5) and done a hundred things(6)
You have not dreamed of — Wheeled and soared and swung(7)
High in the sunlit silence(8). Hov'ring there(9)
I've chased the shouting wind(10) along and flung(11)
My eager craft through footless halls of air.
Up, up the long delirious(12), burning blue
I've topped the wind-swept heights(13) with easy grace,
Where never lark, or even eagle(14) flew;
And, while with silent, lifting mind I've trod
The high untrespassed sanctity of space(15),
Put out my hand(16), and touched the face of God.

NOTES:

1. Pilots must insure that all surly bonds have been slipped entirely before aircraft taxi or flight is attempted.
2. During periods of severe sky dancing, crew and passengers must keep seatbelts fastened. Crew should wear shoulder belts as provided.
3. Sunward climbs must not exceed the maximum permitted aircraft ceiling.
4. Passenger aircraft are prohibited from joining the tumbling mirth.
5. Pilots flying through sun-split clouds under VFR conditions must comply with all applicable minimum clearances.
6. Do not perform these hundred things in front of Federal Aviation Administration inspectors.
7. Wheeling, soaring, and swinging will not be attempted except in aircraft rated for such activities and within utility class weight limits.
8. Be advised that sunlit silence will occur only when a major engine malfunction has occurred.
9. "Hov'ring there" will constitute a highly reliable signal that a flight emergency is imminent.
10. Forecasts of shouting winds are available from the local FSS. Encounters with unexpected shouting winds should be reported by pilots.
11. Pilots flinging eager craft through footless halls of air are reminded that they alone are responsible for maintaining separation from other eager craft.
12. Should any crewmember or passenger experience delirium while in the burning blue, submit an irregularity report upon flight termination.

13. Windswept heights will be topped by a minimum of 1,000 feet to maintain VFR minimum separations.

14. Aircraft engine ingestion of, or impact with, larks or eagles should be reported to the FAA and the appropriate aircraft maintenance facility.

15. Aircraft operating in the high untresspassed sanctity of space must remain in IFR flight regardless of meteorological conditions and visibility.

16. Pilots and passengers are reminded that opening doors or windows in order to touch the face of God may result in loss of cabin pressure.

## Search & Rescue Detachment Maintenance Test Pilots

"In the spirit of *High Flight*, I present this poem dedicated to the Search & Rescue Detachment Maintenance Test Pilots with sincerest apologies to the late John Gillespie Magee."

### High Fright

Oh! I have slipped the surely bonds of ground resonance
And danced the skies on bird-speckled rotors.
Sunward I've climbed and joined the tumbling mirth
Of sudden split cones and vibrated a hundred things
      you have not dreamed of.
Wheeled and soared and swung low in foggy violence
Finally hov'ring there. I've hunted the changing winds along
And flung my meager craft in desperate autos through the air.
Up, up, the long monotonous white beach,
I've topped the oil-swept engines with quesy grace,
Where often gull but never eagle flew.
And, while with obedient lifting collective I've plod
The low unreposing sanctity of airspace,
Put out my hand and signaled for the traffic to stop.

      by Lt. Erl G. Purnell & Lt. Michael S. O'Leary
      Maintenance Test Pilots
      CVT 16 SAR Det
      1972

**Hog Flight**

Oh, I have slipped the surly bonds of Earth
And lurched the sky on greasy, wobbling wings.

Cloudward I've lumbered and joined the tumbling mirth
Of instrument flight and done a hundred things
You have not dreamed of

... slipped and skidded and swung
High in the bombing pattern. Stalling there
I've chased the elusive pipper along and flung
My body down to drop the bomb I know not where.

Up, up the deliriously high pop I flew
And topped the windswept heights with no airspeed
Which neither Phantom nor even Eagle will ever do.

And while, with rudder and stick atwirl, I pivot
To check six, should I not watch my steed,
I'll dip down my wing... and take a divot.

by Dale Hill, with sincerest apologies to
John Gillespie Magee, Jr.

## Ramp Flight

Oh, I have swept the surly floor of earth,
And cleaned the aircraft's laughter silvered wings;
Inside I've climbed and joined the endless chain
Of rampers and done a hundred things
You would not dream of
Heaped and stuffed and crammed
Low in the silent pit. Hunched there
I've passed the passenger bag along and flung
Their heavy bag through footless halls of air.
Up, up the short fluorescent, lighted wands
I've guided the wind-swept jet with easy grace,
When never wing, or even tail should touch;
And, while with silent, solemn mind I've trod
The hot steamy expanse of ramp,
Put out my hand, and picked up the FOD.


## High Glide [skiing or snowboarding]

Oh, I have slipped the surly bonds of friction
And danced the slope on laughter-silvered boards;
Downward I've glided, and joined in tumbling mirth
Of sun-split clouds and done a thousand times what
Many have not dreamed of — carved and soared and sung
High in the sunlit silence. Hovering there
I've chased the shouting wind along and flung
My eager turns through footless bowls of corn
Down, down the long delirious, burning white
I've descended from windswept heights with easy grace
Where never lark, nor even eagle flew
And, while with silent, lifting mind I've slid
The high untrespassed sanctity of powder,
Put forward my face, and touched the stuff of Heaven.

by Peter G. Green

# Types of aircraft flown by John Magee

At the back of John Magee's logbook, there is a list of aircraft flown by him, along with the type of engine. The author has added the Wellington bomber that John had an entry for in his logbook but did not make the list in the back; perhaps John only recorded aircraft that he had flown as 1st Pilot, or Pilot-In-Command (although John's logbook does record "Dual Instruction" and "Night Flying" for the Wellington entries).

| | |
|---|---|
| Reed Rambler | Inverted Gypsy III |
| Fleet Finch II | Kinner R.B. II 125 H.P |
| Stinson "105" and "S-MA" | Lycoming (both) |
| North American Yale | Wright Whirlwind |
| North American Harvard II | Pratt and Whitney Wasp S3H1 |
| Miles Master I and II | Rolls Royce Kestrel, Gypsy VI |
| Supermarine Spitfire I | Rolls Royce Merlin |
| Supermarine Spitfire II | Rolls Royce Merlin XII |
| Miles Magister | (no engine listed) |
| Supermarine Spitfire VB | In logbook, not listed in Aircraft Flown section |
| Handley Page Harrow | In logbook, not listed in Aircraft Flown section |
| Vickers Wellington | In logbook, not listed in Aircraft Flown section |

The following pages contain information on significant aircraft that John flew in his short career as a pilot.

## Fleet Finch[1]

John Magee took his very first flight as a student in Fleet Finch II, number 4688, on January 28th 1941. He flew with instructor Putnam for 40 minutes, covering curriculum elements I and Ia (familiarization with cockpit layout). John continued flying the Finch until his last flight on March 27th, a solo flight for just over an hour, and also his last flight at No. 9 EFTS. He logged 42 hours 45 minutes dual instruction, 50 hours 50 minutes of solo time, and 11 hours 10 minutes instrument/cloud flight.

From what can be gathered from Magee's logbook, he didn't fly any other type of aircraft while at St. Catharines. He may have flown, but not logged, one or more flights in the Reid Rambler.

The photograph below shows Fleet Finch #4725, currently (as of January 2013) located at the Canadian Museum of Flight in Langley, British Columbia. Magee flew this exact aircraft several times while at No. 9 EFTS.

The Fleet Finch was built by the Fleet Aircraft of Fort Erie, Ontario, as a two-seat tandem bi-plane trainer. Along with the Tiger Moth, the Finch trained most of the thousands of aviators who passed through the British Commonwealth Air Training Program.

Magee flew this Fleet Finch II, #4725.

Photo courtesy of Canadian Museum of Flight, Langley, B.C., Canada

## Stinson 105 "Voyager" [2]

In the Aircraft Flown section of Magee's logbook, there is an entry for a "Stinson 105" and a "Stinson SMA." There is also an entry in John's Officer's application which shows two hours in a Stinson, flown in Pittsburgh.

John Magee must have made a trip to Pittsburgh and went flying with his cousin Alan Magee Scaife, (John's first cousin, son of John's Aunt Mary and James Verner Scaife), in Alan's Stinson 105.

Alan Magee Scaife was active in an incredible number of enterprises, including aviation.

The Stinson 105 was known as the Voyager. Introduced in 1939, it was a popular aircraft, owned by Howard Hughes and Jimmy Stewart. A military variant was designated the L-5 Sentinel, and was widely used during WWII.

Alan Magee Scaife and his Stinson 105 Voyager that John took a flight in.
Photo taken at the Latrobe Airport sometime in the 1940s.

John G. Magee Family Papers, Record Group No. 242,
Special Collections, Yale Divinity School Library

## North American Yale [3]

On April 10th 1941, John began his next phase of training at No. 2 Service Flying Training School (SFTS) at Uplands, Ontario, Canada. He started by flying four flights in North American Yale #3440 on April 10th, followed by flights on April 12th and 14th in #3445, #3440, and 3436; the last five were solo flights.

The North American Yale was designed to be the next step in RCAF pilot training. Still considered to be a primary flight trainer, the Yale served as a bridge between the Fleet Finch biplane and the advanced North American Harvard trainer. The Yale had fixed landing gear and smaller engine than its cousin the North American Harvard.

The Yales used by the RCAF were originally built by North American Aircraft Company for the French. After France fell to the Nazis, 119 of the Yales were diverted to Canada, where they were designated as the NA-64 Yale.

This is a picture of the first Yale that Magee flew, #3440.

Public Domain

## North American Harvard[4]

After only 10 flights in the Yale, John's first flight in a Harvard occurred on April 19th 1941, in #2645.

The Harvard and its variants trained the vast majority of pilots for the United States and Canada during WWII. In the U.S., the Harvard was known as the AT-6 "Texan" (Army Air Corps) and the SNJ (Navy). The aircraft was used on active service even in Vietnam, and is still flown today by various organizations.

Magee flew this Harvard, #2658, several times while at No. 2 SFTS.

Public Domain

After one of their Harvards was damaged in 2012, the Vintage Wings of Canada organization decided to recreate one of the Harvards that John flew. The author assisted Vintage Wings in matching the serial number of one of the Harvards recorded in John's logbook with an available photograph. Number 2866 was selected.

Original photograph of Harvard #2866 that Magee flew,
taken in the 1940s.

Public Domain.

Harvard #2866, as recreated by Vintage Wings of Canada.

Photo by the author

## Miles Master I and II[5]

On August 6th 1941, John flew his first flight at #53 OTU on a Miles Master I aircraft, # 8774. He followed this flight the next day on another Miles Master I, # 7890, just before his first flight in a Spitfire. His last flight in a Miles Master II, # 9448 was on September 1st.

The Miles Master was an advanced RAF trainer built by Miles Master Aircraft Ltd. The Master was often the last step on the road to flying a Spitfire, being a two-seat, fully aerobatic aircraft. It was never used in combat, but would have been if the Nazis had invaded England.

Miles Master I.

Public Domain

## Supermarine Spitfire I, II, and IV[6]

Many books and stories have been written and told about the Supermarine Spitfire. During WWII, many tried but few succeeded in flying this legendary fighter. John Magee was one of the lucky ones.

There are several variants of each "Mark," or type, of the Spitfire, with different power plants and armament. John flew the MKI, MKII and MKVB.

During his time at #53 OTU, John flew the Spitfire MKI. Along with the MKII, the Spitfire MKI served as two of the tools that saved England during the Battle of Britain. The MKI paved the way for a long line of legendary Spitfires, the only fighter aircraft in continuous production from the beginning until the end of WWII. Even after WWII, the Spitfire continued on active service with air forces around the world,.

Magee's first flight at 412 Squadron was in a Spitfire MKII, #C7281, on September 25th 1941. He continued flying Spitfire MKIIs until his first flight in a MKVB on October 21st, just after the squadron moved to Wellingore.

On October 14th, 17th, and 19th, Magee flew what appeared to 412 Squadron's problem child: Spitfire MKI, #D6612. All three tests were described as "A/C test," and were apparently very harrowing flights (more detail can be found in the section on 412 Squadron operations).

Spitfire MKIIA, showing the distinctive elliptical wing.

Public Domain

The Spitfire MKVB represented a considerable advance in the type. The MKVB replaced four of eight Browning machine guns with two Hispano 20mm cannons. The engine was larger, and was later equipped with a "negative g" carburetor, allowing for maneuvers which called for the airplane to be "pushed over" (producing negative Gs). In earlier versions, negative G maneuvers would results in the engine cutting out (the more standard maneuver was "pulling up," which produced positive Gs).

The MKVB would be the primary aircraft that Magee flew while at 412 Squadron.

412 Squadron Spitfire MKII at Digby, 1941.

Spitfire MKVB with 412 Squadron markings (VZ-A, serial number AD305).

Both pictures are courtesy of Robert Bracken

## Miles Magister[7]

The Miles Magister was a two-seat basic trainer built by Miles Aircraft Ltd.

Miles Magister #5421 was 412 Squadron's utility aircraft. On several occasions, John flew the Magister, often carrying other squadron personnel (probably support personnel, not pilots) on local area flights including trips to Digby from Wellingore. On October 13th, Magee logged five flights in the Magister, carrying F/O Howe, Cpl Clark, Cpl Miller, A/C Cosway, A/C Davidson, and A/C Taylor.

Miles Magister.

Public Domain

412 Squadron's Miles Magister.

Photo courtesy of Barry Needham.

[1] http://en.wikipedia.org/wiki/Fleet_Finch accessed 2012_12_26.

[2] http://en.wikipedia.org/wiki/Stinson_Voyager accessed 2012_12_27.

[3] http://en.wikipedia.org/wiki/North_American_Yale accessed 2012_12_26.

[4] http://en.wikipedia.org/wiki/North_American_Harvard accessed 2012_12_26.

[5] http://en.wikipedia.org/wiki/Miles_Master accessed 2012_12_26.

[6]
http://en.wikipedia.org/wiki/Supermarine_Spitfire_(early_Merlin_powered_vari ants) accessed 2012_12_26.

[7] http://en.wikipedia.org/wiki/Miles_Magister accessed 2012_12_26.

# Bibliography

## Books

- *Sunward I've Climbed*, by Hermann Hagedorn, published 1942 by Macmillan.
- *High Flight — A Story of World War II*, by Linda Granfield, published 1999 by Tundra Books.
- *Plantagenet Roll of the Blood Royal: The Clarence Volume, Containing the Descendants of George, Duke of Clarence*, by marquis de Melville Henry Massue Ruvigny et Raineval. Published in 1994 by Genealogical Pub Co.
- *John Magee, The Poet Pilot*, by Stephan Garnett. Published 1996 by This England Books.
- *Hugh Lyon—1893-1986—A Memoir*, by Elinor Wright and Barbara Lyon, Privately published in 1993 by Laurence Viney.
- *The Discovery of Poetry*, by P.H.B. Lyon. Published 1932 by Edward Arnold & Co.
- *412 (Transport) Squadron*, by Turner Publishing.
- *The Spitfire Smiths: A Unique Story of Brothers in Arms*, by Squadron Leader RIA Smith DFC & Bar with Christopher Shores. Published 2008 by Grub Street.
- *The AT-6 Harvard*, by Len Morgan. Published 1966 by Arco Publishing Co., Inc.
- *Icarus: An Anthology of The Poetry of Flight*, compiled by R. De La Bere and Three Flight Cadets of The Royal Air Force College, Canwell, Lincolnshire. Published 1938 by Macmillan & Co. Ltd.
- *Immigrants of War*, by W. Peter Fydenchuk. Published 2006 by WPF Publications.
- *Behind the Glory: Canada's Role in the Allied Air War*, Ted Barris. Published 1992 by Thomas Allen Publishers.
- *Spitfire: The History*, by Eric B. Morgan and Edward Shacklady. Published 2000 by Key Books, Ltd.
- *Lost Black Sheep: The Search for WWII Ace Chris Magee* by Robert T. Reed. Published 2006 by Hellgate Press.
- *The Rape of Nanking*, by Iris Chang. Published 1998 by the Penguin Group.
- *Spitfire — The Canadians*, by Robert Bracken. Published 1995 by The Boston Mills Press.
- *Spitfire II — The Canadians*, by Robert Bracken. Published 1999 by The Boston Mills Press.

- *Crucible of War, 1939-1945, The Official History of the Royal Canadian Air Force Volume III*, by Brereton Greenhous, Stephen J. Harris, William C. Johnston, and William G.P. Rawling. Published 1994 by Minister of Supply and Services Canada.
- *Aerodrome of Democracy*, by F. J. Hatch. Published in 1983 by Minister of Supply and Services Canada.
- *Training for Victory – The British Commonwealth Air Training Program in the West*, by Peter C. Conrad. Published 1989 by Western Producer Prarie Books.
- *You Have Control, Sir — My Years in the Commonwealth Air Training Plan (1940-1945)*, by Arnold Warren. Published 1998 by Lugus Publications.
- *The Luftwaffe War Diaries*, by Cajus Bekker. Published 1968 by Doubleday & Company, Inc.
- *Fighter Command War Diaries, Volume 2: September 1940 to December 1941*, by John Foreman. Published 1998 by Air Research Publications.
- *1941 – Part 2 – The Blitz to the Non-Stop Offensive* by John Foreman. Published 1994 by Air Research Publications.
- *The JG 26 War Diary*, by Donald Caldwell. Published 1996 by Grub Street, London.
- *The British Commonwealth Air Training Plan* by I. Norman Smith. Published in 1941 by The Macmillan Company of Canada Limited.
- *The Arnold Scheme*, by Gilbert S. Guinn. Published 2007 by The History Press.
- *RCAF Squadrons and Aircraft* by S. Kostenuk and J. Griffin. Published 1977 by A.M. Hakkert Ltd.

## Magazines

- *After the Battle*, Number 63, article by Andy Saunders.
- *Flying Magazine*, January 1993, article by Mike Jerram.
- *Flying Magazine*, March 1942, poem was printed.
- *Aeroplane Monthly*, November 1995, article by Richard Bentham.
- *This England Magazine*, Winter 1982, article by Dr. A. H. Lankester.
- *Air & Space Magazine*, December 2011, article by Rebecca Maksel..
- *FlyPast*, January 2006, article by Ray Leach.

## Personal Correspondance and Interviews

- Elinor Wright-Lyon, daughter of Hugh Lyon.
- Carlton Weber, producer of USAF *High Flight* television sign-off film.
- Marilyn vos Savant.
- Peggy Noonan, Ronald Reagan's speechwriter.
- Everett Brown, Operations Officer at RAF Digby 1942.
- Robert Bracken, author of Spitfire: The Canadians I & II.
- Hugh Magee, Brother of John Magee, Jr.
- David Magee, Brother of John Magee, Jr.
- Edward Magee, Nephew of John Magee, Jr.
- Linda Granfield, author of *High Flight—A Story of WWII*.
- Barry Needham, Flight Lieutenant, RCAF, 412 Squadron.
- Dr. Alice Birney, Library of Congress.
- Cheryl Fox, Library of Congress.
- Wally Fydenchuk, author of *Immigrants of War*.
- Robert Kosteckas.
- David O'Malley, Vintage Wings of Canada.
- Gary Stein, USAF.
- Brett Stolle, National Museum of the United States Air Force.
- Dr. Katharine Jefferts Schori, Head of the Episcopalian Church.
- David Booth, son of RCAF artist H.H. Booth.
- Dub Pool, son of USAF F-104 pilot Major Lawrence Pool.
- Doug Linton, son of Flight Lieutenant Dwayne Linton, 412 Squadron, RCAF.
- Wendy Noble, sister of Flight Lieutenant Rod Smith, 412 Squadron, RCAF.
- Melodie Massey, widow of Flight Lieutenant Hart Massey, 412 Squadron, RCAF.
- Christopher Shores, author of *The Spitfire Smiths*.
- John Gaertner, former EAA Museum Curator.
- Erl "Puck" Purnell, Naval Aviator and Episcopal Minister.
- Richard Bentham.

# Acknowledgements

This book would simply have not been possible if it were not for the help of an amazing number of people and organizations. Here are some of them:

John Gaertner, former EAA Museum Curator, started me down the research trail during my trip to Oshkosh in 1990. The late Lt. Col. Carlton Weber, USAF, helped with the history of the USAF TV Sign-Off Film (Carlton referred to *High Flight* as "the poem that television made famous." He could be right.). Gary Stein, USAF, located and delivered a copy of the T-38 version of the Sign-Off Film. Dub Pool (son of Major Lawrence Pool who was the pilot of the F-104 featured in the original USAF TV Sign-Off film), provided me information about his father.

Support came from Cheryl Allison with her long letters, Paul Dryer (visit his High Flight Fellowship at www.highflightfellowship.com), Elaine Paterson, Bob Steffanus (Bob was instrumental in locating the Pittsburgh Post-Gazette article on John Magee and *High Flight*), the wonderfully supportive staff at the Library and Archives Canada in Ottawa, Richard Bentham (who graciously gave me access to some of his material regarding JGM and hosted a wonderful visit to his home), Robert Kostecka (pilot extraordinaire, who gave me a great aerial perspective during a flight and a few "circuits and bumps" at Pendleton field, the site of former No. 10 Elementary Flying Training School near Ottawa, Canada), and Dave O'Malley from the Vintage Wings of Canada organization.

Wendy Noble, Pilot Officer Rod Smith's sister, was very helpful, as were Pilot Officer Barry Needham (joined 412 Squadron on nearly the same date as John Magee did), the late author Robert Bracken (*Spitfire: The Canadians*), Erl "Puck" Purnell (Naval Aviator, minister, and son to one of John Magee's Connecticut girlfriends!), and Doug Linton (son of 412 Squadron's Pilot Officer Dwayne Linton).

Catherine Parker took some of the wonderful pictures of the Scopwick Burial Ground and environs. Thanks!

Thanks also go to Martha Smalley and Kevin Crawford from the Yale Divinity School Library in New Haven, Connecticut. During a five-day long research visit examining the John G. Magee Family Papers Collection, Kevin did yeoman work in helping me scan over 1,800 documents.

On a glorious afternoon in May of 2013, I was able to take a look at the original letter from John Magee to his parents that contained *High Flight*. I would not have been able to do so without the help of Dr. Alice Birney from the Manuscripts Division of the Library of Congress. Dr. Birney does wonderful work in protecting that original letter for future generations, and she hopes for a day when a technology may be developed to restore that faded letter to its original state. Thank you, Dr. Birney, for not only allowing me to view the original letter but also for everything you do to take care of it.

Several times, the Experimental Aircraft Association (EAA) has given me the chance to address interested pilots via chapter meetings and during the EAA's annual convention in Oshkosh, Wisconsin (aka "AirVenture").

For their early support, I want to thank Linda Granfield, as well as Hugh, Yvonne, and David Magee.

My spiritual friends and advisors include Richard Bach, Robert Heinlein, Anthony Robbins, James Canfield, Steve Jobs, Timothy Ferriss, Wayne Dyer and many, many others. They don't know me, but I certainly know and have learned from them. Thank you, all.

This book would simply not have been possible if not for Google. Google search, Google maps, Google news, Google images, all have brought me a wealth of information. (I have not been paid to endorse Google... but they are an excellent company in my humble opinion and should be acknowledged for their indispensable research tools!)

Friends. For well over 40 years, Steve Field and Bob Baker have been two amazing friends who have helped me in so many ways. Hank Childers has also provided unwavering support through many years, enduring my countless retellings of the Magee story. Mere words cannot convey my thanks to them. "Friendship is the key to life, and we were friends, and it was good."

A wonderful first draft of the cover art was designed by my good friend and talented artist Anita Comeau. The front cover art that appears on the first edition of this book was created by an amazingly creative person, Brett Latta.

Thank you Trevor Wedge for the first edit of this book; it surely needed it!

There are so many other people and organizations who have helped me along the way, and their names are legion. I am sorry to not be able to name them all, but mostly they know who they are, and every single one of them has my heartfelt thanks.

Finally, this project would have never ended without the help of my amazing wife Julie (I would still be doing research if not for her encouraging me to *finish it*!). She not only did a thorough edit of the book, she has been amazingly patient as I wandered through the ups and downs of research and writing, all the while supporting me in so many different ways, both mundane and magical. She'll never know just how much she helped me, but I will do my level best to make sure she knows how much I appreciate it!

# Afterword: The Author's Journey to Find John Gillespie Magee, Jr.

"It's where we belong, Ray."

Author Richard Bach told me this as I was striving to find a way to thank him for a wonderful flight in his Cessna Skymaster, affectionately called "Daisy." In a way, it was my own personal "*High Flight.*" And really, this statement summed up who I am, and what I do. Though I don't get paid for it, and I don't do it as often as I'd like, I consider myself first and foremost a pilot.

It might be bold to say so, but the sky was where John Magee, Jr., belonged as well. John belonged to that group of people who feel more comfortable flying than they do on the ground. In a way, John, along with every pilot who ever flew, is part of a family whose home is in the sky. How and why this is, I don't know, but I know it to be true.

In 1990 the 50th anniversary of the Battle of Britain was celebrated. I had traveled to Oshkosh, Wisconsin, for the annual convention of the Experimental Aircraft Association (EAA), simply referred to by most as "Oshkosh." Oshkosh is the world's largest airshow, attracting people and aircraft from all over the world. This visit was to be my first.

Months previous to my visit, I had read an article in the EAA magazine regarding a new exhibit they were building. This exhibit was to feature John Gillespie Magee, Jr., author of the poem *High Flight*. I was familiar with the poem, having seen it on late night television, back when TV stations used to go off the air. Before signing off, the station that I watched in Los Angeles would usually play this wonderful film showing a jet taking off accompanied by great music, and then this amazing voice would recite *High Flight*.

I had been fascinated with the Battle of Britain for years. Such an amazing story deserved more attention than it was getting, so my naive self thought that a remake of the 1969 movie "Battle of Britain" should be made. Of course it would be expensive; Spitfires, Hurricanes, Messerschmitts, Heinkels and other aircraft would be much harder to find than in the late sixties, necessitating the extensive use of computer-generated airplanes (CGI).

After I thought about such a movie, I set my sights a bit lower and thought about a book or documentary. I started research, reading everything I could find regarding this key battle of WWII. I thought it would be interesting to include the poem *High Flight* somewhere in this work, so I set to finding out about John Magee and the creation of the poem.

I had not read *High Flight* for several years, so I dug up a copy and read the 14 lines. I read it again, more slowly this time, taking it in. I was struck by just how much I could relate to the words. Having been in love with airplanes and flying for as long as I can remember, I wondered just who this poet was, and how exactly he or she had managed to reach inside of me and extract my exact thoughts and feelings regarding flying.

Well, the author's name was easy enough: John Gillespie Magee, Jr. (although I have seen John's last name appear in many forms such as McKee, MaGee, and so on). In 1990 the Internet was very much in its very beginning, but there was enough there to start finding out things. Coincidentally (the first of many serendipitous events surrounding my journey to find Magee), about that time the EAA magazine published a letter to the editor regarding a recent article on John Magee. I went back and read the original article, which contained just enough information to whet my appetite for more.

Back in 1990, there was relatively little content on the Internet. Nobody had heard of Google. Effective Internet search engines were still a few years away. However, email was around, and I had had an email account since 1976, courtesy of being in the US Navy and involved in a research and development project. (I have been using email continuously since then.) The EAA article that was written by EAA Museum Curator John Gaertner included his email address. I wrote to Mr. Gaertner, requesting more information. He gave me some very useful information along with a couple of links to websites with more information.

And I was off on a journey that I'm still on, and probably will be for the rest of my life.

I checked out the websites, learned what I could. Mr. Gaertner had told me about a 1942 biography that had been written about John Magee, but was long out of print. I started searching for the book, but it would take a while to acquire.

Each contact and website lead me to other information sources. Bit by bit, I was putting together the story of Magee, but there were many discrepancies. Magee was Canadian or British. He died in combat in 1940 or 1942, or during the Battle of Britain. He was a Lieutenant in the Army Air Corps. He was 18, 20, 21, 22, 25. He was inspired to write *High Flight* during a high-altitude test flight in a new model of a Spitfire, or while at 412 Squadron. None of these items turned out to be true. It was hard to even arrive at a consensus.

While doing my preliminary research, the annual EAA Convention at Oshkosh was approaching. I had always wanted to go, and now I had another reason to go. I wrote Mr. Gaertner at the EAA Museum, asking for an appointment to meet him and talk with him about John Magee.

Traveling to Oshkosh from southern California was an adventure in and of itself, and I finally arrived there a week before the official convention started. I met John Gaertner in person at last, and he showed me the material he had gathered on John Magee. It made for fascinating reading. John had a copy of the 1942 Magee biography, *Sunward I've Climbed* by Hermann Hagedorn. I tried to read the entire thing in one sitting since I couldn't take it out of the Museum's library, but didn't quite succeed. I wrote down all the information I could regarding the book.

Also in Mr. Gaertner's files was the information regarding creation of the Museum's Magee exhibit. Mr. Fred Heather of Canada had been a major contributor in terms of information and artifacts. There was an article that was printed in the Canadian Aviation History Society's newsletter by Mr. Heather and Mr. Terk Bayly, both of whom had served with John Magee. Again, wonderful reading. I was finally getting some real information from those who knew. I felt that I was getting to know John Gillespie Magee, Jr. more and more with each passing day.

I spent a very enjoyable two weeks at Oshkosh. The Rolls-Royce Company had sponsored a gorgeous Spitfire MKV to be there in commemoration of the Battle of Britain. There were flying Spitfires adding to the excitement; the sound of the Rolls-Royce engine at full throttle has never failed to raise my pulse and make the hairs on the back of my neck stand up.

Life interfered with my progress on the story. Changes in my marital and job status and living locations were major distractions. I continued doing research as best I could under the circumstances.

Before I knew it, I was in the mid-nineties. Research started becoming dramatically easier with the advent of more comprehensive search engines. I was able to find out more and more information. Unfortunately, my day-job prevented me from doing much travel to the locations where I wanted to go in order to see the places first-hand.

Somewhere along the way (1996?), I started a website which still exists today: www.highflightproductions.com. Through the website, I was able to reach out to more people than ever before.

My daughter was born in 1998, joyously complicating matters even more. Becoming a single dad in 2001 took even more time and energy away from non-essential projects.

However, through it all, I continued using the increasing power of the Internet to dig up more and more information on John Magee and his amazing poem. I spent quite a bit of time emailing different sites, attempting to correct their misstatements regarding John and the creation of *High Flight*. (I am still involved in this never-ending job.)

During my research, I encountered many uses of *High Flight*. So many, in fact, that I felt that it would be nice to create a compilation of these uses. Actually, the major impetus in producing the DVD was the finding and obtaining of the USAF television sign-off film. I gathered what permissions I could, and put together the DVD myself, releasing it in 2003. I have heard from so many pilots and non-pilots with stories of how watching that old sign-off film affected them. One seasoned combat fighter pilot admitted to crying when he saw the film again after decades; he told me that watching the film as a teenager had inspired him to join the Air Force. Many requests have been made to use the sign-off film at memorial services for pilots, and I have been happy to fulfill those requests.

Research continued into the twenty-first century. I had to continue with my day-jobs, which put a crimp into my desire to travel to the eastern U.S. (I was a life-long west-coast guy), Canada and to England. The Internet, though, took me there virtually; through products like Google Earth I was able to find the traces of the airfield in Llandow, Wales, where Magee took off on his inspirational flight, the Magee house in Washington D.C., and so on.

In 2008 I was contacted by Mr. Barry Needham of Wynyard, Saskatchewan, Canada. Barry told me that he believed he might be one of the last surviving members of RCAF 412 Squadron, Magee's combat squadron. I was determined to meet Mr. Needham; he was relatively close to Oregon. In the summer of 2009 my son and I drove the 1,200 miles to Wynyard, where we spent a very enjoyable two days with Barry and his lovely wife Martha. Barry shared with me many stories about life with 412 Squadron, including getting shot down and becoming a German prisoner-of-war. It turned out that Barry and John Magee had joined 412 Squadron on the same day. What a great visit! Barry was excited to hear about my project, and encouraged me not to delay in getting it done, words I have tried to take to heart. It is to Barry Needham that I decided to dedicate this book: He is a supreme example of the "Greatest Generation," and is a hero to us all.

Things happened as they do, and my day-job moved me all the way across the country to North Carolina. NOW I was in closer proximity to the east coast research locations, which I wasted little time in getting to.

I made a memorable trip to Canada, visiting St. Catharines, the CNE in Toronto, the Canadian Forces base in Trenton, Uplands, and the Library and Archives Canada. I flew with Robert Kostecka to the former BCATP field in Pendleton, getting a great aerial perspective. I was able to visit with Richard Bentham, who had written a great article on John Magee.

During a couple of visits to Washington, D.C., I was able to see the Magee home, St. John's church, and the Library of Congress. After much pleading on my part, I was allowed to see and film the original *High Flight* manuscript.

Also, more and more content was available via the Internet. As an example, I was able to download 412 Squadron's combat report for Circus 110 — a copy of the actual typewritten report that was written on November 8th, 1941. Operational Record Books, pictures, personal accounts, all available online.

My pace was accelerating. I was actually putting it all together for the first time: all the facts and figures, people and places, dates and times. After all this time, the story practically wrote itself. But even so... my research continues. To this day. I have several unresolved questions that beg to be answered, and I will do my best to get them answered, whether or not that information ever makes the light of day.

I admit it: by trade, I am not a journalist, nor a biographer; I work with computers and have done so on a daily basis for over 35 years. What I am is a pilot, and I have a passion to find the truth. I look back to discover that I've spent over 24 years in search of the truth about John Magee. I have driven thousands of miles, spent countless dollars and hours, talked to dozens of people, searched libraries and the Internet and many other resources, all in the service of this journey. If nothing else, I am a stubborn and persistent researcher.

I came to the conclusion that it was up to me to tell this story. I waited for somebody else to do it, and though there have been some good efforts, I don't believe that they were truly complete. What you read in the foregoing pages is some of what I have found on this trip (the information contained in this book consists of maybe 10%, 15% tops, of the information I have gathered). I suppose I could have gone on doing research until the end of time, as I love to find things out. However, it was time... no, actually, well past time, that I shared with people what I've learned about that certain young man who wrote one of the most famous poems in the English language.

I've made extreme efforts to authenticate every story contained in this book. The quotes are, in most cases, from the actual letters (reading some of the handwriting was quite the task at times!). Of course, I have much more material than I have been able to include in this book, but I had to stop someplace!

Hope you enjoyed the journey as much as I did!

P.S.

Some 24 years after starting, it's done. I've accomplished what I set out to do: I feel that I truly understand how *High Flight* came to be. After this book is on its way, I will be going down another interesting path, namely: Making this story into a documentary and/or feature film. I believe it deserves to be told to as wide an audience as possible. I'm sure that if I really knew what it took to make a movie, I'd run away screaming... but I don't know better, so I will do it, just like I wrote this book.

I just hope it doesn't take another 24 years....

Ray Haas, Wilson, North Carolina, August 2014

Dr. Alice Birney from the Library of Congress and the author examine the original *High Flight* manuscript in May of 2013.

The author welcomes discussion about John Magee, *High Flight*, flying, airplanes, pilots or any other related topic via any of the mechanisms below:

**Email:** ray@highflightproductions.com

**Web:** www.highflightproductions.com

**Facebook:** www.facebook.com/highflightpage

**Twitter:** @rayhaas

**Google**+: google.com/+Highflightproductions

**Blog:** highflight.wordpress.com/

**Shop:** www.highflightshop.com

CPSIA information can be obtained
at www.ICGtesting.com
Printed in the USA
LVHW060012040322
712610LV00010B/434